POLITICAL THEORY, INTERNATIONAL RELATIONS,
AND THE ETHICS OF INTERVENTION

SOUTHAMPTON STUDIES IN INTERNATIONAL POLICY
*Published in association with the Mountbatten Centre for
International Studies, University of Southampton*

General Editor: Dilys M. Hill

This series was established in 1986 to encourage the publication of
multidisciplinary studies of those public policies with significant
international components or implications. Areas of special interest
include arms control and defence policies, energy policies, human
rights, maritime and space issues, Third-World development questions
and the EEC.

Political Theory, International Relations, and the Ethics of Intervention

Edited by

Ian Forbes
Senior Lecturer
Department of Politics, University of Southampton

and

Mark Hoffman
Lecturer in International Relations
London School of Economics

in association with the
MOUNTBATTEN CENTRE FOR
INTERNATIONAL STUDIES
St. Martin's Press   UNIVERSITY OF SOUTHAMPTON

First published in Great Britain 1993 by
THE MACMILLAN PRESS LTD
Houndmills, Basingstoke, Hampshire RG21 2XS
and London
Companies and representatives
throughout the world

A catalogue record for this book is available
from the British Library.

ISBN 0-333-47376-0

Printed in Great Britain by
Antony Rowe Ltd
Chippenham, Wiltshire

First published in the United States of America 1993 by
Scholarly and Reference Division,
ST. MARTIN'S PRESS, INC.,
175 Fifth Avenue,
New York, N.Y. 10010

ISBN 0-312-09579-1

Library of Congress Cataloging-in-Publication Data
Political theory, international relations, and the ethics of
intervention / edited by Ian Forbes and Mark Hoffman.
p.   cm.
Includes index.
ISBN 0-312-09579-1
1. Intervention (International law)   I. Forbes, Ian.
II. Hoffman, Mark, 1957–   .
JX4481.I54   1993
341.5'84—dc20   92–41320
                                         CIP

John Vincent

John Vincent participated in all of the various workshops and conferences connected with this volume. His interest in the project and his enthusiastic participation in the deliberations, judiciously leavened with the appropriate mixture of insight, optimism, humour and scepticism, did much to make the discussions productive, interesting and enjoyable. His untimely death in November 1990 was a devastating blow to his many students and colleagues whose lives he had touched, including those involved in this project. It was also a major loss to the discipline of international relations and its efforts to forge conversational links with other cognate areas of study, particularly political theory, which John continuously advocated. This book is dedicated to his memory.

Contents

The Mountbatten Centre for International Studies, Southampton

The Centre for International Studies was established within the Department of Politics in the University of Southampton in 1983 and brought together members of the Departments of Adult Education, History, Law and Politics to foster interdisciplinary and multidisciplinary research into the domestic and external dimensions of policy.

Members of the Centre are involved in research on a wide range of issues and the Centre also sponsors research workshops and symposia. Links have been established with the Centre d'Histoire Militaire of the University of Montpelier, the Fondation Pour les Etudes de Défense Nationale, Paris, and the work of the team on Political Culture in Eastern Europe at the Ecole de Hauts en Sciences Sociales, Paris. Members of the Centre have also participated in the work of the European Science Foundation and the International Congress of Historical Sciences.

In 1986 the Centre established the series the *Southampton Studies in International Policy* in collaboration with the publishers Macmillan in London and St. Martin's Press in New York.

Acknowledgements

The chapters in this book are the result of papers, presentations, comments and discussions in a series of workshops and conferences held over a three-year period. The initial meetings were sponsored by the Project on North–South Security at the University of Southampton, funded by the Ford Foundation. Subsequent meetings were held at the University of Southampton and at the London School of Economics. These meetings were funded by the Department of Politics and the Faculty of Social Sciences at Southampton, and the International Research Fund at the London School of Economics. We wish gratefully to acknowledge the financial assistance provided by these various bodies, the institutional support provided by the Department of Politics at Southampton and the Department of International Relations at the LSE, and the initial encouragement for the enterprise shown by John Simpson and his colleagues on the North–South Security Project.

James Mayall's chapter originally appeared in *International Affairs* (Vol. 67, No. 3, 1991). We are grateful to the editor and publishers for permission to reprint the article in this volume.

IAN FORBES
MARK HOFFMAN

Notes on the Contributors

The editors

Ian Forbes is Senior Lecturer in Politics at the University of Southampton. He is the author of *Marxism and the New Individual* and co-editor (with Steve Smith) of *Politics and Human Nature*.

Mark Hoffman is Lecturer in International Relations at the London School of Economics. He is co-editor (with N. J. Rengger) of *Beyond the Inter-Paradigm Debate: Critical Theory and International Relations*.

The other contributors

Anthony Carty is Senior Lecturer in Law at the University of Glasgow. He is author of *The Decay of International Law?: A Reappraisal of the Limits of Legal Investigation in International Affairs*.

John Hoffman is Senior Lecturer in Politics at the University of Leicester. He is the author of *State, Power and Democracy*.

Peter Johnson is Lecturer in Politics at the University of Southampton. He is the author of *The Politics of Innocence* and *Frames of Deceit*.

Michael Leifer is Professor of International Relations at the London School of Economics. He is the author of *ASEAN and the Security of South-East Asia*.

Richard Little is Professor of International Relations at Bristol University. He is the author of *Intervention in British Foreign Policy* and co-author (with Richard McKinlay) of *World Order and Global Problems*. He is editor of the *Review of International Studies*.

James Mayall is Professor of International Relations at the London School of Economics. He is the editor of *The Community of States* and author of *Nationalism and International Society*.

Leo McCarthy is a Lecturer in the Department of Politics at the University of Edinburgh. His main area of research is in international relations theory.

Cornelia Navari is Senior Lecturer in International Politics at the University of Birmingham. She is the editor of *The Conditions of States*.

Barrie Paskins is Senior Lecturer in the War Studies Department at King's College, London. He is the co-author (with Michael Dockrill) of *Theories of Just War* and is currently working on a book on virtue and the just war tradition.

Raymond Plant is Professor of Politics at the University of Southampton. He has published widely in the area of social and political theory and is the author of *Hegel* and *Introduction to Modern Political Thought*.

N. J. Rengger is Lecturer in International Relations at Bristol University. He is co-editor (with Mark Hoffman) of *Beyond the Inter-Paradigm Debate: Critical Theory and International Relations* and (with John Baylis) of *Dilemmas in World Politics*.

Ali Sadeghi is Lecturer in International Relations at Isfahan University, Iran. His main area of research is international political theory.

Caroline Thomas is a Senior Lecturer in the Department of Politics at the University of Southampton. She is the author of *Sovereignty, New States and Intervention, In Search of Security: The Third World in International Relations* and *The Environment and International Relations*.

R. J. Vincent was the Montague Burton Professor of International Relations at the London School of Economics. He was the author of *Non-Intervention, Human Rights and International Relations*, edited *Human Rights and Foreign Policy* and co-edited (with J. D. B. Miller) *Order and Violence*.

Peter Wilson is Lecturer in International Relations at the London School of Economics. His main areas of research are international relations theory and the politics of international economic relations. He is co-editor (with David Long) of *International Relations Theory in the Inter-War Period*.

1 Introduction: Intervention and State Sovereignty in the International System

Ian Forbes and Mark Hoffman

This volume is about the discourse and practice of intervention and non-intervention in international relations and the ethical justifications and interpretations of such behaviour. The essays that follow are the result of a deliberate effort at bringing together the analytical and interpretive skills of theorists of politics and international relations. What follows is a conversation in international theory that focuses on the problems associated with intervention. The basis for such a conversation between scholars from ostensibly discrete subject areas has been identified by Michael Donelan:

> if the starting point of the study of international relations is a world of separate states, a political theorist is right not to be interested in the subject. . . . If, on the other hand, we do not start with this assumption of separate states, there is all the international theory in the world to be done. For there is now a primordial community of [hu]mankind; separate states are but an arrangement of it.[1]

In the course of this dialogue, four major areas of interest emerged as the focal points of this volume. First, our understanding of the nature of the state and state system, the validity of the idea of state sovereignty and the norm of non-intervention are questioned from a variety of perspectives. Second, the applicability of rights arguments is explored, particularly with respect to the possibility of generating justifications for intervention. Third, realist, liberal, critical theory and postmodern conceptions of power, identity and agency in international society are considered. Finally, the universal and particularistic justifications for intervention and non-intervention – both those offered by existing practice and discourse and those which might possibly be generated – are a constant theme in the contributions.

In elucidating these themes, we effectively begin where Hedley Bull's edited volume *Intervention in World Politics* finishes.[2] Our starting point is Bull's conclusion regarding the endemic nature of intervention in international politics. This endemic quality requires that we move beyond traditional accounts of intervention. These have tended to focus on the military–political dimensions of intervention or have dealt with specific case studies. Their working definition of intervention is limited to the military transgression of 'legally' delimited boundaries. Within such confines the question of intervention is usually dealt with as a pragmatic problem for states' foreign policy, and little attention is paid to ethical questions and the implications of intervention for our understanding of the nature of the state, the state-system and political community.

In order to explore these underdeveloped themes, a more encompassing account is required which sees intervention as a discourse and practice which has political, social, economic, psychological *and* moral dimensions. These themes have become all the more relevant given the new dispensation of the international political order. Perceptions of intervention in the international system are no longer filtered through the lens of a bipolar system, nor can specific interventionary acts be construed as epiphenomena of great power interests.

In order to elucidate these themes and aspects of intervention, the volume is divided into four parts: definitions and dilemmas; preliminary theoretical perspectives; hard cases; and concluding theoretical departures. In the process, intervention is not seen as a single, self-contained act, but explored as a social construct of international behaviour which is premised on and instantiates a particular account of the international system. Although the contributions do not adhere to a single view of the nature of this account, this general starting point allows us to highlight the multifarious dimensions of intervention. In particular, the essays examine the intended and unintended outcomes of intervention and explore the standards and norms which are meant to, or might provide particular and universalised justifications for interventionary actions.

PART ONE: DEFINITIONS AND DILEMMAS

The essays in Part One are concerned with definitions and dilemmas relating to the theory and practice of intervention. In the first essay, Richard Little discusses key literature on intervention. In highlighting the strengths and limits of the existing theoretical, empirical and behavioural accounts of intervention, he provides a wide ranging context for the ensuing discussion. The process of context-setting is continued in the chapter by Tony Carty. Here the norm of non-intervention is accounted for as part of the 'discourse' of international law which is premised on an unexplored tension between competing internal and external accounts of the state, the government and the people. The differing accounts within political theory regarding the nature of the state are the starting point for Cornelia Navari's chapter. In her discussion she explores the account of the state in the political thought of Machiavelli, Hobbes, Locke and Hegel, and the implications of each of these for our account of, and justification for, acts of intervention. The final chapter in this section by Peter Johnson argues that the practice of intervention is best interpreted within the context of moral dilemmas understood as self-contradictions.

PART TWO: THEORETICAL PERSPECTIVES

In Part Two of the book a series of contrasting conceptualisations of the theory and the practice of intervention are presented, discussed and critiqued. The question of intervention and non-intervention is approached from definite political and theoretical understandings. In the first essay, Leo McCarthy explores the tensions within the realist account of the state, the international system and, by extension, the theory and practice of intervention. Connecting with elements of Navari's chapter, McCarthy argues that the realist characterisation of the international system as Hobbesian or 'anarchic' in nature is insufficient to support the range of normative positions at which realists tend to arrive. On the other hand, realist accounts which draw on Hegel produce an unacceptably absolutist view of the state. In seeking to account for the reality of intervention, McCarthy sets the stage for subsequent essays in noting that we need to turn elsewhere if we are to develop adequate accounts of intervention.

The next two essays present contrasting 'strong views' on the subject. In her chapter, Caroline Thomas presents an account of intervention which has a strong realist pedigree and results in a strict rule of non-intervention. This entails the view that the autonomy of states is the prime, universal value in international relations. The fundamental problem is that any act of intervention threatens the independence of a particular state, and this in turns threatens the independence of all states. These arguments are replete with moral overtones. The practical moral considerations emerge in any number of ways. First, prudence, and the benefit of hindsight, warns of the inevitability of politically unacceptable or morally undesirable outcomes, whatever the justification or cause of the original intervention. There may be what looks like a just intervention, but it will always turn out badly. Second, intervention serves to undermine the already fragile independence of Third World states. In hindering the development and survival of strong states in the Third World, interventionary activity has the effect of reinforcing inequalities in the international system. Third, and perhaps most important, is the requirement of international order. For the realist approach as presented here by Thomas, state sovereignty and the norm of non-intervention are the *only* guarantors of international order, and must be respected.

The alternative framework offered by Raymond Plant extends a rights-based political theory beyond the usual confines of the state to the realm of international affairs, thereby laying the foundation of a strong case for intervention. The starting point here is the individual as a representative of humanity. Our common humanity rests upon universal human characteristics, and these give rise to rights (both positive and negative). The upshot of this argument is that such rights can generate legitimate claims upon others. Consequently, a valid justification for intervention becomes available, and there will be numerous cases which call for action. Since rights are not dependent upon the existence of the state, so the justification for intervention transcends state boundaries.

Arguing that such strong positions are not capable of capturing all aspects of the subject, the next two chapters develop perspectives that are located between or outside of the dichotomy created by the strong positions articulated in the chapters by Thomas and Plant. In his chapter, Barrie Paskins argues that the ethical aspects of intervention cannot be captured by rules or principles as these ignore the importance of the contexts within which action takes place. However, recourse to Aristotelian notions of virtue provides a basis for theoretical and practical insights into the problems associated with intervention. He argues that the positions developed by Thomas and Plant rely on the virtues of prudence and justice respectively. But, Paskins argues, this ignores the virtue of generosity which provides descriptive and prescriptive criteria for a third discourse on the practice of intervention.

Concluding this section, John Vincent and Peter Wilson take up the challenge offered by Plant's rights-based position. They examine the range of agents and agencies which might fulfil the obligations implied by assuming that a conception of domestic, human and political rights can be actualised at the international level. Such an approach comes immediately into conflict with an international morality based on a limited and narrow conception of state sovereignty. Instead, they draw attention to the transparency of efforts to establish legitimacy by modern states, and therefore the possibility of critical international judgement employing Shue's notion of basic rights. While this does not signal the demise of the sovereign state, it does require a re-evaluation of the basis of both the internal and external legitimacy of states.

PART THREE: HARD CASES

How do these approaches work in practice? Using practical examples, the core theoretical proposals about the validity of state sovereignty can be applied in order to highlight the need for an ethical theory to underpin international action. Four very different cases highlight the practice of intervention in relation to the cross-cutting issues and themes which emerged in the first two sections of the volume. Kampuchea/Cambodia, the Lebanon, South Africa and the Kurds in northern Iraq are the 'hard cases' examined. These 'hard cases' push at the limits and cogency of moral arguments and models for analysis. Each involves a 'state' with dubious claims to legitimacy. Each addresses a similar set of concerns regarding both the idea and practice of intervention and its implications for our understanding of the nature of the state and the state system. Each touches on a related set of questions regarding the ethics of interventionary practices and discourse that are themselves predicated on the legitimacy of the idea of the sovereign state as the basis for international order.

In the case of the Lebanon, intervention has taken place at a variety of levels with relative impunity since the 1970s. As Ali Sedaghi points out, the problem of intervention in the Lebanese case arises partly from doubts that the Lebanese state exists at all. Indeed, so weak is the state that the objections to intervention because it threatens state sovereignty don't seem to fit very neatly. In other words, here is a case of intervention, but not state-to-state intervention. Yet the action is still described as intervention, and there remains a need to be able to judge it politically and ethically. Indeed, the states involved have constructed and offered justifications for their interventions in precisely these terms. Israel and Syria alike intervene in order to impose a state on a country, to give the form the structure and content it lacks. This tells us a great deal about the international system and international order. Order is threatened if the system malfunctions. The Lebanon is anomalous; disorder results and one way of dealing with it is to rectify the anomaly.

Pol Pot's Kampuchea represents another kind of extreme, another 'dubious' state, this time in terms of moral and political legitimacy. It is now generally acknowledged that through its genocidal policies the Pol Pot government abdicated its responsibilities and denied its people equal citizenship. Kampuchea, in other words, stands out as a case for justified intervention on the grounds that positive and negative human rights are not being met. However, as Michael Leifer points out, Pol Pot's downfall was not the result of these gross human rights violations, but Kampuchea's persistent interventions into Vietnam. Rather, it was the Vietnam-sponsored government of Kampuchea and Vietnam alike which subsequently attracted sanctions and the opprobrium of the international community: the latter for the violation of state sovereignty and the norm of non-intervention; the former for its supposed illegitimacy. The justification for this isolation, according to Leifer, was the violation of the cardinal rule of international society: the norm of non-intervention. This hard case exposes what the 'autonomy' of the state means: a sovereign state may react to cross border stimulus but must not act in any positive or corrective sense. The differential application of the rule of non-intervention seems here devoid of moral as well as practical legitimacy.

For John Hoffman, the hard case of South Africa also concerns the moral and political legitimacy of the state. However, this case is quite different from that of the Lebanon or Kampuchea. They were the subjects of intervention; South Africa has been the beneficiary of the rule of non-intervention. Argument and action has revolved around the imposition of economic sanctions. Has South Africa warranted the forbearance of other states?

A state can be legitimate in two ways. Internally, it may be the legitimate authority by dint of the common citizenship of its people. Externally, the state is legitimate if it has sovereignty endowed upon it by virtue of being recognised by the members of the international society of states. On both counts, Hoffman argues, South Africa may be judged to have fallen far short of expectations. The conjunction of colonial origins *and* racist structures manifestly rules out claims to internal legitimacy. Its apartheid constitution made it a pariah of international society. Clearly, the humanitarian case for intervention was available as it was for Pol Pot's Kampuchea. Moreover, it regularly violated the territorial integrity of its neighbouring states and ignored UN resolutions over Namibia. These undermined its claim to sovereignty in the international society of states in the external sense. Nevertheless, this state was protected by the rule of non-intervention.

However, the real test of the concept of the sovereign state concerns not South Africa, but all the other sovereign states. Apartheid South Africa – its existence, its internal conduct and its persistent violations of the sovereignty of other states – challenged the view that there is any such thing as an international society, or international community, or international agreements and law. South Africa stood for some time as a clear case for the necessity and possibility of joint action, of concerted action, of an international package of actions depending on position and power in terms of geography and the hierarchies of influence. To refrain from acting against South Africa may be explained in a number of *realpolitik* ways. To *justify* that non-intervention is another matter altogether. It raises the question of obligations generated by non-interventionary forbearance, and the consequences for states which violate the rule. The hard case of South Africa indicates that sovereign statehood is a powerful fiction.

In the final case study, James Mayall notes that the passing of the Cold War era appeared to create the conditions for the realisation of the liberal dream of a reformed international system. Subsequent events, however, demonstrate that the context of interventionary practice has changed but not the ethical discourse and dilemmas posed. This is nowhere more evident than in the Gulf War and its aftermath. The invasion of Kuwait by Iraq triggered an astonishingly assertive response by an international coalition led by the United States. A huge force was mobilised to re-establish a state of dubious internal legitimacy. Once again, upholding the principle of state sovereignty was deemed paramount.

That principle was almost immediately called into question as a consequence of the situation in northern Iraq. It is the case of the Kurds rather than Kuwait which constitutes the 'hard case'. Under severe pressure from their domestic constituencies, the international coalition violated the sovereignty of Iraq in order to create a safe haven for the Kurdish people. The actions of the international community with regard to the Kurds raise the question of a general basis for humanitarian intervention which can be applied in similar situations.

James Mayall explores the possible justifications for such an extension of international action. Humanitarian concerns, the denial of the rights of autonomous groups, and support for claims to self-determination all might be the basis for modern claims for constructive interventionary action in the 'new world order'. Drawing on Mill's arguments regarding intervention, Mayall argues that the Kurdish case is best understood as an example of imperial responsibility rather than the dawning of a new age of humanitarian intervention. On this basis, humanitarian concerns, rights of groups and claims to self-determination without a tractable imperialist context cannot produce powerful justifications for interventionary activity. Even where imperial responsibility exists, prudence and practicality are likely to militate against intervention.

PART IV: THEORETICAL DEPARTURES

These four case studies underscore a marked reluctance to validate interventionary action on ethical grounds among international relations thinkers and practitioners. This stems from a combination of factors: the morality attached to state sovereignty; the way that moral considerations always add complexity and sometimes clarity but never certainty; the lack of confidence concerning outcomes; and concern over the absence of moral actors to carry out moral actions. Despite the strength of an ethical justification for a potential intervention, despite the acknowledged need or desire for bringing about change in a particular situation, and despite the view that there should not be a general prohibition against moral critiques in international relations, whether that be a silencing of dissent or a disinclination to insist upon standards and norms, the balance remains untipped in favour of justified intervention.

The inadequacy of traditional approaches and accounts of intervention calls for new thinking in respect of the state, sovereignty, the nature of international society and the political discourses employed by theorists of politics and international relations. The three concluding chapters address these concerns and connect with identifiable trends in social and political theory.

In his analysis, N. J. Rengger focuses on prevailing theories of knowledge and the foundational premises at the heart of western explanations of politics and international relations. He identifies the political, cultural and ethical fragmentation which beggars the possibility of producing anything like a set of 'rules' governing intervention. In place of a reliance on the easy certainties of foundationalism, Rengger proposes a contextualist perspective which demands significant change in both the theory and practice of world politics.

The recognition of relativism, however, does not result in an inability to judge and act on ethical grounds. Just as there can be no foundational basis for rules of intervention, the incommensurability of the values in the international system, of course, means that there cannot be a rule of non-intervention either. In effect, Rengger argues that all cases are 'hard cases' requiring decisions which properly reflect the systemic and ethical contexts. For the practitioner and analyst the tasks are clear: substantial reform of the international legal system and the recognition of interdependencies between increasingly porous states. These will change the understanding and treatment of intervention in the context of a transformed state system.

Mark Hoffman demonstrates that it is possible to avoid the foundationalist traps highlighted by Rengger and employ a systematic theoretical approach to address world politics in general and intervention in particular. Taking as his starting point the common factors of agency and identity in the construction of political space, Hoffman focuses on how the contexts of meaning affect and are affected by intervention. This reveals the ambiguities of relations between 'insiders' and 'outsiders' that are routinely disguised by traditional approaches. He argues that an appropriately reflexive political and theoretical method for dealing with these relations can be located in critical international theory.

Adopting such an approach provides the basis for the development and expansion of political communities. This would avoid the dangers of cultural imperialism and embrace an 'ironic cosmopolitanism' which self-consciously acknowledges the possibility of multiple identities. Rather than starting with fixed definitions, this approach entails an understanding of the sovereign state and the anarchic international system as prevailing social constructs which are amenable to change and transformation. It also points to the significance of new forms of political activities and new political spaces which themselves are replete with new distributions of knowledge. Out of such knowledge comes the possibility of new forms of interventionary action, namely third-party mediation.

In the final chapter, Ian Forbes extends the arguments of the previous two chapters to challenge the logocentrism and ethnocentrism of traditional approaches to the state and intervention. Drawing on Foucault's work, power is identified as the key concept for the understanding of interventionary action and a reformulation of the concept of the state and sovereignty and the human subject. Power both disciplines human subjects and creates knowledge structures that constitute international society. By abandoning the notion of power as a possession, and characterising it as a relation, Forbes shows that the state is the result of power relations.

This deconstructive account of the state, which is corrosive of the concept of sovereignty, has implications for the practice and discourse of intervention. It is argued by Forbes that intervention operates as a disciplinary force to maintain the international system of states, through the oppression of individual human subjects. The ubiquity of power relations, however, establishes the certainty of resistance to power and the unpredictability of outcomes. This means that the ostensive regularities and fixities of world politics are best understood as the site of a struggle, mediated as a power/knowledge discourse. The ethics of intervention, therefore, arise out of the struggle itself, conducted at the physical and theoretical margins of the global system, thereby creating the possibility and probability of resistance and countermovements to systems of domination, oppression and exclusion.

In all four parts of this volume, the underlying theme is the contested status of the sovereign state. To argue against intervention is to give to sovereignty a value higher than any other. To argue for intervention is a direct challenge to the value of sovereignty. Since intervention and sovereignty have proved to be so inextricably linked, the adequacy of justifications of intervention have to be set against the adequacy of the justifications for sovereignty. Nor can sovereignty merely be a functional requirement of the international system. It is not enough to say that chaos is the alternative. Rather, sovereignty and intervention are a couple in the moral relationships that states create with one another. They presuppose each other. Intervention is a moral issue because sovereignty is a moral situation.

Notes

1.   M. Donelan, 'The Political Theorists and International Theory' in M. Donelan (ed.), *The Reasons of State* (London, 1979) p. 90.
2.   H. Bull (ed.), *Intervention in World Politics* (Oxford, 1984).

Part I

Definitions and Dilemmas

2 Recent Literature on Intervention and Non-Intervention

Richard Little

INTRODUCTION

This chapter explores some of the recent literature on empirical and normative implications of intervention and non-intervention in the international arena. These concepts are not, of course, unique to international politics. They characterise a wide variety of activities in different social and political arenas. But the role of these concepts in international politics is distinctive because the principle of non-intervention is firmly and now formally embedded in the normative conventions governing international relations. In contemporary international law states are clearly proscribed from intervening in the domestic affairs of other states. Intervention is, under most circumstances, an illegal act. By contrast, the state has extensive rights of intervention within its own boundaries. Indeed, the history of the modern state can be charted in terms of its growing powers of intervention in the lives of its citizens.[1]

Within the state, therefore, intervention is closely associated with the legitimate exercise of sovereignty, whereas in the international arena intervention is generally seen to be a violation of sovereignty, and a threat to world order. As a consequence, intervention beyond the boundaries of the state identifies 'an activity that is not socially approved in the modern international community'.[2] When interventions do occur, therefore, they tend to be ritually condemned and states which intervene are subject to intense international criticism. The critics justify their attack by reference to the growing number of international conventions which proscribe intervention. The principle of non-intervention is embodied, for example, in the Charter of the United Nations, which severely restricts the right to intervene in the domestic jurisdiction of states. The prohibition was strengthened in General Assembly Resolution 2625, unanimously passed in 1970. Here non-intervention is depicted as one of the 'Principles of International Law Concerning Friendly Relations Among States'. The prohibition was reconfirmed in the judgement reached by the International Court of Justice in June 1986 which examined the 'Merits in Military and Paramilitary Activities In and Against Nicaragua'.

The principle of non-intervention, therefore, has played a central role in the evolution of the international order which now exists. But the desirability of this order has come under serious challenge during the twentieth century. A world of independent and sovereign states is no longer unquestioningly regarded as the most desirable mode of organisation for the long-term future of the human race. In recent years, moral philosophers have started to examine and often to question the normative assumptions which underpin the prevailing mode of international order. Given the centrality of the principle of non-intervention in sustaining this order, it is hardly surprising to find that the principle is now being placed under close scrutiny and that the results of this scrutiny are proving to be controversial.

Despite the institutional proscriptions, it cannot be denied that intervention remains an important feature of contemporary international politics. Some of the most dramatic and tragic developments in recent international history have taken the form of intervention by one state into the domestic affairs of another. The research required to develop a general theoretical understanding of intervention, however, is surprisingly limited. The empirical work which has been done is examined in the first part of this chapter. The literature which delves into the normative underpinnings of intervention and non-intervention is examined in the second part. A brief conclusion argues that there are attempts now being made to move away from the rigid distinction between normative and empirical analysis which has tended to prevail in the study of international politics.

THE EMPIRICAL DIMENSION

Intervention has been regarded as a significant feature of international politics. Some major turning points in world history are often associated with specific interventions, while general patterns of intervention have been seen to correlate with structural features of the international system. The start of the Cold War, for example, has often been traced back to the decision to send troops into Russia during the Bolshevik Revolution. The intervention by Italy, Germany and the Soviet Union into the Spanish Civil War in 1936 is frequently depicted as a dress rehearsal for the Second World War. The unsuccessful interventions by the Americans into Vietnam and the Soviets into Afghanistan are seen to demonstrate that there are distinct limits to the power of any state. By contrast, Soviet intervention into Hungary and Czechoslovakia, and American intervention into the

Dominican Republic and Grenada, are often used to illustrate that superpowers can create their own spheres of influence. Interventions by Egypt, Syria, Cuba and Vietnam indicate, moreover, that the behaviour is not restricted to Great Powers. Given this catalogue of intervention, it is unsurprising to find it argued that intervention is a 'built-in feature of our present international arrangements'[3] or that intervention is 'inherent in the nature of international society'.[4] A survey of the empirical literature suggests, however, that this assessment needs considerable qualification.

Many of the important cases of intervention have of course been extensively documented. Indeed, as Raymond and Kegley have noted, most of the literature on intervention consists of historical case studies rather than 'explanations of patterned regularities in interventionary behaviour'.[5] Holsti[6] has suggested that the relative paucity of comparative research on intervention can be accounted for by the inability of scholars to reach an agreed definition of intervention. But this explanation is unconvincing since there are few concepts in the social sciences which elicit a consensus on meaning. Nevertheless, intervention is a concept which does pose particularly knotty definitional problems. Beloff has noted that the term is 'plagued by misconceptions'[7] and Quilter has indicated that it is widely 'misunderstood'.[8] Part of the problem is that by a not-absurd definition, intervention can be equated with the whole of international relations. As Schwarz has observed 'some analysts are inclined to term any foreign policy behaviour as intervention when a power tries to change the behaviour of another power'.[9] Stanley Hoffmann, for example, acknowledges that intervention can be considered 'practically the same as that of international politics in general from the beginning of time to the present'.[10]

During the first wave of the behavioural approach to international relations, in the 1960s, Rosenau, in an important discussion of intervention, argued that while practitioners could legitimately use the concept as a catch-all phrase to cover every form of diplomatic and strategic intervention, from the exercise of military and economic power to the insidious process of cultural imperialism, political scientists cannot be excused for using the term as a 'license for undisciplined thought'.[11] Rosenau insists that progress can only be made if the concept is honed down to manageable proportions. He argues that intervention is characterised by two attributes which distinguish it from other forms of state action. It must, first, provide a sharp break with the established pattern of behaviour between the intervening and target states, and second, it must be consciously designed to change or preserve the structure of the political authority in the target state. Although this formulation has been criticised for failing to accommodate the association of intervention with economic subversion and loss of sovereignty in the Third World today,[12] it has generally been seen as a useful way of illuminating an otherwise protean concept. Schwarz, for example, has demonstrated that it is possible to use Rosenau's formulation provided that the comparisons are at a reasonably high level of generality.[13]

In detailed comparative analysis, however, Rosenau's analytic definition is invariably rejected. It is considered too broad because it can embrace economic as well as military measures and there is a preference for restricting the concept to military activity. This move is often justified on the grounds that 'such a limitation is consistent with the manner in which the word is commonly used with reference to events in international politics'.[14] Moreover, in any empirical venture, as Pearson notes, there is always a desire to ensure that the definition of intervention 'should allow the researcher to observe some form of overt, relatively easily detected behaviour'.[15] Pearson, like most other researchers, concludes that the least ambiguous indicator of intervention is the movement of troops by one country across the border of another.

Even when restricted to military activity, there is still considerable variation in the way intervention is construed. For some analysts, intervention is limited to cases when there is 'blatant use of military force in another country'[16] but where the resistance is not sufficient to constitute war. From this perspective, the hallmark of intervention is that it risks but does not generate a war. Other analysts, however, adopt a much broader focus and extend the definition to include the involvement of an external state in an on-going civil war.[17] Other researchers have chosen to restrict their discussion to intervention into civil wars.[18] Here, of course, the definitional problem is compounded by the need to identify what constitutes a civil war. Intervention, therefore, has been approached from a number of different orientations. Although the task of definition is seen to be important by empiricists, they regard it is only a first step in empirical research and theory building. The main thrust of this research has been to develop a longitudinal perspective to see if there are changes in the pattern of intervention and whether these changes relate to the evolving structure of the international system.

This approach was advanced initially by Kaplan and Katzanbach[19] and it has been systematically tested by Raymond and Kegley, who have looked at intervention in the context of the cycles of power concentration and deconcentration in the international system.[20] The international system is examined from 1816 to 1980 and attention is focused on intervention into civil wars. What the authors find is that there is no consistent pattern to intervention although there is a tendency for the system to be more intervention-prone when power is concentrated in the hands of one state. The interventions, moreover, tend to be undertaken by the preponderant state in support of incumbent governments. However, the analysis also reveals that although there were 106 civil wars during the period under investigation, when intervention could potentially have taken place, there were only 21 specific cases of intervention.

The power concentration model, however, does not explain why a dominant state should wish to intervene. The Raymond and Kegley study also fails to accommodate both the potential for intervention outside civil war situations and the importance which can be attached to the threat of intervention. These possibilities, however, are included in the idea of the imperialism of free trade or informal empire advanced by Gallagher and Robinson.[21] These authors argue that the British, during the *laissez-faire* and apparently anti-imperialist phase in the nineteenth century, used their preponderant power to incorporate large sectors of the globe into the expanding British economy. When necessary they did so by formal annexation. But Gallagher and Robinson argue that the British government preferred whenever possible to promote their economic interests by informal measures which included intervention and the threat of intervention.

Smith goes on to use this insight in a comparison of British and American imperialism in the period after 1815. He draws the general conclusion that 'just as Britain turned a keener eye to Southern affairs at the moment it was calculating shifts in the European power balance, so too Washington was examining the use of Southern nationalism more intently as relations with Moscow deteriorated'.[22] American policy was further conditioned, however, by the geographical recognition that the resolution of local questions had a bearing on the global structure of United States' interests and obligations. The United States began to run into problems because the 'seemingly compelling logic of the geopolitical vision' began to override 'any reading of the logic of local developments'.[23] As a consequence, it found itself intervening, as in Vietnam, to give support to local actors lacking an effective power base.

A rather more detailed account of the structural mechanisms which have precipitated American intervention has been given by Girling.[24] As he sees it, the United States has established a world-wide network of interlocking interests which are designed to promote American security and prosperity. As a consequence, the United States has developed entangling patron–client relationships with a large number of governments around the world. The problem is that there is no 'threshold' between involvement and intervention. Confronted by domestic instability in a client state, the United States has found itself enmeshed in the task of securing a client's survival.

According to Klare, however, American decision-makers found themselves severely constrained in their foreign policy options following the withdrawal from Vietnam. There emerged what Klare has called 'the Vietnam Syndrome' precipitated by the American public's disinclination to engage in further military intervention in internal Third World conflicts.[25] The Vietnam Syndrome came to be seen as a major liability by the late 1970s, when American decision-makers observed the growing capacity for intervention displayed by the Soviet Union. Critics of American foreign policy began to argue that the emergence of the 'human rights' policy in the United States was essentially designed to recreate the country's capacity to intervene by overcoming the internal and external opposition which had built up towards the American interventionary strategy.[26] But a senior State Department official put a rather different and less cynical gloss on this interpretation. He told the *Washington Post* how it had been debated whether the United States had the right to dictate the form of another country's government. It was concluded:

> that some rights are more fundamental than the right of nations to non-intervention, like the rights of individual people . . . There's a growing sense that people's rights include the right to determine their own form of government; that is, we don't have the right to subvert a democratic government, but we do have the right against an undemocratic one.[27]

Whichever view is accepted, however, it remains the case that the United States endeavoured from the late 1970s to improve its capacity to intervene effectively into local wars.

The literature which relates intervention to the structure of the international system focuses, therefore, on the pressures on certain states to engage in intervention. In the nineteenth century, Britain is seen to have engaged in interventionary action in order to maintain its informal empire. In the second half of the twentieth century, the United States is seen to have maintained an interventionary posture in order to preserve the capitalist world economy and prevent states from moving into the Soviet camp. By the same token, the Soviet Union is seen to have pursued a strategy of intervention in order to maintain its sphere of influence and to break the mould of capitalist encirclement.

But there is another body of literature which throws this theoretical perspective into question. Platt,[28] for example, insists that the actions of the British government during the nineteenth century fell a good deal short of energetic promotion and intervention in favour of British economic interests, as described by Gallagher and Robinson. He argues, for example, that the British government refused to become involved in the internal politics of the Latin American states, even if this meant sacrificing British trading and financial interests. Platt notes how non-intervention in the internal affairs of foreign states was one of the most respected principles of British diplomacy and he indicates that the interventionary role which the British government was expected to take in the defence of private business was accepted as being 'extraordinarily limited'.[29] Although it is true that Britain intervened more frequently during the nineteenth century than any other state, these events still prove to be the exception rather than the rule, when all the potential interventionary situations are taken into considerations.[30]

Tillema has made the same arguments in the context of United States intervention in the period after the Second World War.[31] He insists that it is not only necessary to explain why interventions take place, but also why non-intervention so frequently prevails. He examines the period 1946–71. During this period, there were only four occasions when the United States sent troops into domestic conflict. On the other hand, he identifies 139 potential interventionary situations where the United States did not intervene with troops. Tillema argues, therefore, that there must be some major restraints on intervention and that intervention can only occur when these restraints are absent. Critically, the intervention must not involve the possibility of engaging in conflict with the Soviet Union, or necessitate the use of nuclear weapons. At the same time, the President must be willing to override any objections from within his own ranks; there must be no alternative parties available which could take effective action; and there must be a request for assistance in response to intervention by another party. Tillema argues that intervention has only taken place when all these conditions have been satisfied.

In subsequent research Van Wingen and Tillema[32] have made comparative examinations of occasions in the period 1946–80 when troops from one state have intervened into another. They focus on Britain, the United States, the Soviet Union and France. There have been more than seventy occasions when troops have been used in this way. Britain, it transpires, has been responsible for more than half of these interventions. But it can be argued that virtually none of them violate the traditional principle of non-intervention. In subsequent research, they highlight the fact that the United Nations has endeavoured to delimit the cases where the breach to the principle of non-intervention can be justified. Prior to the Second World War, they argue that there were still six instances when intervention was deemed to be legitimate:

(1) in immediate defence of self from actual or imminent armed attack;
(2) in non-self-governing territories administered overseas;

(3)   by consent of the established government under treaty or by specific requests;
(4)   in proportionate reprisal from some illegal acts of others;
(5)   in some cases of hot pursuit;
(6)   under League of Nations sanctions.[33]

By inter-war standards, they argue, 70 of the 71 post-war interventions were legal. They suggest, therefore, that attempts by the United Nations to establish a more absolute principle of non-intervention have not been endorsed by state practice.

But this finding does not disturb the general proposition that there is a reluctance to intervene militarily in other states, and particularly into civil wars. The proposition needs to be qualified, however, when attention is paid to military activity short of sending troops. Duner, who has made a study of intervention in the 1970s, establishes a twelve-point scale of military involvement which ranges from the supply of troops down to the use of territory as a military sanctuary.[34] When military intervention is differentiated in this way, it becomes apparent that activities like supplying arms and providing military training are the dominant forms of intervention. Duner reveals, however, that there are clearly thresholds in military intervention, and the evidence does not suggest that the supply of arms gives rise to a commitment which induces higher levels of intervention. The findings also reveal that at every level of military intervention, the developing countries were much more heavily involved than the developed countries in civil wars around the world.

The empirical literature suggests that intervention is neither an accepted nor a recurrent feature of the international arena. Nevertheless, thinking about the virtues of non-intervention became more fluid in the Cold War era and a debate opened up among political actors in the international arena. While Third World countries were anxious to strengthen their boundaries against external intervention, the United States and the Soviet Union began to claim a right of intervention. Indeed, Franck and Weisband argued that it was possible to observe an 'echo effect' between the United States and the Soviet Union when the Johnson Doctrine was reformulated in terms of the Brezhnev Doctrine.[35] These two doctrines gave the superpowers extensive rights to intervene within their own immediate spheres of influence. But despite these doctrines, both the United States and the Soviet Union pursued relatively cautious interventionary policies.

It has been left to more traditional analysts to explore the nature and implications of the doctrines and perceptions of political actors. Behavioural researchers have tended to focus only on behavioural indicators.

Traditionalists acknowledge the need to examine the complex relationship between perception, doctrine and practice. The static, ahistorical conception of intervention employed by the behaviouralists is considered inadequate as a means of understanding interventionary activity. A theory of intervention, it is argued, must embrace the view of the world held by the political actors involved. But to encapsulate this view, it is also necessary to confront the normative issues at stake in any interventionary situation.

THE NORMATIVE DIMENSION

In recent years there has been an upsurge of interest by normative theorists in questions relating to intervention and non-intervention. This interest has emerged partly in response to the conflicting features of the international arena identified in the previous section. On the one hand, during the twentieth century there has been a growing conventional commitment to the principle of non-intervention, while, on the other, intervention has persisted as a characteristic feature of international relations. Normative theorists have been acutely conscious of both these features but their assessments of them have been very different. Two schools of thought have emerged. One is related to individual rights theory and the other to the theory of state sovereignty. The schools disagree, first, about the basis on which the principle of non-intervention should be established. For some theorists, the principle of non-intervention rests on the inherent right of states to lay claim to sovereignty and independence; others argue, however, that the principle must be grounded on the rights of individuals to self-determination. The controversy between these theorists, therefore, revolves around the question of whether rights in the international system inhere in individuals or states. The competing answers to this question lead, in the second place, to very different assessments of the interventions which have taken place. Although the two schools of thought acknowledge the need for a principle on non-intervention, they also recognize that the principle cannot be absolute. It is acknowledged that under some circumstances intervention can and must be justified. The potential must exist for interventions to take a legitimate form. But the two schools, of course, come to different conclusions about what constitute legitimate grounds for intervention. Those theorists who base the principle of non-intervention on the rights of states establish the grounds for intervention on a more restricted basis than do the theorists who base the principle on the rights of individuals.

This debate amongst normative theorists is not new: it draws upon a long history of thinking about intervention and non-intervention. But it is particularly pertinent at this time because the principle of non-intervention has come to be so universally acknowledged in the international arena. The study of non-intervention by Vincent[36] has proved to be particularly influential, therefore, because it provides one of the most comprehensive discussions of the way that thinking about non-intervention has developed. On the basis of Vincent's analysis, it is possible to trace the two contemporary normative approaches back to earlier thinking about the concept. Theorists still influenced by medieval ideas considered that the law of nations applied to individuals rather than states. The application of international law to states rather than individuals required a significant mental leap. It was in the writings of eighteenth-century thinkers like Wolff and Vattel that the normative consequences of treating the state as a sovereign institution first began to be worked out. Vincent shows how Wolff and Vattel came to recognise that states must observe a principle of non-intervention because acts of intervention necessarily violate the sovereignty of the state. These theorists reached this conclusion by establishing an analogy between individuals and states. They argued that because all individuals have a right to their independence, so, by analogy, all states have a similar right. Intervention was seen to be a violation of that right. On the basis of this formulation, Vattel identified an international legal framework which coordinated an international society composed of independent states 'closed in or sealed off from one another'.[37] By the end of the eighteenth century, therefore, international jurists had come to view the state as an autonomous entity with rights grounded in international law, just as individuals have rights which are grounded in municipal law. From this perspective, then, international law was only seen to regulate relations between states. It came to be accepted, almost by definition, according to Levitin, that a state's internal affairs must lie 'outside the purview of international law'.[38]

By the beginning of the nineteenth century, the virtues of non-intervention had also come to be regularly acknowledged by practitioners. Henry Brougham, a British Cabinet Minister, referred in 1826 to 'the salutary political maxim of not interfering in the internal concerns of other countries', adding that it was 'indispensable to the peace of the world and the general liberties of mankind that such a maxim should be acted upon as the rule of our foreign policy'.[39] The British led the way in propagating the principle of non-intervention. This became particularly clear after the Napoleonic Wars, when Britain found itself out of step with Austria, Prussia and Russia; those states wanted to establish a general right of intervention into any revolutionary situation. But the difference was not, in practice, categorical. As Castlereagh observed, 'no government can be more pre-

what constitutes a just cause. It was in response to the dwindling authority of the Church and the burgeoning power of the state that Wolff and Vattel recast the legal framework to embrace states rather than individuals.

There have been two rather different reasons given for abandoning the identification of international law with society conceived in terms of states. In both cases, however, the effect is to require either expunging or redefining the principle of non-intervention. In the first place, it has been suggested that we are living in a transnational and interdependent world where the idea of non-intervention has become redundant. Farer has suggested, for example, that the necessary conditions for sustaining the principle of non-intervention no longer apply. As he sees it, non-intervention can only serve as an appropriate norm for regulating relations between states in a world where there is genuine economic and political independence. No state in today's world possesses independence of this kind, he argues, with the result that the principle of non-intervention 'floats out of reach like some halcyon dream we attempt on awakening to recapture'.[44] But this argument is only appropriate when intervention is defined in economic or political terms. If it is associated with military activity, however, then the growth of interdependence has no effect on the identification of intervention as a distinctive category of behaviour.

The second reason which is put forward to justify reformulation of the principle of non-intervention is that it fails to take account of the increase in and growing concern about the violation of human rights. It is argued that in 1945 the principal preoccupation of the United Nations was to identify ways of outlawing the use of force. The importance attached to the principle of non-intervention can in large part be related to this desire. But the consequence of the blanket condemnation of the use of force, according to Levitin, is that there is no possibility of discriminating, on a normative basis, between divergent uses of force. As currently constituted, it is argued, there is no way of distinguishing between the Soviet use of force in their intervention in Czechoslovakia in 1968 or the Tanzanian intervention in Uganda in 1977, which removed Idi Amin. In the first case, the human rights of the citizens were clearly violated by the intervention, whereas in the latter case, the effect of the intervention was to promote the human rights of the citizens. From Levitin's perspective, therefore, the principle of non-intervention is becoming increasingly irrelevant. After the Second World War, he insists, the concern with war was legitimate. But today, the danger of world war has faded, while the large-scale violation of human rights has become a regular feature of world politics. Levitin wishes to see thinking about the principle of non-intervention revised, therefore, because he believes that if the international law is to be more relevant it must become 'more nearly congruent with its moral bases'.[45]

A similar line of argument has been made by Teson. However, he identifies a 'congenital tension' between the concern for human rights and the notion of state sovereignty. He sees these as two of the major pillars which support international law. Teson believes that the tension generates a major dilemma for everyone concerned about the normative dimensions of international relations, because if intervention is prescribed to promote human rights, then the door is opened to 'unpredictable and serious undermining of world order'. But if intervention is proscribed, even to curb violations of human rights, then the principle of non-intervention entails a 'morally intolerable position', whereby it becomes impossible to 'combat massacres, acts of genocide, mass murder and widespread torture'. To deal with this dilemma, Teson argues, it is necessary to reformulate our conception of international law.[46]

At the heart of Teson's argument is the assertion that it is only individuals who have rights. Sovereignty, therefore, does not constitute an inherent right of the state. He associates legal theories which endeavour to defend the autonomous moral standing of states and government with the Hegelian myth that states have inalienable rights. The legitimacy of the state can only be justified if it promotes the rights of all its citizens. If the state fails to perform this task, it loses its legitimacy and the protection afforded by the principle of non-intervention. Under these circumstances, other states are perfectly entitled to intervene in order to rectify the violations of human rights which have taken place. From one perspective, therefore, Teson is only wanting to open up another exception to the principle of non-intervention. However, from another perspective, he is endeavouring to reorient the established conception of international law, returning more to the position adopted by Grotius, whereby intervention is always permitted, provided that the cause is just. Teson is, in fact, building on the work of a growing body of theorists who have adopted an increasingly permissive attitude to the need for intervention[47] and who are unconcerned about the traditional justification underpinning the principle of non-intervention.

Teson is also contesting the views of theorists such as Walzer who accept that the legitimacy and sovereignty of states 'derives ultimately from the rights of individuals',[48] but who have drawn back from the open-ended consequences of this position. Walzer argues that there are few, if any, states which could claim that the rights of none of their citizens have been violated. Pressed to the extreme, non-intervention is rendered completely void by such a principle of just intervention. Walzer goes on to argue, therefore, that intervention can only be justified in extreme cases where massacre, genocide or enslavement are involved. But as Slater and Nardin have suggested, once Walzer has acknowledged the legitimacy of humanitarian intervention 'he can provide no plausible argument for drawing the line as restrictively as he does'.[49]

Slater and Nardin think that Walzer's critics are 'insufficiently sensitive to the considerations of national diversity, political prudence and international order'.[50] Their aim is to extend the boundary which morally justifies humanitarian intervention, while at the same time taking countenance of the restraints which underpin the principle of non-intervention. They begin by arguing that because circumstantial considerations vary from case to case, it is not possible to specify how substantial and systematic violations must be in order to justify external intervention. Nevertheless, from the moral perspective, for a very wide range of cases, 'intervention cannot be ruled out as a matter of principle'.[51]

To be morally justified, however, armed intervention must satisfy four conditions. First, less drastic remedies must already have been tried and failed; second, it must appear likely that the intervention will end the abuse of rights; third, the costs of the intervention must be proportional to the scale of the rights violations; and finally, the disruptive effects of the intervention on international stability must be minimal. It is argued that these conditions are only likely to be satisfied in a very limited number of cases. Slater and Nardin do not favour changing the established conventions prohibiting intervention in order to accommodate their view that intervention can be morally justifiable. They conclude, instead, that it is possible to hold that 'international law should not permit humanitarian intervention without being forced to conclude that such intervention is always without moral justification'.[52] In other words, intervention may be moral, on occasions, and yet remain illegal because the 'requirements of effective law and sound morals are not the same'.[53]

CONCLUSIONS

The distinction drawn in this chapter between empirical and normative analysis is a conventional one which derives from the epistemological position often referred to as positivism. Positivism presupposes that a line can be drawn between facts and values. A division of labour is thereby established between social scientists and moral philosophers who have the task of identifying principle which should guide behaviour in a civilised society. For positivism this division of labour is not simply a matter of academic convenience. It is argued that a failure to keep normative and empirical discourse in separate domains can only lead to a distorted understanding of both reality and morality. The social scientist has to rely on systematic observations to validate or invalidate claims about the world. Empirical investigation can be used, for example, to determine whether the rate of intervention is increasing or decreasing. Normative questions, on the other hand, involve metaphysical or deontological claims which are not amenable to empirical testing. A statement which rests on a normative claim can only be discussed on the basis of reasoned argument which is unaffected by observed facts. Empirical information, for example, cannot undermine the validity of the normative statement that one state does not have the right to violate the domestic jurisdiction of another. By the same token, the moral philosopher makes no claims about whether a moral course of action will promote the interests of a social actor. The two factors are seen to be unrelated. As Lackey has put it, there is a 'logical gulf between the demands of morality and the dictates of self-interest'.[54] Positivists assert, therefore, that there are two categories of truth. First, there is a deontological form of truth which is unaffected by activity in the real world, so that if a social actor fails to follow a moral injunction, the truth of the injunction is in no way affected. Second, there is an ontological form of truth: in this case, if social actors fail to conform to a predicted pattern of behaviour, then the truth of the prediction is immediately put in doubt.

The distinction outlined here between normative and empirical claims has been widely accepted by both social scientists and moral philosophers. It is often regarded as axiomatic that they are engaged in quite separate endeavours and that any attempt to conflate the two activities would be detrimental to both. Yet the social scientist and the moral philosopher are also seen to be standing apart from reality. They are both, in a sense, passive observers, who have no direct effect on the world they are examining.

This position has always been challenged by Marxists who have viewed positivism and the putative neutrality of social scientists and philosophers as part of a fiction of bourgeois ideology. Most social scientists, however, have accepted the basic tenets of positivism and they provide the basis of what Bernstein has called the mainstream approach to the analysis of social reality.[55] But these basic tenets of the mainstream position are coming under increasing and wider scrutiny. It is argued, for example, that underpinning a discipline such as social psychology has been a deep-seated and unrecognised ideological set of assumptions associated with individualism.[56] Major social theorists such as Giddens argue, therefore, that social scientists cannot assume that they are external and neutral observers; they must accept that they are part of the system they are describing.[57] Sayer has extended this line of argument and asserted that social scientists cannot give a complete explanation of the world they are describing without adopting an overtly moral stance. For example, he asserts that social scientists would be offering incomplete analyses and explanations of events in South Africa if they failed to explain why apartheid is based on a set of morally flawed premises.[58] Social scientists, therefore, are being encouraged to adopt a much more critical and reflexive posture.

Some moral philosophers are coming to a similar or at any rate related conclusion. It is, of course, still widely accepted that moral philosophers should adopt a deontological position. Lackey, for example, accepts that the task of the moral philosopher is to identify principles which are universal and are applicable across time and space and which provide a benchmark against which social activity can be measured. On this basis, it is possible for moral philosophers to tell the politician or the expert when they have violated a moral code. But if the politician asks what must be done 'the moral critic simply replies, "You must think of something else" '.[59] But a second school of thought is questioning this external and passive posture. Cohen argues that moral philosophers cannot work on the basis of these abstract and moral principles. There are now attempts being made to explore the consequences of any action before pronouncing on its moral status. Cohen argues that this new breed of moral philosopher is using the tools of the social scientist in the 'attempts to construe, predict, and assess these consequences'. He asserts that the aim is to 'narrow the apparent gulf between self-interest and morality and, thereby, to generate morally better policy options'.[60]

Most of the recent attempts to ensure that morality embraces ontology have occurred in the work of moral philosophers who have grappled with the paradoxes and dilemmas associated with nuclear deterrence. But it is clear in the work of analysts such as Slater and Nardin that there is a growing interest in developing this approach in the context of intervention and non-intervention. Central to the approach is the recognition that it is not possible to make absolute or abstract pronouncements about intervention and non-intervention. Any moral posture has to be formed in the light of the consequences of the policy adopted. Any assessment of the consequences of intervention and non-intervention must be premised by an understanding of what has happened in the past. Far from operating on different planes, as the positivists have traditionally alleged, social scientists and moral philosophers are locked in a complex and symbiotic relationship.

Notes

1. See, for example, the debate amongst historians on this issue. J. Brebner, 'Laissez-Faire and State Intervention in Nineteenth Century Britain' in 'The Tasks of Economic History', *Journal of Economic History, Supplement VIII* (1948) pp. 59–73; and A. J. Taylor, *Laissez-Faire and State Intervention in Nineteenth-Century Britain* (London, 1972).
2. E. Luard, 'Collective Intervention' in H. Bull (ed.), *Intervention in World Politics* (Oxford, 1984) p. 157.
3. H. Bull, 'Conclusion', ibid., p. 181.
4. A. Guelke, 'Force, Intervention and Internal Conflict' in F. S. Northedge (ed.), *The Use of Force in International Relations* (London, 1974) p. 122.
5. G. A. Raymond and C. W. Kegley, 'Long Cycles and Internationalized Civil War', *The Journal of Politics*, Vol. 49, (1987) pp. 481–99.
6. K. J. Holsti, *International Politics*, 2nd edn (Englewood Cliffs, NJ, 1972) p. 278.
7. M. Beloff, 'Reflections on Intervention' in *The Intellectual in Politics and Other Essays* (London, 1970) p. 225.
8. J. H. A. Quilter, 'Editor's Foreword', Special Issue on Intervention, *Journal of International Affairs*, Vol. 22 (1968) pp. ix–x.
9. U. Schwarz, *Confrontations and Intervention in the Modern World* (New York, 1970) p. 84.
10. S. Hoffmann, 'The Problem of Intervention', in H. Bull (ed.), *Intervention in World Politics* p. 7.
11. J. N. Rosenau, 'The Concept of Intervention', *Journal of International Affairs*, Vol. 22 (1966) p. 173.
12. C. Thomas, *New States, Sovereignty and Intervention* (Aldershot, 1985).
13. See Holsti, *International Politics*, p. 278–9; and Schwarz, *Confrontations and Intervention*, pp. 83–5.
14. R. Macfarlane, 'Intervention and Regional Security', *Adelphi Paper*, No. 196, 1985, p. 2.
15. F. S. Pearson, 'Geographic Proximity and Foreign Military Intervention', *Journal of Conflict Resolution*, Vol. 18 (1974) pp. 432–60. See also F. S. Pearson, 'Foreign Military Intervention and Domestic Disputes', *International Studies Quarterly*, Vol. 18 (1974) pp. 259–90.
16. J. Van Wingen and H. K. Tillema, 'British Military Intervention', *Journal of Peace Research*, Vol. 17 (1980) p. 291.
17. F. S. Pearson, 'Foreign Military Intervention and Domestic Disputes' and 'Geographic Proximity and Foreign Military Intervention'.
18. M. Small and J. D. Singer, *Resort to Arms: International and Civil Wars* (Beverley Hills, 1982).
19. M. A. Kaplan and N. de B. Katzanbach, *The Political Foundations of International Law* (New York, 1961).
20. See G. A. Raymond and C. W. Kegley, 'Long Cycles and Internationalized Civil War'.
21. J. Gallagher and R. Robinson, 'The Imperialism of Free Trade', *Economic History Review*, Vol. 6 (1953) pp. 1–15.
22. T. Smith, *The Pattern of Imperialism: The United States, Great Britain and the Late-industrializing World Since 1815* (Cambridge, 1981) p. 190.

23.   Ibid., pp. 174–5.
24.   J. L. S. Girling, *America and the Third World: Revolution and Intervention* (London, 1980).
25.   M. T. Klare, *Beyond the 'Vietnam Syndrome': U.S. Intervention in the 1980s* (Washington DC, 1981).
26.   J. Petras, 'U.S. Foreign Policy: The Revival of Interventionism', *Monthly Review*, (Feb. 1980) pp. 15–27. See also the introduction to R. Highway (ed.), *Intervention or Abstention: The Dilemma of American Foreign Policy* (Lexington, KY, 1975).
27.   L. Pratt, 'The Reagan Doctrine and the Third World', *Socialist Register* (1987) p. 82.
28.   D. C. M. Platt, 'The Imperialism of Free Trade: Some Reservations', *The Economic History Review*, Vol. 16 (1963) pp. 296–306; and D. C. M. Platt, *Finance, Trade and Politics in British Foreign Policy 1815–1914* (Oxford, 1963).
29.   D. C. M. Platt 'Further Objections to an Imperialism of Free Trade', *The Economic History Review*, Vol. 26 (1973) pp. 77–91.
30.   See R. Little, *Intervention: External Involvement in Civil Wars* (Oxford, 1975).
31.   H. K. Tillema, *Appeal to Force: American Military Intervention in the Era of Containment* (New York, 1973).
32.   J. Van Wingen and H. K. Tillema, 'British Military Intervention', *Journal of Peace Research*, pp. 291–303.
33.   H. K. Tillema and J. Van Wingen, 'Law and Power in Military Intervention: Major States After World War II', *International Studies Quarterly*, Vol. 26, No. 2 (1982) pp. 220–50.
34.   B. Duner, *Military Intervention in Civil Wars: The 19702* (Aldershot, 1985).
35.   T. M. Franck and E. Weisband, *World Politics: Verbal Strategy Among the Superpowers* (New York, 1971).
36.   R. J. Vincent, *Nonintervention and International Order* (Princeton, NJ, 1974).
37.   Quoted in A. Carty, *The Decay of International Law? A Reappraisal of the Limits of Legal Imagination in International Affairs* (Manchester, 1986) p. 89.
38.   M. J. Levitin, 'The Law of Force and the Force of Law: Grenada, The Falklands and Humanitarian Intervention', *Harvard International Law Journal*, Vol. 27, No. 2 (1986) p. 651.
39.   Quoted in R. Little, *Intervention: External Involvement in Civil Wars*, p. 25.
40.   D. L. Hafner, 'Castlereagh, the Balance of Power, and Non-Intervention', *The Australian Journal of Politics and History*, Vol. 26 (1980) p. 75.
41.   Ibid., p. 80.
42.   J. A. Perkins, 'The Right of Counter-intervention', *Georgia Journal of International and Comparative Law*, Vol. 17 (1987) pp. 171–227.
43.   Levitin, 'The Law of Force', p. 632.
44.   T. J. Farer, 'Harnessing Rogue Elephants: A Short Discourse on Foreign Intervention in Civil Strife', *Harvard Law Review*, Vol. 82 (1969) p. 532.
45.   Levitin, 'The Law of Force', p. 651.
46.   F. R. Teson, *Humanitarian Intervention: An Inquiry into Law and Morality* (London, 1987) pp. 3–4.
47.   See, for example, C. R. Beitz, 'Bounded Morality: Justice and the State in

World Politics', *International Organization*, Vol. 33 (1979) pp. 405–21; C. R. Beitz, 'Nonintervention and Communal Integrity', *Philosophy and Public Affairs*, Vol. 9 (1980) pp. 385-91; G. Doppelt, 'Walzer's Theory of Morality in International Relations', *Philosophy and Public Affairs*, Vol. 8 (1978) pp. 3–26; and D. Luban, 'Just War and Human Rights', *Philosophy and Public Affairs*, Vol. 9 (1980) pp. 160–81.

48. M. Walzer, *Just and Unjust Wars: A Moral Argument with Historical Illustrations* (New York, 1977) p. 53.
49. J. Slater and T. Nardin, 'Nonintervention and Human Rights', *Journal of Politics*, Vol. 48 (1986) p. 91.
50. Ibid., p. 87.
51. Ibid., p. 92.
52. Ibid., p. 95.
53. Ibid., p. 95.
54. D. P. Lackey, *Moral Principles and Nuclear Weapons* (Totowas, NS, 1984) p. xvii.
55. R. J. Bernstein, *The Restructuring of Social and Political Theory* (Oxford, 1976).
56. M. Billig, *Ideology and Social Psychology* (Oxford, 1982).
57. See, for example, A. Giddens, *Central Problems in Social Theory* (London, 1979).
58. A. Sayer, *Method in Social Science: A Realist Approach* (London, 1984).
59. D. P. Lackey, *Moral Principles and Nuclear Weapons*, p. 219.
60. A. Cohen, 'Lackey on Nuclear Deterrence: A Public Policy Critique or Applied Ethics Analysis?', *Ethics*, No. 97 (January 1987) p. 457.

3 Intervention and the Limits of International Law

Anthony Carty

This discussion of intervention begins with the adoption of a reductionist view of international law. This suggests that international law can be reduced to what international lawyers understand by international law and how they apply it as international lawyers looking at international relations. International lawyers, unlike municipal lawyers, are quite a diverse and mobile group of individuals on the international scene. They may be professors in universities, but they also act as counsellors before the International Court of Justice. These same professors may even serve on the International Court of Justice itself. This international legal community provides the recruiting pool for the foreign offices of many countries. These foreign offices then tend to rely upon what the professors in the universities say, and governments in turn draw upon this advice. This results in a kind of self-referencing discourse about the nature of international society. It is a form of discourse that has historical roots in obscure and arcane political theorising about international relations and in particular about the state.

It should be noted that this is not a view of the subject that most of the international legal community takes. Their view is that of legal positivism: international law is law, it is 'out there' and it consists of legal rules that have been enacted or formulated or set down by legally constituted authorities which are states. Sometimes these states act together in international organisations or in the form of treaty-making conventions. Most frequently they produce law through state practice and custom. Lawyers see themselves as describing 'the law'. They express their opinions about what is going on, but this only counts as secondary evidence. It has no basis in legal authority, which is the obsession of lawyers. Most of the time they are talking about what they have said about the subject and commenting on and criticising one another. But this discourse is not sufficiently related to the types of concrete situations which are my concern.

In the *Corfu Channel* case, the International Court of Justice denounced any pretended right to intervention in international law: whatever the defects in the organisation of international society, respect for the principle of territorial sovereignty was seen as one of the essential bases in international relations.[1] The principle has been equally forcefully stated in a General Assembly Declaration on the Principles of Friendly Relations Among States in 1970.[2] Indeed, it is stated in remarkably absolute terms, that no state has any right whatsoever to intervene in any way whatsoever in the affairs of other states. Yet it remains a well-known fact that interventions are a persistent feature of international relations. How is the jurist to react to this phenomenon?

Any response must question received ideas of law and not merely offer reasons for, or causes of, the illegality of state conduct. For instance, it is, in my view, incongruous to write as Noel does in his review of the issue that the explanation of the contradiction between law and practice escapes the scope of the law.[3] Noel identifies the problem of regional powers consistently seeking regional hegemony, to say the very least, but he leaves this fact in the air. He doubts whether many Latin American states are worthy of the name, given the extent to which they are economically and culturally penetrated by the United States. Yet he reaffirms the absolute nature of the duty of non-intervention as confirmed by contemporary international law in spite of the practice which he describes.[4] How has a conventional rule of law come into existence despite the admitted determination of superpowers to disregard it consistently, particularly as it applies so frequently to entities which are clearly already penetrated by powers greater than themselves?

The nature of the problems associated with this positivist legal discourse can be illustrated and highlighted by setting out and commenting critically upon the judgement of the International Court of Justice in the case of *Nicaragua* v *The US*.[5] The reason for focusing on this particular judgement is that the judges in this case actually came to grips with the question of the nature of intervention, that is, when it is legal and when it is illegal (which it nearly always is). They gave their views on these subjects in what appears to be a fairly orthodox presentation of the point of view of an international lawyer. Their position was almost unanimous and even the dissenting judgement of the American judge does not differ from the position adopted by the majority concerning the question of intervention. But the judgement is problematic in its reliance on the orthodox approaches to the subject of intervention and international law.[6]

The judgement was meant to be binding on the United States – it is not an advisory opinion, it is a categorical judgement against the United States. The opinion of the majority is to be found within Paragraphs 205 and 241 of the judgement. One of the essential findings of the judgement was that the United States, by training, arming, equipping, financing and supplying the Contra forces or otherwise encouraging, supporting and aiding military and para-military activities in and against Nicaragua, has acted against the Republic of Nicaragua in breach of its obligations under customary international law not to intervene in the affairs of another state.

There are questions put as to the motives for the US intervention and particularly whether it was solely to interdict Nicaraguan intervention in El Salvador. The majority treated two facts as being decisive: (1) that the United States gave assistance to the Contras; and (2) that the Contras in turn intended to overthrow the government of Nicaragua. These two essential facts, which the Court considered incontestable, were the basis for the judgement that this act of intervention had occurred, whether or not the United States's objectives were as far-reaching as those of the Contras. It did not matter whether the Contras intended to overthrow the government of Nicaragua or just to change its policies. The relevant principle of law is that intervention must bear on matters in which each state is permitted by the principle of state sovereignty to decide freely for itself, such as the choice of its political, economic, social and cultural system and the formulation of its foreign policy. The definition of intervention that the court relies on is contained in a General Assembly Resolution of 1970 on 'The Principles of Friendly Relations Among States'. This covers specifically support for 'subversive armed bands operating from the territory of one state against another'.

One of the reasons it is an interesting judgement is that the majority went on to consider whether there could be justifications for the intervention which would be legally compelling. The Court could not countenance providing aid to an opposition group, even if a request had been made. It went on to note:

> Indeed it is difficult to see what would remain of the principle of non-intervention in international law if the intervention already allowable at the request of the government of the state were also to be allowed at the request of the opposition. This would permit any state to intervene at any moment in the internal affairs of any other state.

The majority went on to consider at length the question of whether the support of the Contras could be justified by reference to the conduct of the government of Nicaragua towards its own people. It devotes ten important and highly contestable paragraphs to this issue. The starting point is that the matters raised in respect of the conduct of the government of Nicaragua towards its own people are normally within the domestic jurisdiction of a state provided it does not violate any obligation under international law. The Court says that 'every state possesses a fundamental right to choose and implement its own political, economic and social system'. A state could enter into a legal commitment to modify this right and so the question was whether or not Nicaragua had in the present context entered into an international legal commitment to modify the conduct of its own internal affairs.

The majority looked at the Charter of the Organisation of American States. Article 3 requires a 'political organisation based on the effective exercise of representative democracy', but the majority threw against this Article 12, which says that every state has the right to organise itself as it sees fit, and Article 16, which says that 'every state is allowed to develop its culture and economic and political life freely and naturally'. The Court then went on to consider the legal significance of a resolution of the OAS in 1979, 'The Plan to Secure Peace', whose acceptance by the Nicaraguan government had been communicated to the OAS. The resolution referred to the installation of a democratic government in Nicaragua, including the principal groups which were opposed to Somoza, 'a government which would reflect the free-will of all people', and a promise to call the first free election in Nicaragua. The Sandinista Government of Reconstruction accepted and ratified the proposals of the OAS. The question was whether this commitment by the Sandinistas to the Resolution of the OAS constituted a legal commitment with respect to its own population. The majority said that it could find nothing in this which amounted to a legal commitment: 'The 1979 Resolution stressed that the solutions to the problems of the Nicaraguans was a matter for the Nicaraguans themselves exclusively, while it was merely based on certain general considerations'. There follows a passage in the judgement indicative of the confusion of the ICJ and the international legal community about the problem of agency, or international legal personality. The Court opinion says:

> The Nicaraguan Junta of National Reconstruction planned the holding of free elections as part of its political programme of government following the recommendation of the 17th Meeting of Consultation of the Foreign Ministers of the OAS. This was an essentially political pledge made not only to the OAS but also to the people of Nicaragua who were intended to be its first beneficiaries. But the Court cannot find here a legal instrument with legal force, either unilateral or bilateral, whereby Nicaragua has committed itself in respect of the principle or the methods of holding elections.

The Court jumps from one characterisation of the legal personality to another without realising it is doing so. In a single paragraph it has moved from the Junta of Reconstruction, to the people of Nicaragua, to Nicaragua. That move takes place and it is fundamental but it is not recognised by the lawyers. The Court continues:

> In any case, if there was such a legal obligation, it would have been an obligation to the OAS and not towards the US. Even if the latter could look at the view of the OAS, it could not use methods which were not open to the latter and so it could not be authorised to use force. Of its nature, a commitment of this kind comes within a category that cannot justify the use of force.

They go on to consider the question of human rights in Nicaragua. They point out: 'It is alleged in the US Congressional finding that the Nicaraguan government has taken significant steps towards the establishment of a totalitarian Communist dictatorship'. The response of the majority of the Court here was categorical:

> However the regime in Nicaragua could be defined, adherence by a state to any particular doctrine does not constitute a violation of customary international law. To hold otherwise would be to make nonsense of the fundamental principle of state sovereignty on which the whole of international law rests. Consequently, Nicaragua's domestic policy options, even assuming that they correspond to the description given to them by the US Congressional finding, cannot justify on the legal plane the very actions the respondent complained of.

The Court considered the 1985 Congressional finding that Nicaragua had violated human rights and said that even if there was no Nicaragua commitments to the OAS it could not with impunity violate human rights in international law. Again the wording of the response of the Court is important:

> However, where human rights are protected by international conventions that protection takes the form of such arrangements for monitoring or ensuring respect for human rights as are provided for in the conventions themselves. The political pledge made by Nicaragua was made in the context of the OAS, the organs which were consequently entitled to monitor its observance. Nicaragua had ratified the American Convention of Human Rights and invited the Inter-American Commission on Human

Rights to visit Nicaragua. The OAS could have, if it wished, taken a decision on the basis of these rights.

Even if the US wished to form its own evaluations of the situation, use of force would not have been an appropriate method to monitor such respect of human rights. Again, the wording of the Court may be noted: 'With the regard to the steps actually taken, the protection of human rights as a strictly humanitarian objective cannot be compatible with the mining of ports, the training, arming and equipping of Contras'.

That is the position of the Court. I would now like to suggest some criticism of the majority reasoning. I think it is worth focusing on because it is a fairly representative statement of a virtually universally held view of international law among international lawyers.

It is difficult or maybe uncomfortable to attempt to deconstruct an argument when I very much prefer the conclusions that have actually been reached in the particular case. However, I would like to stress that the majority characterisation of the legal issues is bound up with a language of power. As a lawyer it is difficult if not impossible to go beyond this legal approach to the actual crisis surrounding Nicaragua.[7] My criticisms are more concerned to present the nature of the maze created by the legal language in this case than to give comfort to American positions which the majority rejected.

A linchpin of the Court's argument is that the principle of non-intervention is an integral part of customary international law. Now this is a hardly surprising conclusion. The Court could comfortably reaffirm the position which it had taken in the *Corfu Channel* case. Although the principle is not spelled out in the Charter of the United Nations, it is generally understood to be a corollary of the principle of the sovereign equality of states. However, the Court itself would recognise, if asked directly, that these assertions are not legally authoritative. The Court's own decision in the *Corfu Channel* case is merely secondary evidence of what is supposed to be the customary practice of states. It is not authoritative in itself, and logical deductions from abstract propositions such as 'the principle of non-intervention follows from the principle of sovereign equality' are not permissible in an empirically based legal positivism.

It is not surprising, and indeed it is encouraging, to find a full statement from the Court as to the orthodox method of deriving legal rules, such as those with respect to non-intervention. The Court reiterates that there are two elements of customary international law: legal conviction and actual practice. It states firmly: 'The mere fact that states declare the recognition of certain rules is not sufficient for the Court to consider these as being part of customary international law and applicable as such to those states'. Bound as it is by Article 38 of its Statute to apply international custom as evidence of the general practice accepted by law, the Court may not disregard the general role played by practice. The litmus test is whether this apparently empirical approach will allow practice or the real world or those outside the international legal community to speak up and disrupt a dominant discourse. The language that the Court applies is quite clear in this respect. The Court assumes that the rule which it is investigating, such as the rule of non-intervention, actually exists already. The Court finds itself thoroughly entangled in this academic or doctrinal debate: can states have a legal conviction that they are bound by a rule as foundation for a practice, which practice is itself regarded as creative of the source of the rule? This is a fundamental conundrum for international lawyers when talking about the nature of customary international law.

The explanation is that a practice is only allowed to confirm an established discourse. In the passage of the judgement which follows there is inevitably a play on the word rule, as the Court, in a fairly academic judgement, first sets out how rules of customary law are to be found. The Court says:

> In order to deduce the existence of customary rules, the Court deems it sufficient that the conduct of states should, in general, be consistent with such rules and that instances of states' conduct inconsistent with the given rule should generally have been treated as breaches of that rule, not as an indication of a new rule.

In exactly the same vein, the Court confirms the existence of a customary rule of law against intervention. The Court accepts that it must assess whether the practice is sufficiently in conformity with state declarations for it to matter to customary international law. The following passage of the Court's judgement, attempting to cope with this question of intervention, needs to be quoted at length.

> The Court has to consider whether there might be indications of a practice illustrative of a belief in a kind of general right of states to intervene in support of an internal opposition in another state whose cause appears particularly worthy by reason of the political and moral values with which it was identified. For such a general right to come into existence would involve a fundamental modification of the customary principle of non-intervention. The significance for the Court of cases of state conduct *prima facie* inconsistent with the principle of non-

intervention lies in the nature of the grounds offered as justification. The United States authorities have on occasions clearly stated their grounds for intervening in the affairs of a foreign state for reasons connected with, for example, the domestic policies of that country, its ideology, the level of its armament or the direction of its foreign policy. But these were statements of international policy and not an assertion of rules of existing international law. In this case the United States has not claimed that its intervention, which is justified in this way at the political level, was also justified on the legal level where it has used legal arguments to justify its intervention solely by reference to classical rules of collective self-defence against armed attack.

In my view, the interpretation of the Court is correct up to a point. States are unwilling to give formal, principled or coherent declarations in favour of intervention. Yet in this case, the Court has very clearly confined itself to an idea of customary international law which consists solely of such declarations, despite the fact that no substance is thereby given to the practice element of custom, which the Court itself admits that it should be trying to bring to light. Its approach is that favoured predominantly by Third World states which treat UN Declarations as statements of the legal conscience of humankind. It might easily be said that the court ignores the two obvious alternatives of legal intention and legal custom which derive from Western concepts of jurisprudence. The first notion may well be attached to any conduct which is serious in its implications and refers to a matter normally regulated by law. For example, if a state is actually providing material and military support for an intervention in another country, what it says about this action is not as important as the fact that it is acting in violation of what one might have thought to have been a rule. One must interpret that as having some legal significance. Second, the notion of custom itself has usually been understood to mean that law within an uninstitutionalised society, such as international society, should arise out of the actual conduct of the members of that society rather than merely form their declarations. In some cases the conduct may be taken to have no legal significance. However, that one should begin and end with quasi-institutional state declarations as to the law means definitely abandoning any attempt to grapple with practice as such.

I would maintain that the Court is giving exclusive prominence to the expressed wishes of those entrenched in positions of power. The Court's interpretation ignores the true character of customary international law which is to reflect the non-institutionalised character of international society. The latter notion means simply that the existing state and governmental system was not put in place by the law, at least not in any positivist sense. Given the essentially anarchic nature of international society, a concept of law for such a system should allow reflection upon the actual experience generated by the system. Yet the Court cannot undertake such an invest-igation without going beyond the official declarations of established state authorities and looking into the dynamics of the people actually involved. As the Court itself puts it: 'It has no authority to ascribe to states legal views which they do not themselves advance. It will not try to interpret the conduct of the United States in any other terms other than those put out in its legal declarations'.

The Court inevitably starts with a right not to be subject to intervention with respect to the internal affairs of a state. Turning to the commitments that the Sandinistas may have made to their people or to the OAS, for example, we can again quote the Court:

> The question as to whether the Nicaraguan government is said to have entered into a commitment is a question of domestic policy. A state's domestic policy falls within its exclusive jurisdiction provided of course that it does not violate any obligation of international law. A state which is free to decide upon the principle and method of popular consultation within its domestic order is sovereign for the purposes of accepting a limitation of its sovereignty in this respect. This is a conceivable situ-ation for a state which is bound by institutional links to a confederation of states or indeed to an international organisation. But within that context or framework, Nicaragua clearly has not, in the Court's view, accepted any legal limitation to its sovereignty.

The Court's examination of the possible legal nature of the commitment to hold free elections simply conflates the Nicaraguan *junta* with the state of Nicaragua. The people are somehow simply separate, intended to be the beneficiaries of a purely political and therefore non-binding commitment to hold free elections. In other words, the state is not the population, it is not to be equated with government. The Court takes no cognisance of the manner in which the Sandinista regime came into existence or the character of its present relationship with the people in the country. The nature of the historical association of the US with the previous regime and its relations with the Contras are simply not matters to be investigated. The Court takes as given the abstract international legal order: Nicaragua exists and the question of what Nicaragua *is* does not arise. There is no possibility that law could grow out of or be a response to a concrete situation. It might seem just as well for Nicaragua that the Court took this approach.

However, the question still remains – not least for the lawyer – who or what is Nicaragua? It is the Court's treatment of this aspect of the case which can be used to explain its whole approach to the law as custom. The Court simply adopts the quite unfactual theory of an international legal system as a hierarchy of competencies with the state somehow given and in possession of an unlimited series of competencies which it may however choose to modify in the light of an international legal space or regime.

In my view, there is no way that state practice or a system such as international law can have produced this notion so deeply embedded in the language of international legal discourse. Rather, it is the case that the discourse of international law shares its historical origin with the development of political thought. This is an epistemological point. From it derives the development of a formalist concept of the state as autonomous from its social, political and economic contexts. Although this view is usually attributed to Hegel, Hobbes is also considered responsible for the conception of a sovereign which is somehow distinct from both the governed and the governors. In this view Hobbes is opposed to Locke, who distinguished the sovereign from the governors but not from the governed. This explains more than anything else the ferocity with which so much of the American international legal community rejects the judgement of the ICJ and is rather indifferent to the fact that the Regean administration chose to defy it. One of the most illuminating American appraisals of the Court's judgement, in *The American Journal of International Law*, is by Fernand Teson. He links what he calls the Hegelian myth embedded in international law with the 'true Lockean basis for governmental legitimacy':

The Court supposes that states are somehow moral agents just as individuals. The notion of autonomy is a human quality which cannot be applied to the concept of the state. Only persons can pursue rational ends but states are not persons and although governments are made of persons their moral rights *qua* governments are not grounded in any mystical quality of the state as Hegel and the Court thought, but in the consent of their subject. Thus the assertion of a fundamental right of the state to choose its political system is no more than a defence of the legitimacy of any use of political power. The transmutation of words has now become the rationalisation of oppression. The 'freedom', 'independence', 'sovereignty', 'equality', 'liberty' of the state means carte blanche for tyrants to exercise arbitrary power and deny individual freedom, that is freedom in its original sense.[8]

The international legal community has committed itself almost unanimously to a particularly Hegelian conception of the state. It is around the validity of this preference that the real intellectual battle appears to rage.

Notes

1. *Corfu Channel* case, ICJ Reports (1949) p. 35.
2. GA Res. 21311, 20 UNOR (1965); and GA Res. 2625, 25 UNOR (1970).
3. 'Cette discordance entre la *réalité* et le droit ne peut s'expliquer que si l'on se place sur le terrain politique'. J. Noel, *Le principe de non-intervention: théorie et pratique dans les relations interaméricaines* (Paris, 1981) pp. 221–2.
4. Ibid., p. 219.
5. ICJ Reports (1986) p. 1.
6. Restriction of space means that I am unable to discuss the mostly hostile reactions to the judgement by American international lawyers which were published as a hefty collection of papers in *The American Journal of International Law*, Vol. 81, No. 1 1987).
7. This is supposing that there is a single trustworthy way of characterising the situation. For a discussion of this, see the chapter by N. J. Rengger in this volume.
8. F. R. Teson, 'Le People, C'est Moi! The World Court and Human Rights', *The American Journal of International Law*, Vol. 81, No. 1 (1987) pp. 173–83.

4 Intervention, Non-Intervention and the Construction of the State

Cornelia Navari

Why are we bothered by intervention? What kind of.a problem is intervention? Intervention involves altering the balance of power in a state. In order to differentiate intervention from a constant process of influence we need to develop a theory of intervention which distinguishes alteration from mere influence. Such a theory would demonstrate the various ways in which such alterations may be achieved and the conditions under which they are likely to occur. This is a process of building middle-range theories of international relations. But intervention also raises questions of a first-order kind which entail something more than middle-range theories.

THE STATE AS POLITICAL SPACE

The intervention question may be posed as the responsibility of outsiders to insiders. The status of outsiders and insiders is affected by the way that political action is justified. There are various ways to justify political action. An anthropologist might say that individuals have a limited altruism outside of an approximate social group. Alternatively, a political scientist might argue that the power of a state is (functionally) needed to implement decisions on the distribution of resources, and that citizens should act through state agencies. Others, such as Marxists or anarchists, might argue against this and say that the state is an inappropriate framework for achieving justice and that the state needs to be transcended. Each of these justifications give rise to assignments of responsibility, justifies action and names certain social groups or agents as appropriate actors. Each also gives rise to a definition of a relevant political space. Implicit in the very idea of intervention is an outsider's entrance into a political space.

Traditionally, what demarcates the internal and the external space, and differentiates insiders from outsiders, is the concept of the state. Certain obligations are deemed to fall on citizens that are not relevant for non-citizens, and it is agents authorised by the state that are usually considered 'intervenors'. It is for this reason that, for most people, the state is a matter of moral necessity: it necessarily imposes obligations of certain sorts on its citizenry, and others. This involves certain assumptions about the purposes and functions of states. It is also, and very importantly, a set of practical arrangements which provide for actual living space. One of the reasons we are concerned about intervention is the external disruption to the real circumstances within which we live and the way we organise our activities.

The state is more than a practical or moral necessity, however. It is also an arena of moral choice and has been put forward as the most important setting for ethical life. It is not the only possible such arena: other possible candidates are the family, the church or even the international community. But at the heart of the ethics of intervention is the ethical status of the state. Indeed, the two are logical correlates: intervention only becomes a moral problem if we assume that the state is an arena, indeed *the* arena, of moral choice. Conventional international relations theory makes just such an assumption, as does a good deal of political theory. Such an assumption is scarcely unchallengeable, however, and whether it is warranted is one of the most pertinent questions we might ask about intervention.

At the heart of our thinking about intervention, therefore, is the problem of the state: what is a state and what is a state for? These are the fundamental questions that should constantly be addressed when considering intervention. In addressing these questions, political theory offers several major accounts of the state as an ethical order. Alternatively, the legalist paradigm offers a view of international society with a more low-level but extremely user-friendly concept of states as legal agents. Legalism, realism, cosmopolitanism and post-realism all have preferred models of the state. Indeed, these schools of thought in international relations largely define themselves by the way that they draw upon accounts of the state. Accordingly, each school may be judged by the ability of its chosen model to make sense of the question of intervention. On this basis, we may possibly identify new modes of explanation; we may also prefer certain developments in explanation to others.

MORAL NECESSITY v. MORAL CHOICE

The state is a moral arena, political theory tells us. To disrupt such a realm involves the possibility that a meaningful ethical life cannot be lived. Not just any set of political arrangements qualifies, however, as a true moral realm. Nor is any state proof against intervention on account of its ethical status. There have to be certain requisites present in order for the realm to be achieved. Our perception of the ethics of intervention will thus depend on what is required to produce the moral realm. Political theory tries to provide a check-list against which we can measure actual political arrangements. The problem is that the form of the state as an arena for moral choice has always been undergoing change.

The development of the idea of the state in the western political tradition reveals a movement from a fundamental Christian foundation towards a secularised, bureaucratic machine that now serves its own interests. In broad terms, Hobbes provided certain of the key moves, Locke another set, Hegel yet a third.[1] Weber added the insight of the pre-Weberian state. The result is a variety of perspectives on what the state has to look like in order to provide a moral realm.

For Hobbes, morality without the state was impossible because, he argued, obligations in an unlegalised social condition could not be maintained. Indeed, he held that no recognisable social order could exist without the state. Hence, it is often held, the mere existence of a state is sufficient to guarantee the moral realm. But Hobbes also had a rather strict definition of the state, centring on a particular notion of sovereignty. For Hobbes, the sovereign or legal power had to be located in a sovereign person or body which held all of the law-making right, and which had the power to impose its laws. It was only under such conditions that peace could be achieved, obligations maintained and promises kept. The mark of the good state was, therefore, coherent government and a 'legally perfect' administrative system.

Citizens have certain rights in this account, notably the right to judge whether the sovereign is maintaining public peace, and whether it is possible to 'treat others as one would like to be treated'. Equally, however, they are dissuaded from making any too-hasty judgements (unless another sovereign is waiting in the wings to quickly re-establish domestic order). The moral state was, thus, not only the orderly, unified state but one whose citizens recognised its necessity. It was the disruption of the sort of state which entailed moral risk.

For Locke, of course, 'society' exists. He argued that a natural order pre-existed the state. This was a complex natural order, of families, corporations, judgements and executions. This is a pluralistic society in which the state exists to service naturally emerging requirements on the part of a number of diverse individuals and groups, rather as if citizens were clients. According to Locke, natural society did a good many things for itself, and indeed should be allowed to do so; the state was founded to deal only with the 'inconvenience' ensuing from a variety of social impulses. Hence, the proper state was the limited state. By this account, the good state is one with responsive rather than self-serving government. The primary feature of a moral social order is not merely, or even primarily, coherent government, but a responsive political process which limits itself to responding to individual and group definitions of need. In the Lockean view, in direct contrast to Hobbes, a state which tries for more may be worse than no state at all.

For Hegel, on the other hand, the client state invaded by individual interests was invidious. He held that there was no such thing as 'society' in the Lockean sense; there were only particular societies in which particular norms, beliefs and traditions held sway. The society of states was hence a society of discrete culture groups. As for Locke's 'civil society', that was a particular historical culture, recently developed, which allowed individual needs and wants to be satisfied. But it was the state which provided the conditions of a corporate existence that could transcend the potential selfishness of mere need and want. According to Hegel, the transcendent was always located in the particular. Unlike Locke, the ethical community was seen as one in which particular groups put their needs aside, where they made sacrifices. The culture group underlay the state, in that it formed a potential community, but it was in establishing the legal order of the state that people evoked their willingness to make sacrifices for the community to which they belonged; that they were prepared, indeed, to create a real ethical community. Hence, the state assumes a moral meaning: it is a realm of willing a greater good. But only in particularity. For Hegel, the good state was akin to the nation-state, the state that served the collective will of a specific community.

The Weberian contribution centred on a materialist concept of scientific reason, accompanied by a Nietzschean scepticism of the basis of knowledge. Weber saw science as providing the only fully legitimate, and hence moral, basis of political action, because it was the only legitimate basis for knowledge. Everything else – natural law, community, religion – was so much superstition. Nor, in consequence, could the (Hegelian) cultural community provide for the rational ends of the state. Accordingly his state took form: the proper state was that with a rational, knowing, technocratically oriented bureaucracy which served the state's purposes – the purposes of a collective organisation of multiple needs and definitions, comprehended rationally. This essentially western cultural product was counterposed to the 'irrational' state. 'Pre-Weberian' states serve pre-articulated prejudices, outmoded religions, superstition and prejudice. Only Weber's rational state is the good state.[2]

DISRUPTING THE MORAL REALM

Intervention is an interference which disrupts the established moral realm. However, the various ethical propositions identify disruption somewhat differently, and provide distinctive justifications for its avoidance. By Hobbesian categories, for example, intervention consists in encouraging dissension or civil war, and this is heinous because, in disrupting its order, one is threatening a return to a state of nature in which no real morality is possible at all. For Locke, however, the good state is akin to the model of the liberal-democratic state. In this view, interfering disrupts the correct messages from getting through, messages from an assemblage of free individuals and associations. In the Hegelian view, the state must not be interfered with because such interference disrupts the expressive moral acts on the part of a morally constituted community.

Accordingly, political theorists deliver a variety of injunctions to behaviour of both a positive and negative sort. But if we expect political theory to deliver authoritative injunctions against intervention in any circumstances, we will be disappointed. On the one hand, the notion of the state as an ethical order prohibits intervention. On the other, the notion that the state may be the only ethical order available legitimises, indeed requires action to preserve or reinstate it. The debate over boycotts against South Africa draws moral force from both of these injunctions.

At issue is the definition of a 'bad' intervention; what is 'bad' differs, in some instances radically. For Hobbes, any intervention is bad because it challenges the absolute authority of a Leviathan. Any action which encourages the division of the sovereign power or which is directed against the machinery of the state is wrong. In Locke, however, this is not necessarily a bad thing. Here, 'bad' intervention is distinguished from normal intervention, which is conceived of as a new, legitimate category called 'influence'. For the most part, in liberal theory, intervention as influence is a naturally occurring phenomenon, a construct of a multiplicity of needs and judgements, many of which will quite legitimately come from 'outside' the state, and will be criticising the state. State agencies are licensed to sort out such complaints (indeed, that is their job), not to protest against them. Intervention, in the Lockean account, is the kind of interference which prevents the political process from being responsive. In Hegel's account, wrong action differs again: it is that which prevents such a self-determining legal process from emerging, as in an imperial suppression of a nationalist movement, or which interferes with a particular community's constitutional prerogative, such as in preventing a community from throwing off a monarchy and establishing a republic.

These diverse theories also legitimise different sorts of agency. In the Hobbesian construction of political space, outsiders and insiders are distinguished legally; intervenors are who the governments says they are. And there is a no serious moral distinction to be made between insiders and outsiders except perhaps for the distinction between traitors and spies. Unity is either there or not there; to encourage disunity is woeful in any case and merits the same treatment. Once the division has occurred, however, intervention ceases to exist, even as a legal category, and 'outsiders' are legally, morally, as well as necessarily, free to support whom they will. The only injunction upon them, and it is a logical injunction upon everyone, is to direct their behaviour to encouraging the re-establishment of a sovereign power as soon as possible. Locke, on the contrary, distinguishes agency by purpose. When a problem of mutual social concern arises, from whatever source, then 'outsiders' become insiders. They become part of the concerned public on whose behalf state arrangements exist. Intervenors are those from outside who prevent responsiveness. In Hegel's view, however, it is always a particular people – Nigerian, or Israelis, or Palestinians for example – which develops through struggle with itself (or others), through myths and stories, and ultimately sacrifices, and the state is the framework of a specific people's struggle and the evidence of its sacrifice, its ethical life. Such a community is, by definition, self-serving. Hence, ultimately, there is a cultural determination of outsiders and insiders.

Hobbes's categories are powerful ones and fit with certain of our intuitions. In the Lebanon, for example, where the sovereign power has vanished, intervention seems difficult to identify. And we would certainly share his belief that it is better to move toward the reconstruction of this state as soon as possible, almost irrespective of who wins. However, not everyone has been satisfied with Hobbes's injunction that judgement is the prerogative of the sovereign alone, or that this receipt for moral order is the best that is possible. Moreover, in a particular sense, the presence or absence of unity does not fit with many circumstances in the modern world. At what point can we say that the sovereign power has ceased to exist and at what point do we pass from the morally heinous to the morally neutral?

Locke's categories seem to fit better with a good deal of activity which characterises actual politics, as well as international relations. The actions of others may be the subject of legitimate concern within our political space, and foreigners can have claims if their innocent collective and individual goings-on are adversely affected. Also, every claim made upon the state, either ours or someone else's, is not to be interpreted as encouraging civil war or dangerous dissidence. And where 'unity' seems a difficult concept to define and hence protect, responsiveness seems more capable of being identified and judged. The problem with the Lockean, liberal view arises in attempts to prioritise the multiplicity of claims that are being made upon the state. Does one do as well to serve foreigners as one's own citizens? To what community, precisely, is the Lockean state to be responsive? Locke gives us no clear criteria for evaluating a mass of claims emanating from outside a given order. And there are difficulties with prioritising claims within given orders.

Hegel's view expresses perhaps our most widespread understanding of why intervention is such a bad thing. Simply put, intervention prevents self-determination on the part of the political community, which is the only 'place' self-determination can be achieved. (We must be sure, of course, that self-determination is what is being pursued.) Hegel's view contains a sociological and historical understanding as well as an ethical perspective. We know that consciousness develops, we know that it has a communal basis, and that 'peoples' are created out of historical processes of evolution. But evolution also ensures few neat 'natural' lines around cultures. Inevitably, more than one actual and potential culture will always occupy a political space. There is also Hegel's unilinear notion of progress. He was sure that things would get better, whereas part of our historical understanding is that we know they can get worse. As such, we cannot trust cultural evolution in the way Hegel seemed to, or suppose that all cultures are engaged in ultimately beneficent movements forward.

It would be tempting to see such a body of thought as potentially unifying, delivering a multiplicity of authoritative judgements. Certainly, in so far as our ideas on intervention are profoundly influenced by, if not derived from these ideas, they are delivering judgements of a sort. We could, perhaps, treat them as different instances of intervention and pick and mix accordingly. Such a method has its limits, however. Weber's pre-rational bureaucracies might need to be sorted out, particularly if, in Lockean terms, they are seriously hampering political responsiveness. However, Hegel suggests that long historical processes may be required for a community to develop 'reason', so to suppress them may prejudice our own moral orders.

Political and moral theory leads to a deeper understanding of the questions regarding intervention and the state, but it provides no fixed point for authoritative judgements. This has prompted international relations to employ quite different notions of the state.

THE LEGALIST CONSTRUCT OF THE STATE AND INTERVENTION

The discourse of international relations has evaded some of the problems of ethical theory by employment of the legalist paradigm. This model assumes that the state has, *sui generis*, a moral personality located in and expressed by an internationally endorsed sovereign power. This is a moral personality in the sense that it carries out duties and enjoys consequent rights, like signing treaties and enforcing the rules of GATT. In this legalist interpretation, all states operate on the assumption that all other states are such personalities. They are all sovereign, independent agents capable of directing action so endorsed. Even if they are not, they have to act 'as if' they were. The existence of a number of such independent responsive agents with duties and rights then becomes the basis for the provision of an international order, which is justified because it protects such right-and-duty fulfilling agents. As the legal order changes, moreover, new duties and injunctions are entered into; and this is deemed a coherent legal system because duties and injunction ultimately arise from the legal agents of the state which are the empowered legal agents of the system.

The 'cardinal rule' of such an order is the independence and primacy of the territorial integrity of the state. Otherwise it could not fulfil its legal obligations. This rule provides both for the legalist definition of intervention and the justifications for its avoidance: interfering with territorial sovereignty and the undercutting of international order. The 'cardinal rule' is also held to provide the basis for an international legal norm of non-intervention, and justifications for both a universal and an individual injunction. For any independent state, intervention on its own part is to be avoided because of the precedent which is created. Equally, any act of intervention threatens the independence of a state, which threatens the independence of all states and, therefore, all governments have a general interest in opposing all interventions for the sake of international order.

This approach is very persuasive up to the limits of its explanatory application. States in international law are legal corporations and the international order is certainly based on their being endowed collectively with a capability for legal acts. They must also be free to carry out these acts for the system to work.[3] This certainly entails inhibitions on their behaviour towards one another, as a matter of fact as well as principle, and part of that sense of inhibition is well expressed by the legalist paradigm. State agencies are concerned with precedents in many of their approaches to international law and many of their refusals to sanction others' intervention arises from concern with their own sovereignty in potential future circumstances. Moreover, international law certainly does absorb changing ideas which it converts into injunctions.

One problem with it, however, is that the international legal order does not develop in a coherent way. It contains numerous diverse criteria, incorporated over time, not least of all concerning the state itself. In international law, the state is among other things a mechanistic order-keeper, the expression of a collective will and the body responsible for satisfying rights: separate parts of international law have separate means of addressing each of these aspects of the state. Thus the state is enjoined to maintain order but also to protect human rights; to avoid intervention but to speak for its citizens; to protect human dignity but avoid intervention.

Such diverse criteria clearly affect this order's perception of when and in what respect intervention becomes problematic. If the state is seen as the mechanistic order-keeper, for example, intervention becomes a problem only to the extent that it disturbs the mechanistic balance-of-power order. If the state is an expression of collective will, however, then intervention itself starts to become problematic. Yet a further order of difficulty arises if the state transgresses rights when it is meant to provide for the realisation of rights: this injunction positively invites intervention.

The standard reply might be that international law, like all law, changes due to a variety of influences. However, its modification does not occur in the same manner as domestic law. For example, one device for sorting out conflicts of law in the domestic order is the general principle that the later law takes precedence over the earlier interpretation. But such a legal principle is scarcely achievable in the unconstitutionalised context which is international relations. Moreover, the international legal order cannot provide the basis for attributing competencies to states and legitimising setting them up anew. Hence, it does not develop in such a way as to solve the problems of intervention in the way that we require.

In addition, if we look at state practice we would rightly wonder about the status of the implied norm of non-intervention: states are constantly intervening in one another's affairs along the whole range of the definitional criteria so far mentioned. Raymond Cohen's argument concerning the 'drama of diplomacy and the diplomacy of drama' may well be relevant for the norm of non-intervention. He characterises some diplomatic exchange as a form of 'ritualised noise' which goes on in certain situations and may result in point-scoring, but that has little meaning at all outside of the very particular institutional culture in which it occurs.[4] In the case of non-intervention, that institutional culture is the United Nations. But such ritualised noise can scarcely be used to deliver any authoritative normative or legal injunctions.

The conclusion to be drawn is that the international legalist paradigm is of little help in sorting out the problems of intervention. Its 'as if' reasoning – treating international law as if it were a form of domestic law and less-than-sovereign entities 'as if' they were fully sovereign states – serves only to conceal the point that they are not those things. This form of reasoning cannot deal with the normative, legal and moral problems created by a variety of bodies operating together in a uninstitutionalised context. More-over, such reasoning is incapable of developing greater subtlety in respect of the real circumstances of international politics.

THE REALIST STATE IN AN ANARCHICAL WORLD

Realism provides another discourse for the interpretation and generation of ethical rules regarding intervention. Realism, of course, asserts the primacy of the power-state. But it arrives at its defence of the power-state, and its insistence on realism, through an ethical doctrine. Indeed, it is an ethical discourse which asserts the ethical primacy of the power-state. Realists argue that the essential purpose of political action is the preservation of the good state. Hans Morgenthau, like Hegel, argued that ethics is a cultural phenomenon, protected by the state. The only way to stop the marginalisation of ethics is to try to preserve the goodness within one's own state. But, because the international system includes bad states, power must be used for self-preservation. Thus does 'power defined as interests' become the goal of every 'proper' state.

As Machiavelli has demonstrated, there is also a morality in the employ-ment of power, a prudential morality, perhaps, but one entailing important criteria of right action. Power must be used in certain ways. The Prince must aim for limited and achievable ends; suitable means should be available, as should the means to monitor and control initiated action, or provide for orderly withdrawal if the enterprise becomes too costly. The Prince can never control all the consequences of actions, but is enjoined to try to predict as accurately as possible the probable consequences of behaviour. A virtuous Prince, once committed, is responsible, ahead of time, for unfore-seen events, however unfortunate. Realism thus requires a disciplined bal-ancing of practical and prudential considerations.

Moreover, in engaging in the realist mode of thought, one is not simply defining, or choosing among, interests in a random way. It is not the case that *any* definition of a state's interests will do. Discipline in the use of force leads necessarily to a disciplined consideration of the proper ends of action. Also, realist thought forces us to ask whether a declared end really does serve the interests of the state. Concern with goals is central to realist thought. The analyst must define the goal of action in order to understand why the state behaves as it does; and realist thought requires those who engage in it to identify clearly the goals which are present in any enterprise – whether the enhancement of the power of the Prince, the general good, or some sectoral interest – since it is only through the definition of the goal that sense can be made of action. This inevitably leads realists into constant discussion of the appropriateness of goals as those goals relate to the state's wider purposes.

Realist thought also has the advantage of a coherent and powerful analytic method in the form of rational choice theory, a theory which can both deal with disputed ends and account for behaviour. The central element of rational choice theory (and modern realist thinking is a form of rational choice theory) is the determination of goals, in particular how people change and redefine their goals. This is placed within the theory of rational behaviour and marginal incrementalism. According to this theory, most people generally have multiplied goals which they must choose between. That goals are disputed does not matter; indeed, they are important because they are disputed. What then becomes interesting is how priorities and goals change, which is related to the gaining of advantage in changing circumstances. In this way, rational choice theory provides a powerful analytic mode of comprehension of behaviour, as well as criteria for calculating its appropriateness.

That realist thinking can be used both to describe what people are doing and as a guide to what they *ought* to be doing is its major strength. It is also, however, the most potent source of its weakness. It tempts the realist into creating pseudo-worlds of 'oughts' which are portrayed as existent worlds. And realists are constantly falling into the trap. They set up rules of prudence, they describe the world as one in which states are pursuing national interests, and then they are constantly discovering states that are getting their national interest wrong or not even pursuing that sort of interest at all. The Prince must never believe his own jargon; that is consistent with the realist view. It is also consistent with the realist view that Princes are prone to go astray. It is therefore incumbent on the realist to define what it is that Princes are actually doing. But this mode of analysis already tells us what the Prince is 'actually doing'. In fact, realism is a guide to action. It is not a description of behaviour.

Ironically, when it comes to 'actual' behaviour, behaviour which does not accord with the model, the realist is confounded. In the pure form, this mode of analysis gives no category but 'interests'. No other way of explaining behaviour is available. For the realist, United States intervention in

Nicaragua was either rational, that is, in the service of America's 'real' interests, or it is incomprehensible. Realism is thus not so much a theory of action as a theory of right action. But the realist is no better placed than any other moral theorist when it comes to elucidating America's, or any other states's 'real' interests.

Yet realism's understanding of the international arena can open other modes of analysis. Because it forces us to elucidate the conditions under which, among other things, constant and endemic intervention occurs, it can lead us into speculation about the underlying conditions which promote intervention. Indeed, it even provides one answer: the weakness of states. This can lead to questions about the conditions of the prevailing weaknesses of Third World states. Theories can be elaborated to explain weak states and to assign agency and even responsibility for weaknesses. Western responsibility for the intended and unintended promotion and continuation of such weaknesses can be examined. In consequence, entirely new theories might be developed in which intervention is precisely not a matter of intention but one of structure. This could lead to the view that new and different political and economic practices ought to be developed to transform the nature of international relationships as a way of addressing the problem of intervention.

However, any potential endemic weakness of Third World states, and the possibility that such weaknesses are a product of 'global structures', also challenges realism. It raises the question of the degree to which traditional realist notions of the state and state power are any longer appropriate for comprehending the state. If power, after all, is the efficient secret of the state, how did such weak states come to be created and what purpose do they serve? This in turn encourages a reconceptualisation of what statehood means in the Third World and why, precisely, it is desirable to promote autonomous states in the Third World. And if the realist's answer is 'to create strong states', then this calls for an explanation of how realism's global ethic, which legitimates intervention, can possibly contribute to the development of the strong state.

A further question concerns whether the notion of the 'strong state' is an adequate conceptualisation of the purposes of statehood. It is presumably not the case that any type of state is desirable. And what does a strong state mean anyway? The difficulty of such a category is evident in the case of Kampuchea under Pol Pot. That state met very few criteria for a 'strong state'; it has been characterised as functionally incompetent. Yet this functionally incompetent state was able to move two million people out of the cities into the countryside, resulting in hundreds of thousands of deaths. Similarly, South Africa is problematically defined as a strong state. On the one hand, it can be seen as a modern, rational, bureaucratic, Weberian edifice in that it is technologically sophisticated and behaves like a modern superpower in the region. On the other hand, it has disciplined and controlled its population through fear, myth and pseudo-scientific theories of racial superiority.

THE COSMOPOLITAN STATE IN A WORLD SOCIETY

According to the cosmopolitan ethic (and many of our intuitions derive from cosmopolitanism), a state's basic legitimacy is the guarantee against intervention. The question then becomes: What are the criteria for assessing state legitimacy? Is the state to be considered as an end in itself? Or is it important, rather, because it guarantees a basic quota of human rights, or provides some other list of basic human needs? If the state is considered an end in itself, argues the cosmopolitan, then everything becomes a servant of the state. If, on the other hand, there are ends to which the state is merely instrumental, then the state relates to and must be judged by such conceptions of ends as, for example, developing conceptions of ourselves as bearers of rights, or the instrument of evolving human consciousness. In particular, if rights are held by individuals, then corresponding duties are also held by individuals, and it is to individuals that we must look as the agents of action or inaction, and the bearers of responsibility, not 'states'. In many circumstances, it may be more efficient for those duties to be organised into collectivities which we call states. But there is no particular moral significance in such an organisation.

The morality of states, in the cosmopolitan view of the state, is contingent on their being efficient guarantors of something else, such as for example, the word of God.[5] The state as a political entity is not problematical in this view, nor are borders to be respected merely because the state exists.

However, the problem with cosmopolitanism begins with its 'merely instrumental' view of the state. In most cosmopolitan views, the state may be a mere instrument but it is a fairly vital instrument because, while the state may not be the end, the end appears to be unattainable without it. Thus, it too must be protected, along with the needs for which it was founded. This gives rise to the familiar paradox of, for example, rights-based theories of the state: namely, that the agency which allows us to transcend oppression is at the same time an agency of oppression. The first and basic condition of the state's existence is that we conceive of ourselves as citizens. If this is so, how can such a state serve as a vehicle for the movement which will allow us to transcend that limited conception of ourselves as mere citizens and to realise ourselves as humans in the cosmos?

The problem with simple cosmopolitanism is its argument that the state cannot be made the basis for international morality. Having adopted such a position, it is incumbent upon the cosmopolitan position to identify what sort of political organisation it would sanction. The question then becomes: What kind of moral problems are associated with this new, and better, form of political organisation, and how are they any different from those associated with the state?

THE POST-REALIST STATE AND CULTURAL SYSTEMS

Let us return to the problems raised by realism for a moment. As we noted, the realist view offers a very powerful mode for understanding causes and consequences of intervention. Its major weakness, however, is that intervention always appears to be the same sort of thing (a disruption of the state), caused by the same sort of thing (a threat to state interests), engineered by the same sort of thing (the rational state incrementalising its interests), with the same sort of *realpolitik* consequences (reinforcing the interests of states). To differentiate intervention, in particular, morally to differentiate behaviour, a theory is required which produces differentiated accounts of intervention, that is, which distinguishes one thing from another.

Political culture theory and theories which relate the state to civil society allow us to differentiate interventionary behaviour. When, for example, we decide that America's intervention in Nicaragua cannot be fully accounted for by rational action, then accounts of institutions, long-held beliefs and political impulses and how these affect political behaviour are brought into play.

That cultural systems matter is, in any event, central to our views of intervention. After all, the fact that we have a problem with intervention derives largely from our view of the nation as an organic cultural entity. Where we see an entity which has a history, a language, and a duration over time, then we get nervous about intervention. In this sense, there are echoes of a nineteenth-century ideology of nationalism. But we seldom seem to ask whether, in the Third World for example, the congruence between the state and such organic entities actually exists. In fact, many Third World states are characterised by an absence of a shared core culture and little agreement on the rules of the political game; there are complex social, religious, ethnic and linguistic divisions which are intermeshed with political authority in many ways, some of which are scarcely conducive to political stability. Indeed, it is the existence of such mixtures that actually invites intervention. There is an overwhelming association, for example, between the military intervention of the period following the Second World War and civil, religious, tribal or separatist wars in the Third World.

How a community envisages political participation is an important part of political culture. In particular, in thinking about the distinction between Europe and Africa, some pre-Weberian contexts are necessary to appreciate accurately and empirically Third World politics. Rational, incrementalising values like economic growth cannot be assumed to be the sole principle that Third World peoples bring to their political struggles. It was not simply a question of material well-being, after all, that led them to choose statehood, but matters of human dignity, of citizenship, of status, of emancipation from subordination.

The nineteenth-century liberal had a theory uniting individual right and national right. Much modern sociology is concerned with collective rights and the place of the individual in the modern state. This suggests that it is important for Kampucheans to have collective rights, and that individual Kampucheans might enjoy more rights in such a context than in a colonial situation. One of the advantages of the nineteenth-century theory of national self-determination was that it united methodological individualism and structuralism. So, too, does the modern twentieth-century sociological theory on the origins of nationalism. It allows us to relate individual wants and needs to diverse social movements and state forms. It should allow us to make sense of intervention in a way which neither justifies it, nor which forces us to suppose that the nation-state is the final end of all political action.

In relating state forms to social movements, intervention as a unified concept begins to break up. Intervention begins to look like quite different things, with quite different impulses, between quite different states, not all of which are justifiable, even by the criterion of states' interests.

This leads on to the argument of a post-realist kind which relates the notion of domestic space to system effects. The means of understanding the relationship between one thing and another are better now than in the past: there are sophisticated ways of monitoring the consequences of, for example, pollutant emissions on climate or the impact of a hegemon's banking system on the international monetary order. This allows for more differentiated and precise assignments of responsibility than was available in the past. Indeed, such responsibilities are unavoidable even though they were previously opaque. Another consequence of understanding the relationship between one thing and another better is that it calls into question what exactly domestic space is, and engenders wider concepts of community responsibility than the community of the state. The phenomenon of system effects does not necessarily bring all domestic space, and what occurs in it, legitimately into the purview of others, but we can begin to see why others might be concerned with the particular and often haphazard construction of our domestic spaces.

CONCLUSIONS

International relations is locked into an obsession with the state while having rather simple concepts of it. Such simple concepts may be useful in certain contexts, such as calculating the relative power balances between states, but they can scarcely help us in thinking about the problems raised by intervention. This is because intervention is not peculiar to the state but characterises politics *per se*. In challenging conventional notions of norms of intervention and non-intervention, we are challenging a certain prevalent view of politics, not merely of international relations.

If the state is taken to be the supreme or at least universal value, then we need a much better account of the differences between states. This needs to be developed in a way that will invite their comparability with one another. One such account is *modernisation theory*, which relates states along somewhat mythical lines. But it also allows states to be distinguished in a number of complex ways, including political culture and social structures. Other accounts are the new *historical sociology* which views the differences between states as a function of their origins and development within a statesystem which is, itself, changing, and *development theory*, akin to modernisation theory, but which sheds the mythical historical line and uses the idea of 'obstacles to development' to highlight structural characteristics (and different structural characterisations) among states. Such accounts, if developed, would have important implications for our thinking about intervention. In such accounts, intervention could scarcely be a universal category. On the contrary, it would become a variety of quite different things that happen between quite different states.

Most cases of intervention raise exactly the question of what sort of state against what sort of state, whether advanced against backward, whether self-interested against religiously motivated, whether communist against liberal (or vice-versa). Moreover, what a particular states does or does not do about sanctions or genocide reflects on the nature of the state in a way that distinguishes it from other states. Such actions say a great deal about what the state is, how it validates itself, and where it is morally and politically, as well as historically, located. Intervention and non-intervention also engender and entail moral responsibilities for the state and this leads inevitably to discussions of the nature of their legitimacy.

What makes intervention interesting is that it stands at the threshold between international and domestic politics. We not only have to make up our minds about what should apply between states, but we also have to come to grips with notions of legitimacy and authority that have traditionally belonged to the domain of domestic politics, and not to international politics. But it is precisely the questions of authority and legitimacy that are central to discussions of intervention.

Within the confines of the politico-administrative realm we call a state, there are rules, purposes, a framework of law and an administrative system. Given the role of administration, it is possible to ascribe responsibility both for action and inaction. The definition of agency, the responsibilities given it and its relation to ourselves, allows us to provide action and inaction with moral characterisations. The ascription of agency reflects the relationships between the individual, a corporate body and society. Corporations in domestic society are, after all, bearers of duties and the officers within them can be found at fault. It is equally possible to ascribe responsible agency to a state. Indeed, international law does so.

The problem for international relations as a discipline is to get some kind of agreed account of what states are, what they are for and within which system of rules they operate. Such an account is by no means readily available, at least in contemporary political thought, as the discussion above demonstrates. Nevertheless, it will only be once international relations has developed a much more sophisticated characterisation of the state that we can even begin to work out questions of responsibility and the consequences for which states may be held accountable, both in relation to actions and inactions. The characterisation of the state is the fundamental issue for international relations and political theory alike.

Notes

1. The story is of course much more complex than this selection might indicate. The choice here reflects the conceptions of the state that dominate international relations theory. Apart from alternative readings of the development of the state (which might stress Rousseau and Nietzsche), there are also political sociological accounts of the state (Marx, Gellner, Mann).
2. On whether it was universalisable Weber passed no final judgement.
3. See R. Higgins, *International Law and the Reasonable Need of Governments to Govern*, Inaugural Lecture, London School of Economics, 1982.
4. R. Cohen, *Theatre of Power* (London, 1987).
5. Theocracy is a form of cosmopolitanism, as is the notion of a rights-based theory of the state, implicit in R. Plant's contribution in this volume.

5 Intervention and Moral Dilemmas

Peter Johnson

In philosophy it is often the case that the end of one story is the start of another. This is true of many attempts to provide a moral justification for the intervention by one state in the affairs of another. Such attempts frequently lead to the conclusion that there is an inherent contradiction in the argument: either states possess the right of self-determination or there is a morally justifiable basis for intervention. In other words, an object, in this case, the state, cannot be both self- and other-determined without self-contradiction. Now a self-contradiction is what it is by virtue of its claim that X both is and is not the case. Not all self-contradictions are moral dilemmas, but a moral dilemma is a kind of contradiction. In a moral dilemma we are being asked to make a choice in a situation of moral conflict in which the moral values involved are mutually exclusive. If contradictions are logically empty, and if dilemmas are varieties of contradictions, then the theoretical and practical seriousness of this conclusion for discussions of the moral basis of intervention should be quite clear. It creates a logical obstacle to the derivation of rules governing the moral basis of intervention, its nature, occasion and degree. If this inference is to be questioned we have no alternative but to challenge the conclusion on which it seems to rest. Quite properly, what appears to be the end of an argument is actually the start of another.

If we ask what it is about a dilemma which specifically creates the difficulty there are at least three interrelated aspects. The first identifies the problem as the intrinsic character of conflicting values. In other words, it is in the nature of the values concerned that conflict between them is irresolvable. They are necessarily incommensurable. It is, of course, true that many have tried to ascertain a universal currency against which values may be measured. It is also true that we may try to reduce the degree of conflict by saying, for example, that an increase in equality may reduce liberty in some respects but may increase it in others. It may very well be that a move of this kind will prove attractive as the basis for a moral theory of intervention. But what needs to be emphasised is that whatever merits such arguments possess they do not depend on any logical capacity to break down incommensurable values into their more basic components. They do claim that such values are to be checked against an independent standard like utility or preference, but this is not because any reduction has taken place. In contrast with this, the dilemmas posed by intervention positively require further analysis. The second aspect locates the difficulty in the situation in which the conflict of values takes place. The precise claim involved here varies, but the general argument is that distortions in the social environment create the dilemma, not the nature of the values as such. In different circumstances the same values would be consistent. For example, in the case of intervention it becomes necessary to ask who bears the rights of political sovereignty. Is it the individuals who make up the state or the government which claims legitimate rule? What moral functions need to be fulfilled for the right of political sovereignty to exist, and under what circumstances is such a right forfeited? These questions certainly make the dilemma more elaborate in many different ways. The third aspect finds the source of the dilemma in the agent. What is wrong is not the value or the situation, but the agent's thinking about these things. The dilemma, therefore, has no objective existence.

MORAL DILEMMAS AND INTERVENTION

At this stage we need a more precise identification of the type of dilemma we have to examine, and I want to start by describing those I am going to exclude. Firstly, there are cases where the disagreement is between a moral value on the one side and some prudential advantage or interest on the other. Such cases may not be easy to resolve, but it is clear that they are not instances of a specifically moral dilemma. However, it may be objected that the disagreement could be between a moral value and a specifically political interest or advantage, and that this would bring it closer to the problems commonly encountered in providing a moral justification for intervention. I think there is some force in this objection, and I would like to deal with it in two ways. One, what counts as a specifically political interest or advantage would have to be derived from principles of justice for it to be included in the category of moral dilemma in which I am interested. A simple assertion of national self-interest would not be sufficient. Two, even if this condition were satisfied, the dilemma which results may not be specific to the moral problems raised by intervention.

This leads on to the second category of dilemma I wish to exclude. This does involve a moral choice between two incompatible moral values, but in a way that has no direct bearing on the moral standing of states. Indeed, there is no reason in theory why it could not be discussed completely independently of this. The incompatibility involved finds its roots in the ambiguity in Aristotle's distinction between complete and partial justice. In broad terms, the dilemma is generated by the large-scale incompatibility between the value of impartiality, or equality of respect, which presses towards the acceptance of general obligations, and the value of individual liberty which presses towards the necessity of limiting the moral demands which can be made. It may be the case that there are no convincing reasons for thinking that this conflict is essentially irresolvable. This may lead to arguments which defend a systematic restructuring of international political and economic arrangements and which are based on a revised form of distributive justice.

However, even if such arguments were persuasively constructed it is not clear how they would bear specifically on the moral problems of intervention. One reason for this is that the incidence of morally justified intervention may not be sufficient to satisfy the requirements of the agreed standard of distributive justice. Another reason is that the logic of intervention presupposes the existence of states, and it may very well be that if the dilemma is to be removed then states will have to be removed too. But this is to beg the question of the moral status of states, and, in any case, is tantamount to the claim that we can remove the pain of family life simply by abolishing the family.

The third and final category of dilemma I wish to exclude are those whose moral character makes them only indirectly related to the problems raised by intervention and which push us towards a different area of moral philosophy. We get a clearer idea of this by mentioning the kinds of action which most usually provoke discussion along these lines. These include various forms of what might be called pre-emptive intervention whose purposes range from legitimate self-defence to the protection of the citizens of one state when they are within the boundaries of another. Now I do not wish to deny that these three areas present governments with dilemmas which are often extremely difficult to resolve. However, there is no reason to think that the moral problems involved are exclusive to intervention, or that it is intervention which is the source of the moral difficulty. Nothing has so far been said which explains why this should be the case. On the contrary, the moral terms used to understand such dilemmas derive their sense from traditional difficulties in moral and political philosophy. If this is true then there is no obstacle to our discussing these cases in the characteristic language of political morality, in other words, in terms of the various senses of the means/ends relationship, the 'dirty hands' and 'clean hands' problem, the idea of the lesser of two evils, and the distinction between doing and threatening to do. However, even if we grant this, the specific moral problem of intervention remains obscure.

An interesting and serious effort to deal with this obscurity is the argument that what makes intervention morally puzzling is the strong element of risk, luck, or unpredictability involved in establishing its outcomes. Sidgwick, for example, has argued that even morally justified intervention should be kept within narrow limits, given 'the danger that – being designed, or believed to be designed, to further the aggrandisement of the intervening State or States – it may arouse the jealousy of others, and cause an extended war'.[1]

The difficulty here is not simply that of a just action or policy producing more harm than good. The precise problem is how we are to attach moral significance to actions or policies whose outcomes are indeterminate. On this view, the moral problems raised by intervention are firmly within this area and have the following implications. A general implication is that the context for the argument is that of political morality which has affinity with questions raised regarding moral luck. A specific implication is that it is necessary to see the moral status of intervention in the light of the dimension between internal and external risk.

Thinking about intervention in terms of moral luck involves two major weaknesses. First, questions of moral luck may be seen as variants of establishing the limits of rights-based moral theory. In other words, saying that someone has a right in respect of something tells us little or nothing about the moral conduct which follows from such an attribution. This is because rights may be insisted upon, waived or overridden. There is, therefore, a logical gap between rights and right conduct, to use Melden's expression. This has an obvious application to the problems of intervention, but it tells us nothing about the moral basis of the rights of either individuals or states. As such the specific problem raised by intervention is once more left obscure. Second, the line of argument we are considering is quite properly concerned with the moral status of luck in human decisions. But in the case of intervention we are given no answers to the questions: What creates the risk? What gives the risk its moral significance? With these weaknesses before us we have to conclude that the moral problems of intervention are not in a sub-class of political morality, and therefore the dilemmas of the latter do not help us to identify the dilemmas specific to the former.

RESPONSES TO THE MORAL DILEMMA OF INTERVENTION

We are left, therefore, with the problem of identifying the moral dilemma specific to intervention. The specific dilemma posed by intervention is in the form of a conflict between the moral significance of the state and the claims of humanity; between autonomy and justice. Some solve the dilemma by diluting the moral significance of the state. They may, for example, doubt the ethical significance of states because their boundaries are often ambiguous and open to dispute. National frontiers are contingent and take the form that they do because of historical accident rather than moral design. As the moral problem of intervention turns on the justification which can be given for the various ways in which these boundaries may be crossed it would be an advantage to show that from the moral point of view they are arbitrary. An example of this can be found in Pascal. He writes:

> What basis will he take for the economy of the world he wants to rule? Will it be the whim of each individual? What confusion! Will it be justice? He does not know what it is. If he did know he would certainly never have laid down this most commonly received of all human maxims: that each man should follow the customs of his own country. True equality would have enthralled all the peoples of the world with its splendour, and lawgivers would not have taken as their model the whims and fancies of Persians and Germans in place of this consistent justice. We should see it planted in every country of the world, in every age, whereas what we do see is that there is nothing just or unjust but changes colour as it changes climate. Three degrees of latitude upset the whole of jurisprudence and one meridian determines what is true. . . . It is a funny sort of justice whose limits are marked by a river; true on this side of the Pyrenees, false on the other.[2]

It is obvious that Pascal does not see the conflict as the clash between respect for the moral autonomy of states, on the one side, and the obligations imposed by universal justice, on the other. For Pascal the contingent character of state boundaries diminishes their moral authority. But if this is true then there is no moral dilemma since the state has had its moral character arbitrarily removed.

We find a different view of this dilemma in Kant. Here the principle of the mutual recognition of autonomy is basic to the idea of international right. However, two problems present themselves at this stage. First, not all states will satisfy the requirements of justice provided by Kant's liberal republicanism. Second, it is difficult to say which of the actions of free and independent states do or do not concern others. Both these points would seem to encourage intervention to a considerable degree. However, on Kant's view, to say that this is morally permissible must mean that the principle of the mutual recognition of autonomy ceases to have a universal claim. For this reason Kant attempts to bypass the moral problems posed by intervention, and concentrates instead on the obligations of forbearance and hospitality, and the development of cultural and commercial co-operation. The validity of those arguments depends on Kant's views concerning the rationality of history and the nature of moral progress. If these views are doubted, and if the value of the co-operative virtues in international politics is not the central issue here, then it must follow that Kant does not fully address the specific moral dilemma posed by intervention.

There is another position that attempts to bypass the central moral dilemma of intervention. Here the moral justification of intervention requires reference to a moral rule or principle. For this to be derived we need a way of distinguishing between which of a state's actions affect other states and which do not. Since interdependence means that action always affects others, then it must follow that the moral problem posed by intervention is not one of principle but of degree. This move introduces the difficult problem in moral philosophy of how we make moral evaluations or decisions when the differences are (a) large-scale, and (b) matters of degree. In other words, we can rule out callous indifference and philanthropy without having any persuasive rational basis for where we locate the point of moral obligation. As long as this argument is not misused as a basis for moral quietism I think we are right to place it on the agenda at this point. In addition, the emphasis on degree implies a recognition of the virtue of prudence in the sense that the disparity between harm and benefit in some cases of intervention may be such as to rule them out as cases of obligation.

Nevertheless, the argument that the problems of intervention are best understood as moral problems of degree is seriously misleading. To begin with, it is certainly true that there are many different issues involved in questions like 'Where do we draw the line?' But it does not follow from the fact that there are difficult cases that the line is impossible to draw. In theory this would be the case whatever the empirical incidence of interdependence. Further, no reasons are given for or against the view that the moral line should be equivalent to the boundaries of states. Finally, as Mill has pointed out, if the problems of intervention are seen as moral problems of degree to be checked against the primary virtue of prudence, then there is nothing here to prevent us applying the same argument to non-intervention. The consequence for Mill is that:

> non-interference is not a matter of principle . . . . When you abstain from interference, it is not because you think it wrong. You have no objection to interference only it must not be for the sake of those you interfere with; they must not suppose that you have any regard for their good. The good of others is not one of the things you care for; but you are willing to meddle, if by meddling you can gain anything for yourselves.[3]

Another possibility is to adopt some form of moral individualism. On this view, states and individuals are not the same logical animal, since states may be reduced to their components in a way that is not possible for individuals. States are not sources of moral ends in the same sense as individuals. The state is a moral fiction, and so in logic cannot possess the same kind of moral autonomy that we would ascribe to an individual. If this is true then the rule in favour of non-intervention is mere prejudice.

There are two problems with this view which demonstrate that we cannot assume *a priori* that individualism as such casts irresistible doubt on the idea of non-intervention. The argument merely assumes that individualism is essentially anti-statist. It says nothing about those political philosophies, say, utilitarian or contractarian, which do claim to give an account of the moral nature of the state in a way which is consistent with their individualist foundations. Even though moral individualism diminishes the independent moral significance of the state, it does not follow that it cannot rule out unwarranted intervention. What it means is that the account of its exclusion is not in terms of the violation of communal integrity or national self-determination, but in relation to the undermining of individual rights. The argument may be that states are morally secondary to a notion of international distributive justice which takes the well-being of individuals as its basic component. It is impossible to imagine the global administration of such a standard without a juridical authority. This is because the material redistribution involved would derive its moral legitimacy not simply from its being intrinsically obligatory but also from the source and method of its application. This does not mean that the moral problems of intervention are solved. What it means is that they are switched to another level of moral philosophy. Moreover, there are many well-known positions in political philosophy which argue that a political community is a necessary location for the expression of individual aspirations. It is a mistake for individualism to wish these away in the course of some well-aimed criticisms of Hobbesian pictures of international politics. Second, the argument does not remove the dilemmas posed by intervention. It simply transfers them to individuals.

MORAL JUSTIFICATIONS FOR INTERVENTION

One attempt to overcome the difficulties with individualism is to argue that the moral significance of the state is derived from the idea of the common good and the moral community. The moral dilemma arises not because of the existence of states but of entities that fall short of statehood. This is the view of the dilemma we find in a neo-Kantian position. Here the principle of the mutual recognition of autonomy is basic to the idea of international right. However, not all states will satisfy the requirements of justice necessary to be accorded this right. Therefore, the principle of the mutual recognition of autonomy ceases to have a universal claim. This might seem to encourage intervention to a considerable degree.

There are strong and weak versions of this neo-Kantian position. Both resist the individualist assumption that if the dilemma is to collapse it will be because of the discovery of a commensurable standard which undercuts the conflicting values. Instead, they draw out the logic which it is claimed is, in different degrees, and in different respects, internal to the idea of the state. The strong view is implied in Green's comment, 'I count Czarist Russia a state by courtesy only', and in his remark that:

> It is nothing then in the necessary organisation of the state but rather some defect of that organisation in relation to its proper function of maintaining and reconciling rights, of giving scope to capacities, that leads to a conflict of apparent interest between one state and another.[4]

But if a state is not fully a state then what follows in Green's terms is not that intervention would thereby be justified, but that the question is left open. In which case, nothing follows regarding either the occasion or the degree of justifiable intervention.

The weak version tries to avoid this difficulty by being more specific about the identity and function of the state and therefore the kind of justifiable intervention which would be consistent with them. A good example of this position is found in Michael Walzer's *Just and Unjust Wars*.[5] Walzer argues that it is the difficulty of the moral 'fit' between a community and its government which creates the dilemma of intervention. Intuitively the absence of 'fit' creates a *prima facie* case for morally justified intervention. But this language is highly ambiguous. We are told nothing regarding the extent of intervention, and we are asked to assume that the idea of *prima facie* obligation is sufficient to resolve all cases of moral conflict which occur. Walzer's attempt to deal with these problems owes something to Mill's view in *On Liberty* and the essay on non-intervention. While being strongly anti-paternalist in tone, they do not exclude multiple forms of non-coercive relationships between states. They allow, as Mill puts it, for the existence of anomalous cases, and they attempt to justify coercive interference with liberty only in the name of liberty.

The connection with Mill ceases, however, when we are confronted by a logically complex idea like the state. This leads Walzer to adopt the following basic approach:

> The principle that states should never intervene in the domestic affairs of other states follows readily from the legalist paradigm and, less readily and more ambiguously, from those conceptions of life and liberty that underlie the paradigm and make it plausible. But these same conceptions seem also to require that we sometimes disregard the principle; and what might be called the rules of disregard, rather than the principle itself, have been the focus of moral interest and argument.[6]

Walzer allows three cases where, as he puts it, '[t]he ban on boundary crossings is subject to unilateral suspension'.[7] First, there are cases of secession where there are two or more political communities within one territory, and one of these or the government is forcibly preventing the other from secession.[8] Second, there are cases of counter-intervention in which one state has the right of intervention where one state has already intervened, for example, in a civil war, and the right of intervention is gained from the need to balance the force of the first. Finally, there are cases of humanitarian intervention to prevent the massacre, genocide or enslavement by a government of its own citizens. When, and only when, one of these conditions is present can foreign military intervention be morally justified.

Now as far as the moral basis of the position is concerned it is clear that the three cases pull in different directions. In the first two cases it is the existence of political sovereignty which is in doubt. The dilemma posed by intervention is that some identifiable moral good can only be achieved at the expense of another. But if political sovereignty does not exist then the price does not have to be paid and the dilemma vanishes. The model here seems to be the case where a promise can only be kept by sacrificing some other equally powerful moral obligation. On Walzer's view, this conflict is removed by eliminating the promise or showing that the action is actually required by the principle. This can be done by saying that it was made under duress or that there was a tacit understanding about the limits of keeping it. This case presupposes the existence of overriding moral considerations and that they can be used as a basis for weighing the alternatives. The risk here, of course, is that we allow too much, with the consequence that the original principle is irreversibly weakened. That this is Walzer's fear is clear from his account of the specific interventions which the rules of disregard allow. This also explains why, on his view, a state may possess the right of political sovereignty independently of the character of its political arrangements.

But there are other kinds of dilemma which are outside Walzer's model. There are, firstly, tragic moral dilemmas in which an agent may justifiably think that whatever he chooses to do will be wrong. There are conflicting moral requirements and neither succeeds in outweighing the other, and so whatever choice is made regret or remorse will result. It may be argued that Walzer's primary non-intervention rule is strengthened if the problem is seen in this light. But this would simply mean that where the conflict is not simply between incommensurable values but between different ways of life the dilemma is much more acute. The second kind of dilemma exists where individuals justifiably claim that they have been badly treated as a result of the choice that has been made. This is much more political in character and has an obvious bearing on the problems of intervention. Here, in cases of secession, for example, both action and inaction may provoke reasonable complaints of interference or neglect. With regard to humanitarian intervention the difficulty is more straightforward. This only makes moral sense if it rests on something like universal human rights. But this leaves the right of political sovereignty in limbo, and, without further specification, could be consistent with intervention greater than that allowed by the original rules of disregard.

These are not the only problems raised by Walzer's argument. We may question the claim that unfree states possess a right of political sovereignty which has moral force. If the argument allows intervention for self-determination then why not also for self-government? As few states satisfy the individual or communal rights on which Walzer claims their right to sovereignty is based, it is inconsistent to retain a firm limit on morally justifiable intervention. Either this should be increased or further arguments need to be provided for the general moral value of national autonomy in international relations. Here the argument rests heavily on Mill's claim that it is for the inhabitants of a state 'to brave the labour and danger necessary for their liberation',[9] if freedom from the oppression of their own government is to be achieved. But why should anti-paternalism apply in cases of struggles for self-government when it does not apply in self-determination? Further, and less powerfully, individuals may request assistance, in which case it seems odd to say that the non-intervention principle is morally sufficient to justify not providing it. Now Walzer is, of course, right to say that there are many examples of the immorality of intervention. It may stunt a people's political capacity for self-determination. It may unleash a chain of political and military consequences which involve considerably more harm than good. It may be based on economic advantage, and depend on motives which are mixed or whose impartiality may be doubted. However, it might be argued that these still leave more room for morally justified conditional intervention than is allowed by Walzer's principles. There is something to be said for this criticism, but it does imply that the kinds of moral dilemma posed by intervention will extend far beyond the boundaries of Walzer's theory. This is because the problem is then one of assessing the moral significance of *de facto* states in relation to that of individuals and communities.

From the standpoint of theory this has the consequence of pushing the ethics of intervention in three different directions. One, there is a strong pressure to see it in the light of dilemmas of political morality, which are not specific to it. Two, individualist theories, such as contract, rights or utility, which notoriously pull in opposite ways when it comes to intervention, have to be redrawn to account for the morality of communal aspirations. Three, the character of different forms of human association may be plural and diverse in a way which makes it a source of moral value.

CONCLUSION

Dilemmas of the kind I have discussed will persist because the conflict they involve cannot be removed without loss. What this does not mean is any reduction in the seriousness of moral value for international politics. It may be argued here that moral pluralism is incompatible with radical social and political action. To say that the obligation to intervene and the respect for a society's way of life are irreducible is to say nothing beyond quietism as far as conduct is concerned. But this view has little empirical or theoretical evidence to support it. The requirement that cosmopolitanism – if it is to have any value – issue guidelines which are direct and free from contradiction makes demands which it is impossible to satisfy outside utopianism; in which case we have no alternative but to reconstruct the relation between the moral aspirations of intervention and its practice: but that, as they say, is another story.

Notes

1. H. Sidgwick, *The Elements of Politics*, 2nd rev. edn (London, 1897) p. 262.
2. Pascal, *Pensées*, trans. with an introduction by A. J. Krailsheimer (Harmondsworth, 1976) pp. 45–6.
3. J. S. Mill, 'A Few Words on Non-Intervention', in *Dissertations and Discussions*, III (London, 1973) p. 159.
4. T. H. Green, *Lectures on the Principles of Political Obligation* (London, 1941) p. 173.
5. M. Walzer, *Just and Unjust Wars* (London, 1978) pp. 86–108.
6. Ibid., p. 86.
7. Ibid., p. 90.
8. There are particularly intransigent majority/minority problems here, but a discussion of these would take us away from the main line of the argument.
9. Mill, 'A Few Words on Non-Intervention', p. 173.

Part II

Theoretical Perspectives

6 International Anarchy, Realism and Non-Intervention

Leo McCarthy

INTRODUCTION

The Realist school of thought considers international relations to be essentially anarchical in nature. The absence, and indeed the impossibility, of world government provide the basis for Realism's understanding of the ethical dimensions of world politics. In a straightforward sense, the existence of international anarchy is indisputable; a myriad of utopian projects aside, the human race insists stubbornly on organising itself in discrete political units. We shall see, however, that this circumstance is insufficient to support the range of normative positions on intervention to which the Realist perspective leads.

The features of international anarchy which Realism identifies as the determinants of international morality help explain why the study of international relations and the study of political theory have generated little common discourse. The widespread presumption that normative political theory has little relevance for international relations has helped sustain Realism as the predominant approach to understanding states' actions, both in scholarship and practice. Realism's depreciation of the importance of ethical questions helped preserve its credibility in an era of 'scientific' understanding of international relations.

The central concepts of political theory – justice, rights, liberty, equality, democracy – have been raised and developed within the context and confines of the state. In turn, questions about the legitimacy of the state, questions which have been taken to define political theory as a form of enquiry, have been articulated in terms of these concepts. Intervention, which may be understood as the use of coercion (ranging from diplomatic or economic sanctions to military intervention) by a state or group of states against another with the intention of changing the domestic policy or political constitution of a state against the will of its leaders, presents problems for political theory.[1] Intervention, especially when defended on humanitarian grounds, certainly raises questions about the legitimacy of the state, but these questions are posed outside the state; they are not resolved in terms of its relations with civil society.

REALISM AND THE ABSENCE OF INTERNATIONAL SOCIETY

In 'domestic' political theory (except for anarchism), the concepts of 'state' and 'society' almost invariably entail each other. The state is the condition of civil society (Hobbes); or the state enhances and secures social co-operation and coexistence (Locke); or the state transcends human particularity and egoism in civil society (Hegel); or the state is itself determined by relations of dominance within society and exercises its power in such a way as to reproduce those relations (Marx). Realism denies the existence of an international society, where 'society' is understood to imply states co-existing in mutually recognised interdependence, according to common and binding rules and with a significant degree of shared moral and cultural understanding.

On some Realist interpretations, no international society can exist because there is no world state. The Hobbesian paradox – how anyone could rationally enter into the covenant which creates the state when the binding force of any such agreement presupposes the state's existence – is insoluble at the level of international relations (although somehow it was solved in the case of the state). In the opposite view, the absence of any significant degree of international society precludes world government. Some realists believe that such a society may develop or be resuscitated in the future.[2] All are agreed that plans to create a 'community of humankind' through supranational institutions or through the growth of functional agencies are utopian delusions. The degree of systematic intervention in the jealously-guarded affairs of the sovereign state which such schemes would evidently require is unthinkable. In the contemporary international system there can be no intervention which is expressive of the common purposes of international society, because no such society exists.

Because states have no common superior, their actions and outlooks are of necessity egoistic. States are like men in Hobbes' state of nature; they cannot be expected to behave justly towards one another in the absence of any higher authority to enforce reciprocal behaviour. International law is viewed by Realists as being in essence no more than the expression of the sovereign wills of states signatory to the particular treaties and conventions which compose it. It has no binding force beyond the volition of states; nor is any centralised or mandatory machinery for the enforcement of the provision of international law against recalcitrants possible.[3]

JUSTICE v. ORDER

Principles of justice in the relations of state[3] which include the principles of non-intervention and self-determination, are given different importance by writers in the Realist school. But it is fair to say that such principles are, where acknowledged, considered to be precarious in their observance and ambiguous in their nature. The introduction of 'moralism' into the discourse of international relations is usually viewed by Realists as an attempt to disguise the stark facts of national power. A state's interest and ambitions come to be presented as an absolute requisite of 'international justice', which is thereby reduced to a rhetorical sham.

Realists are agreed that intervention, whether it be the action of a single state or 'collective' intervention, does not require any special legitimacy by reference to some shared principles of global justice superior to the justice which is ordained by states. No such principles are believed to exist. Attempts to enshrine principles of justice in international agreements, which might then be used to justify intervention in a variety of guises, are condemned as naive, and subversive of international order. Efforts to provide for collective intervention to safeguard international security, even where (as in Chapter VII of the UN Charter) no other principles supportive of such intervention are allowed, are similarly disparaged. Intervention as an activity is viewed by most Realists as quite outside the competence of international law either to regulate or to legitimise. Intervention is purely political action, from which the machinery of international law is by definition excluded.

Realists hold the state to be the principal, and in some accounts the unique, constituency of human justice. For Hobbes, as we suggested, justice only has meaning where a sovereign authority has been established. The primacy of the state in securing just conditions is elsewhere defended in Realist literature in terms of a supposed 'fit' between political systems and the culture of the societies to which they belong. Furthermore, the existence of representative political institutions through which interests can be articulated, and of a legal system capable of enforcing rights and justice-claims – including those prescribed by international law – is seen to presuppose the state.[4] These features of the state are held to be unique to it; they could not be reproduced even if a 'higher' political order could be created.

While Realists differ as to how appropriately the Hobbesian 'state of war' analogy describes contemporary international relations, there is general emphasis on the primacy of order as a value in international relations. The balance of power and the persistence of war as necessary mechanisms of international order are stressed, and the prospects for any viable system of collective security doubted. Though Realists are usually loath to describe intervention in terms of justice or injustice, they nonetheless deprecate it as a source of international disorder, against which the principle of state sovereignty must be asserted. The paradox is that the very mechanisms which international order is said to require rule out any binding principle of non-intervention.

The realist response is that the mechanism of the balance of power serves to protect the independence of states in general, in that it prevents the emergence of any state with such overwhelming power as to threaten the existence of its neighbours (or conceivably of all other states), at the unavoidable cost in an imperfect world of extinguishing sovereignty in the particular instance. Thus, in Europe we can count on the debit side the historical partitions of Poland, the annexation of the Baltic states, and the severely restricted sovereignty of most of the states of Eastern Europe in the decades before the *annus mirabilis* of 1989. On the credit side, the balance of power has guaranteed the independence of other states against powerful neighbours. Historical examples include Belgium and the minor principalities of southern Europe, and the post-1945 independence of Austria.

The point is that non-intervention, which in its ultimate form is the right to be protected against absorption by another state, is, while being an essential corollary of the principle of sovereignty, nonetheless subordinate to sovereignty as the *general* organising principle of world politics. Non-intervention must, on occasion, be sacrificed in the interests of an international system which preserves the sovereign state.

THE MORAL CHARACTER OF STATES

We shall simply note rather than further explore this paradox of intervention, because a deeper contradiction in Realist theory exists, and to some degree underlies the one just noted. In a world where there is no higher authority than the sovereign state, the Realist characterisation of the problem of security is at bottom a 'zero-sum' one. The image of Hobbes's state of nature, sometimes faint, sometimes clear and stark, stands behind the various Realist theories of international relations. To be sure, this condition is somewhat ameliorated in the relations of sovereign states.[5] States are not as vulnerable as individuals; some degree of interdependence and the pragmatic necessity of the mutual accommodation of interests among states, even traces of shared moral values, are recognised in all but the most ferocious of Realist accounts. States are also thought to be innately more prudent, if not more moral, than individuals in the face of the possibly appalling costs of resorting to violence to settle conflicts.[6]

However, the acceptance of a state of nature image of international relations necessarily entails the principle of self-help as the core of a state's policy. It is not surprising that some Realists have made the recognition of the primacy of the national interests, together with the eschewing of moral commitments and optimistic assumptions about the conduct of other governments, both the dictate of prudence and the moral obligation of politicians.[7] At the same time, the position of the state as the primary or only constituency of justice establishes its unrivalled moral significance. It leads Hegel to accord to the state the character of a moral absolute: its function, its very nature, can be replicated by no other institution. But the principle of self-help and the presumptive moral value of the state are ultimately in radical conflict.

Given the wide range of ethical perspectives within the Realist literature, the ambiguities in the thought of some of its main proponents, and the undoubted difficulties in reducing its underlying philosophy to a manageably small set of principles, it might be thought that this conflict is only one of ideal types, and that a middle way between the two elements of Realism is possible. In fact, no philosophically consistent middle way is open.

In Hobbes's state of nature, the natural right of self-preservation is the only right that individuals, and by his own analogy states, can be said to have. Hobbes's classic description of the moral dimension of the state of nature is as follows:

> [I]n this law of Nature, consisteth the Foundation of Originall of JUSTICE. For where no Covenant hath preceded, there hath no Right be transferred, and every man has the right to every thing; and consequently, no action can be Unjust. But when a Covenant is made, then to break it is *Unjust*: and the definition of INJUSTICE, is no other than *the not Performance of Covenant*. And whatsoever is not Unjust, is *Just*.
>
> But because Covenants of mutuall trust, where there is a feare of not performance on either part . . . are invalid; though the Originall of Justice be the making of Covenants; yet Injustice actually there can be none, til the cause of such feare be taken away; which while men are in the naturall condition of Warre, cannot be done. Therefore before the names of Just, and Unjust can have place, there must be some coercive Power, to compell men equally to the performance of their Covenants . . . [8]

The natural right of self-preservation necessitates the establishment of a sovereign; but where there is none, this right makes prudence the main criterion of action. Hobbes is not merely saying that the state alone can ensure compliance with the principles of justice, though this he clearly believes; he insists that it is meaningless even to speak of those principles as hypothetical imperatives outside the state. Outside the state there exists only a moral vacuum.

This belief is reflected by writers such as George Kennan and Hans Morgenthau in their insistence that the duty of the statesman to safeguard the 'national interest' with which he is entrusted is the ultimate moral principle of international conduct *faute de mieux*. The Hobbesian image of international morality is visible also in Morgenthau's attempt to delineate a distinct realm of 'political ethics'. This leads him, however, into all the problems of Machiavellian ethical dualism which Hobbes avoids by simply shutting out ethics altogether from relations between states.

The problem of the legitimacy of intervention is evidently modified when no state, in the sense of an institution with a sufficient degree of monopoly of force to be able to guarantee the terms of the Hobbesian Covenant, exists within the affected territory – as, for example, in the case of Lebanon. It might be said that we should only consider actions as constituting 'intervention' when such a state does exist. On this view, intervention only becomes morally problematic when the sovereign power which guarantees the conditions of justice among its people is itself under threat. This might be construed to mean that the moral significance of the integrity of the state depends upon its securing the welfare and the rights of its citizens. In other words, the moral character of the state is derivative, but is all the more significant for being so.

But such a construction misses the point. *No* sort of interventionary activity is problematic from a Hobbesian viewpoint, because there can be no binding principles in states' relations with each other. The moral vacuum does not exist only where men live without a state. States define the spheres of moral action of their constituent members. Beyond this sphere is only natural right. Nor is it possible to interpret Hobbes as attributing a derivative character to the moral 'personality' of the state. On the contrary, the unique moral property of the state in sustaining domestic conditions of justice does not 'spill over' into any special moral standing or claims against other states, for none can arise in the state of nature existing among them. Most importantly, the nature of the state provides it with no moral guarantee against intervention by other states.

It is not perhaps surprising that other Realist theories of the state indicate a recoil from the starkness of Hobbes's moral theory. If the Leviathan is the 'negative' condition of justice, many Realist writers are anxious to supply a more positive account of the relationship between justice and the state. We have noted arguments concerning the supposed cultural 'fit' between states and societies, and the role of the state in sustaining representative political institutions. But most importantly, for those who stress the 'essential contestability' and cultural relativism of the concept of justice, the state's authority provides a means of avoiding incessant and destructive conflicts over issues of justice and rights.[9] Other writers have sought a synthesis between a Hobbesian scepticism about the significance and coherence of moral claims between states, and a positive assertion of the state as a vehicle for human progress. The moral exclusiveness of the state is defended as a condition of this.[10]

Moral scepticism as a comprehensive form of doubt about moral claims in international relations may be distinguished from the tradition of the 'morality of states'.[11] In the latter, the several strands of the natural law tradition are woven together to produce varying forms of the analogy of states and persons. While classical natural law tradition conceded that states have rights and other moral claims only because the individuals who compose them do, the 'morality of states' tradition came to identify the moral personality of the state as more than and even qualitatively different from the aggregate of the moral personalities making it up.[12] Then nineteenth-century legal thought established the personality and rights of the state as being *sui generis*; they were no longer derivative of anything.

A casual review of Realist literature might suggest that most of it fits in the category of 'moral scepticism'. But the distinction given above is not a tidy one. It is true that the consistent Realist cannot make use of a direct analogy of states and persons, since similar moral relations might then be seen to exist among states as among individuals, and it is the core of the Realist argument that the moral conditions of domestic society are not present in world politics. However, arguments for the unique value of the state as the realm of human justice which would be very familiar to the classical natural law theorists are also encountered in Realist literature.

Michael Walzer defends the principle of non-intervention on the grounds that the state constitutes the physical sphere and the means of protection of a common way of life shared by a people. Although human rights and cultural autonomy are the basis of the state's moral character, the presumption that there is likely to be a closer moral and cultural empathy between a state and its society than exists between the values of that society and the values and motivations of an intervening power gives the state a presumptive moral value. That value is lost where there is evidently no sort of 'fit' between state and society, and where rebellion is justified. But, following

J. S. Mill, Walzer maintains that internal injustice within a state cannot serve as legitimate grounds for outside intervention; political emancipation and social justice can be secured by a society only through its own efforts.[13]

Walzer cannot be counted as a Realist, because he maintains that non-intervention is a binding principle of justice among states. Intervention is equivalent to aggression against the person. It is always morally wrong because it forces people to risk their lives to protect their rights and their common way of life.[14] Yet he is in the company of Realist writers as disparate in their philosophical outlook as Carr, Morgenthau and Kennan in assuming a correspondence between the forms of most actual states and their societies, which lends to the state a special value.

CONCEPTIONS OF STATES, SELF-INTEREST AND MORALITY

The deeper contradiction of Realism should now be evident. The negative defence of the state made by Hobbes provides no restraints on one state's interference in the affairs of another. The positive ethical defence of the state, however, explains and defends the state's moral character by reference (direct or indirect) to the rights of the people within it. The moral consequence of this is (or ought to be) a strong presumption against intervention.

Another way to express this is to say that the principle of sovereignty as a defence against intervention has two distinct meanings within the Realist perspective. For the Hobbesian, sovereignty is merely a description of effective political authority. The essential character of the state – its capacity to safeguard the rights of its citizens – is insufficient to generate rights on its part against other states. Hobbes's is a moral defence of sovereignty in its internal aspects only.

For those concerned to make a more positive and extensive ethical defence of the state, sovereignty is the attribute of the state through which its unique moral capacity is recognised. It is clear that, while Realists agree on viewing the state as the primary arena of justice, and in their scepticism about the meaning of, and prospects for, extensive moral claims in international relations (such as the doctrine of the 'sovereign equality' of states, or human rights, or international distributive justice), they must disagree about the moral importance of non-intervention as a particular instance of a principle of international justice. Scepticism about the defence of the only constituency of justice thought to be available threatens to degenerate into moral nihilism.

This tension in Realist perspectives has engaged a number of its proponents. The contradiction between the principle of self-help and non-intervention is part of a larger debate concerning self-interest and the legitimate claims of others. Morgenthau seeks to resolve the tension by arguing that

> it is exactly the concept of interest defined in terms of power that saves us from both moral excess and . . . political folly. For if we look at nations, our own included, as political entities pursuing their respective interests defined in terms of power, we are able to do justice to all of them. And we are able to do justice to all of them in a dual sense; we are able to judge other nations as we judge our own and, having judged them in this fashion, we are then capable of pursuing policies that respect the interests of other nations, whilst protecting and promoting those of our own. Moderation in policy cannot fail to reflect the moderation of moral judgement.[15]

All this seems problematic, given that Morgenthau remarks just before this passage that 'the state has no right to let its moral disapprobation . . . get in the way of successful political action, itself inspired by the moral principle of national survival'.[16] The expressions 'national interest' and 'national survival' come to be used by Morgenthau almost interchangeably. However, we ought to require a lot of persuading that states should be allowed *carte blanche* to decide what is necessary for 'national survival'.

In any case, self-interest simply is not a form of morality. The very idea of a moral principle is that it constrains the pursuit of self-interest by enforcing the recognition of a transcendent purpose (the 'good of society' or the 'Law of God') which takes priority over the gratification of the individual will. Attempts to show that all moral judgements are in fact reducible to expressions of utility preference, or some other mundane imperative, fail to account for the complexities of moral choice, inescapable dilemmas, and the effect of our moral beliefs on choices of ends as well as of means.[17]

There is nothing in Morgenthau's attempted reconciliation of self-help and respect for others' legitimate interests that enables us to address the extreme moral complexities to which intervention gives rise. The balance of power, whose manipulation has been historically the central concern of great powers, has, as we noted, led to the annihilation of the sovereignty of other states. Perhaps a moral case can be made for saying that the preservation of the independence of the many justifies destructive intervention against the few. But it is at best ahistorical to suppose that when we have weighed up our own best interests, moral moderation must inform us that respect for others is always compatible with securing those interests.

The most perspicuous feature of intervention as an international activity is, indeed, that there is no comfortable reconciliation to be effected between states' self-interest and the moral consequences of their actions. It is in some respects more honest to posit a radical separation of the sphere of the moral and political, as does Benedetto Croce, than spuriously to differentiate 'political ethics' and ethics 'as a whole' as Morgenthau attempts to do.[18] At least the ethical consequences of action are not measured by more lax, and therefore inferior, moral principles than are other types of action. But one might still ask, if moral principles cannot be used to judge political action – the most significant form of action for humankind – then of what use are they?

The most extreme form of intervention is war. Hegel thinks that war is itself inevitable: 'If states disagree and their particular wills cannot be harmonised, the matter can only be settled by war',[19] and that this is in itself no bad thing. The transcendence of the egoistic interests of the individual in civil society that is accomplished by the state is most apparent in the identity which war creates between subjective purposes of the individual and those of the state. Thus Hegel writes:

> This destiny whereby the rights and interests of individuals are established as a passing phase, is at the same time the positive moment, i.e., the positing of their absolute, not their contingent and unstable, individuality. This relation and the recognition of it is therefore the individual's substantive duty, the duty to maintain this substantive individuality, i.e., the independence and sovereignty of the state, at the risk and the sacrifice of property and life . . . [20]
> Sacrifice on behalf of the individuality of the state is the substantial tie between the state and all its members and so is a universal duty.[21]

However, one can have too much of a good thing:

> The fact that states reciprocally recognise each other as states remains, even in war – the state of affairs when rights disappear and force and chance hold sway – a bond wherein each counts to the rest as something absolute. Hence in war, war itself is characterised as something which ought to pass away.[22]

The state is not the condition of man's moral obligation or faculties, as it is for Hobbes, but is rather the highest stage in the development of moral life. Hegel's account differs further from that of Hobbes, who makes self-preservation the ultimate criterion of right, and from those Realists who make the unique relation of state and society the ground for the defence of the exclusivity of the state. Hegel insists that the goals and interests of the individual should be subordinated to the purposes of the state, not simply as contingent necessities of its physical defence, but as a consequence of its very idea. This must raise doubts about the likelihood of war 'passing away'. Nor is it clear how the state, given its absolute moral self-subsistence and consequent boundless egoism, comes to accommodate its interests and actions in the face of the 'absoluteness' of the other. It is not, of course, even logically possible to conceive of a sovereign power existing to judge between absolutes, for then they would no longer *be* absolutes.

The contradiction, then, is between two conceptions of the state. In the Hobbesian conception, the state is the condition of moral action, even the source of moral values, but it exists in a moral vacuum within which this value of the state cannot be translated into any principle governing relations between states. In the Hegelian conception, the state is an institution uniquely adapted to promoting moral values, albeit one which is not itself the progenitor of those values. The latter conception stresses above all the moral *efficiency* of the state as the source of its primacy, but since the state is not on this view the *sine qua non* of moral action, this account of the value of the state insists upon translation into principles of respect and recognition for other states which perform the same functions with respect to their citizens.

The pure egoism of Hobbes's state, the depreciation to a lesser or greater extent of the validity of moral claims between states, and the simultaneous assertion of the defence of the integrity of the state as constituting in itself a moral principle, are elements which exist in different combination, more or less uneasily, in Realist thought. As we have seen, attempts to find a middle way between egoism and mutual moral respect are problematic. This is of the first importance for the Realist understanding of intervention, since intervention provides the clearest example in international relations of the clash of interests of states and the wills of their leaders. It is also the activity in which those leaders find it most urgent to employ moral arguments, however, disingenuously, to support their action. That there is difficulty in establishing common discourse between the main themes of Realism suggests its limits as a moral theory of politics.

GROUNDING NON-INTERVENTION

The central problem is that the two conceptions of the state on which these themes are formulated are both inadequate. The relevance of Hobbes's image as a description of the modern international system has been acutely criticised by several modern writers.[23] It needs only to be added here that what there is of descriptive and explanatory value in Realism is transformed by its inadequate moral perspectives into a set of misleading normative conclusions.

Hobbes's account of the origins of justice and injustice provides, as we have already remarked, no way of escaping from the state of nature. *A* cannot insist to *B* that justice requires the honouring of the promise which is contained in the original covenant when it is only as a consequence of the entering into that covenant that the sovereign authority, which is the unique source of the meaning of 'justice' and 'promise', comes into being. It is a wholly counter-intuitive description of the nature of justice. The state is evidently the guarantor of those rights of the individual which are legally enshrined, whether they be rights to certain civil and political freedoms and equality of treatment, or economic and social rights to certain resources and opportunities.

But the philosophical defence of rights can also be grounded in a theory of individual personality and moral agency.[24] Moreover, the three canons of distributive justice – rights, merits and needs – can be examined and defended quite coherently without the assumption that a state is actually there to impose a pattern of distribution in accordance with a particular interpretation of those canons.[25] The correlative ideas that no one has any just claims before the state, and that what is to count as just is quite simply laid down by *fiat* by the state, run counter to the deep moral significance we attach to the concept of justice, a significance which even the utilitarians were forced to acknowledge. These ideas also run counter to the unquestionable functional necessity of socially understood principles of justice.

The moral egoism of Hobbes's state fails because self-interest is not a kind of morality, because moral rules define and delimit the legitimate spheres of self-interest and render their protection mutually compatible. If we want to keep Hobbes's natural right, only a thorough-going moral scepticism will suffice. If this is to be avoided, the indifference to intervention, to which Hobbes's characterisation of the state of nature leads, must be rejected.

The principle of non-intervention is more persuasively defended on the basis of relations between states and civil society, provided that this defence is intended to base the legitimate claims of the state, including the right to territorial integrity and immunity from intervention, in the state's protection of the interests of its citizens, and is not intended to lead to a crude and arbitrary analogy of states and persons. The important feature of this approach is that, in contrast to the Hobbesian situation, the rights and other claims of citizens must be considered as existing independently of their state. Moreover, the defence of the state must depend upon its actually securing the rights and justice-claims of its people to a higher degree than could result from any transformation of the domestic political order which could be achieved through intervention. Positing this as a condition of the ethical defence of the state is not of course to claim that all (or even most) states are the effective guarantors of their people's welfare. Many states are an evident menace to the people of whose interests they are supposed to be the trustees.[26] Nor is it to underestimate the extreme difficulties encountered in predicting and evaluating the costs and benefits of intervention in particular circumstances.[27] Nonetheless, *in principle* the securest foundation of the principle of non-intervention is a corollary of a positive moral defence of sovereignty.

If the ultimate moral defence of non-intervention in the particular instance does not rest on the recognition of pre-existent rights and interests on the part of individuals and upon the specific nature of the state's role in securing them, then the terms of debate about intervention become once again structured around the premise of moral egoism, which, as we have seen, keeps a sterile silence on the questions of intervention and non-intervention.

CONCLUSION

The postulation of the pure moral egoism of the state inhabiting an international state of nature is a self-contradiction. The state has available to it no arguments to prohibit intervention against itself, and so must deny the moral significance of its own predication. It collapses into moral nihilism. The positive defence of the sovereignty of the state appears to make the welfare of its citizens the primary ground for upholding a principle of non-intervention. The Realist who holds to this can avoid the tendency of the natural law theorists to regard states and persons as analogous, with all the ethical complications of international relations such a view entails. However, Realism's scepticism about the ethical dimensions of international relations militates against a defence of non-intervention as a principle of international justice. The Realist does not trust *any* such defence, since the wider interests of international order requires the sacrifice from time to time of the twin principles of sovereignty and non-intervention. Realism's valuation of sovereignty as a moral principle depends on the view that the defence of the 'national interest' by the leaders of a state is the highest moral obligation. Therefore, there is no means of comparing the relative moral consequences, so far as actual human beings are concerned, of the continued sovereign independence of one state rather than another.

Since one variant of Realism ends in self-contradiction, while another threatens to end in ambiguity and even incoherence, it is unsurprising that the attempts we have reviewed to steer a middle path between the implications of the two have proved unsatisfactory.

The persistence of intervention in the real world, and the self-serving and spurious defences which its instigators usually manage to produce, inclines the weary Realist towards a Hobbesian conception of the essential amorality of international relations. However, this gives no consistent means of philosophically defending the principle of non-intervention, which must be valued as the corner-stone of the system of states. Realism therefore inclines also towards a positive defence of sovereignty grounded on the moral effectiveness of the state. In the end, the two positions are incompatible. The Realist's intuitions are that the philosophical defence of non-intervention is impossible, because the Hobbesian view of how international relations actually are is closest to the truth. In either variant of realism, the refusal to consider ethical questions beyond the state as anything other than peripheral in their relation to human values leads to the state being treated as an absolute. Any serious understanding of intervention as dependent for its moral legitimacy upon its actual effects upon the rights and welfare of individuals is precluded from within the Realist framework: one must start elsewhere.

Notes

1. For a concise and illuminating discussion of the nature of intervention, see S. Hoffmann, 'The Problem of Intervention', in H. Bull (ed.), *Intervention in World Politics* (Oxford, 1984).

2. Hans Morgenthau argues that the sense of a world community is an indispensible condition of the emergence of a world state. He decries the 'public' conduct of international relations in the new era of 'nationalistic universalism', and looks forward (and back) to an era of more formal, careful and private diplomacy as a means of effecting accommodation between states' interests, and thereby of facilitating the re-emergence of a world community. See Hans J. Morgenthau, *Politics Among Nations*, 6th edn with K. W. Thompson (New York, 1985) pp. 29–32.

26. A highly sceptical response to the argument that the supposed 'fit' between states and societies justifies *prima facie* a general prohibition of intervention is to be found in D. Luban, 'The Romance of the Nation-State', *Philosophy and Public Affairs*, Vol. 9, No. 4 (1980) pp. 392–97.
27. There are, indeed, many arguments of a consequentialist nature in support of non-intervention as a customary principle of international relations, particularly in regard to the unpredictable and highly dangerous effects of military escalation, effects which often pose serious threats for international order in a much wider context than the immediate locality of intervention.

7 The Pragmatic Case Against Intervention

Caroline Thomas[*]

In this chapter the case against intervention to promote human causes is put forward. Fundamental to this position is the fact that the state is *the* common value in international politics. If an international community can be said to exist, it is through the recognition of international rights and duties inherent in statehood that this is so. International law and diplomacy, in which non-intervention in the domestic affairs of other states plays a key role, are designed to serve the state and the state system. The rights and obligations which exist in the international sphere are the rights and obligations of states and not of individuals, with the possible exception of the right to self-determination. Yet even the latter is generally recognised only within the established territorial boundaries of existing states; a movement for national self-determination which threatens the territorial integrity of existing states is outlawed by the community of states. Any attempt to establish a basis for interventionary action premised on a universal formula of human rights, even if this could be achieved in theory, cannot be translated into state practice for three simple reasons: state sovereignty, heterogeneity within the system, and the hierarchical nature of the system.

First, individuals are not the stuff of international politics in the present state system – states are. The world is divided into territorial states, which under international law are sovereign. There are two aspects of state sovereignty. Externally there is a formal sovereign equality between all states; internally the state holds the highest decision-making authority within the land. This state system of ours is quite special, precisely because of the 'keep out' signs which are explicitly erected around state borders. This democratisation is unique in history.

Second, given the heterogeneous nature of the state system in which politics must be played out, interventions cannot be justified in universally acceptable terms (excepting self-defence, of course); they will always be concerned with promoting state interest. The present state system is far less homogeneous than the European system of the nineteenth century. This suggests that the idea of an international community had a greater validity within the context of that system than it has within our own. We do not have a transcultural set of human rights accepted both at the level of rhetoric and practice. Some advocates point to the Universal Declaration of Human Rights as just such a set of universal values and rights. Does it make sense to speak of universal human rights in such circumstances? The Declaration springs from the Western liberal tradition, and smacks of ethnocentrism. Moreover, as Michael Akehurst has noted, it 'took twenty-eight years to convert the "soft-law" of the Universal Declaration into the "hard-law" of the Covenants, and at the end of 1981 less than half the states in the world were parties to the Covenants'.[1] If there are any transcultural values within the international system, then those values must derive from recognition of sovereignty and national self-determination.

Third, the hierarchical nature of the present state system and the gross inequalities within it means that power will prevail. This is especially dangerous given the crusade mentality typical of a superpower. The superpowers perceived the rest of the system as the spoils, as potential converts to their way of life. Thus Third World states found themselves to be pawns in the superpower competition. The idea of wars being fought not for rational limited ends, but for ways of life, for good against evil, adds a very dangerous element to international relations. Moreover, superpowers are not alone in their desire to seek converts for a particular way of life, as the Gulf War has shown. In these circumstances, any efforts to justify intervention are fraught with danger.

This may not be how the world *ought* to be, but this is how the world *is*. It is this reality that we have to work with in our efforts to make this a less horrific world in which to live. The case is stated here quite bluntly: the heart may dictate that moral judgement must play a significant role in the relations between states, but the head says otherwise. This is a very genuine moral dilemma. Given the importance of the state, and the heterogeneity, and hierarchical nature of the state system, it can be argued, and demonstrated, that most of the time intervention will do more harm than good. In international affairs, sovereign statehood is itself rooted in a moral conception, and experience suggests that the morality of states does not result in any greater hardship to people than the international moralities which have been propounded during this century. If states act out of moral considerations other than those flowing from the morality of sovereign statehood itself, the flood gates will be opened for intervention motivated by particularistic interpretations of human rights. The easiest way to explain this claim is by reference to examples.

INTERESTS, MORALITY AND CONSEQUENCES

The first example is that of the Tanzanian intervention in Uganda in 1978–9 which precipitated the fall of Idi Amin.[2] Tanzania was not militarily superior to the state in which it intervened. Arguably, this example comes nearer than any other this century to being dictated by humanitarian concerns. Although the Tanzanian government statements regarding the intervention were loaded with humanitarian reasoning, this was *never* officially offered as a justification for its action. Nyerere's public justification for the intervention was self-defence: Ugandan forces had invaded Tanzanian territory and attempted to annex the Kagera Salient. Under international law, Tanzania had a right to act in self-defence and drive out the Ugandan invaders. Some would argue that there was a *prima facie* right of proportionate retribution or punitive action against Uganda. Indeed, this right was claimed. But Tanzania had no right under international law to remove the leader of another state.

At the time of the Tanzanian intervention, Nyerere's actions seemed appropriate.[3] How could the international community stand by and watch these atrocities being perpetrated by Amin against the citizens of his own state? The inaction of the UN, the OAU, and the Commonwealth appeared morally feeble and their condemnation of Tanzania was unjustified. All kinds of states (including the major Eastern and Western states, the Muslim Arab states, Israel) had at various times over the previous seven years been deeply involved with the Amin regime despite the atrocities that were being committed in Uganda. They acted on the basis of state interests during Amin's hold on power; they continued to act on that basis during and after the Tanzanian invasion. Nyerere, on the other hand, acted initially in the interests of the Tanzanian state, then acted on the basis of the interests of the people of Uganda as he perceived them. In so doing he challenged the conventional wisdom that sovereignty is the highest priority in the international system at all times. Instead, he acted in the name of justice. This was not the only occasion on which Nyerere placed human morality above the morality of the state. His attitude to the Biafran tragedy, and to the role of the OAU in general, all represented a call for individual rights to be the concerns of all states.

Carried away with this notion of individual rather than state morality, he failed to foresee the consequences of his action, even though some of them were quite predictable. Apart from the immediate problems, such as divisions within the new government, the lack of a police force or army, and the continued presence of Tanzanian troops which these necessitated, with hindsight the longer term problems which emerged cast doubt on the utility of the Tanzanian intervention. Since the intervention several Ugandan governments have come and gone. Amnesty International reports suggested that repression by some post-intervention governments has been on a scale possibly as widespread as that suffered during Amin's rule. Certainly before his removal by the military, Obote's record was as poor as his record in pre-Amin days.[4] During the civil war between the military government and the left-wing Ugandan People's Movement, the government actually brought back Amin's troops from exile in neighbouring states such as Zaire and used them in the struggle against the guerillas.

The adverse consequences of the intervention were not all on the Ugandan side. The material cost of the intervention to Tanzania, one of the poorest states in Africa, has been huge and disastrous. It is difficult to understand how Nyerere could have imagined that he could carry out a successful intervention in Uganda. What type of outcome imposed from outside would be generally regarded as fair and preferable and just by Ugandans who, after all, did not form a united nation? Unless Nyerere was prepared to back by the force of arms a government of a particular complexion in Uganda, internal divisions were bound to cause massive problems. Installing a government of his own choice in Uganda was something that Nyerere was loath to do. Such action would have transgressed principles of human freedom which Nyerere wanted to uphold, laid Tanzania open to charges of cultural imperialism and in violating the Organisation of African Unity Charter would have created a dangerous precedent. Yet without such action, the complexity of domestic political alignments in Uganda negated any chance of peace.

While interventions may alleviate immediate indiscriminate terror or the persecution of a particular group, they can also result in the substitution of one oppressor by another, or of new uncertainties and dangers emanating from a different geopolitical configuration. Thus Kampucheans, freed from the terrible excesses of the Pol Pot regime, found themselves totally dependent on Vietnam and diplomatically isolated from the rest of the world.[5] They faced the added threat of the Khmer Rouge, backed by the West, on the Thai border. Moreover, they suffered the added insult of the seating at the UN of the government in exile, the Coalition Government of Democratic Kampuchea, which was basically the Khmer Rouge dressed in diplomatically more acceptable garb by having Prince Sihanouk as its president. Bangladeshis, freed from the excesses of the Pakistani Government and army, find themselves subject to Indian sub-imperialism.[6] Can any of these cases be genuinely characterised as humanitarian interventions? The answer is no. Michael Walzer, in his major study on just wars, commented on humanitarian intervention: 'I have not found any but only mixed cases where the humanitarian motive is one among several'.[7] Interestingly, in the many cases of intra-Third World interventions, justifications are never couched primarily in humanitarian terms, but always within the logic of the state system, that is, in terms of self-defence. It is easy to understand why – state interest takes precedence over human concerns. States outlaw intervention as an insurance policy for their own futures.

The lesson to be drawn from these examples is that states' interests are best served by the outlawing of intervention. Conscious of the political realities of the world in which they must survive, small states have been particularly anxious to elevate the status of sovereignty and non-intervention. This is a common theme in the inter-American treaties, in the Arab League, in the OAU,[8] and in UN resolutions such as the Charter of Economic Rights and Duties of States.[9] All states know that in the absence of an independent international arbiter and agreed sanctions, the rules are often disregarded. Nevertheless, the recognition of the rule of non-intervention at least gives weak states some legitimacy in their protestations against the activities of stronger states. Third World states know only too well that if the principle is abandoned, it is they who will suffer most. For them the notions of sovereignty and non-intervention bring a degree of equality and *hope* to their existence. Without such notions, they have no chance of any degree of autonomous decision-making. After all, that is the point of self-determination, which finds its most potent expression in nationalism.

This raises an important question: is it realistic to press for a higher morality than that of the state while nationalism remains such a pervasive force in the international system? Can international political activity be governed by universal values which ignore the vitality of the ideas of the nation-state and self-determination? An international morality based on the individual is misplaced in the present international system and has as much if not more potential for harm than for good.

MORALISING IN THE INTERNATIONAL SYSTEM

The dangers of imposing an international moral framework are exemplified by the tide of liberal moralism which led to the Versailles Settlement. The ideas were completely out of touch with international political and economic reality. This led Keynes, in *The Economic Consequences of the Peace*, to castigate Woodrow Wilson and his fourteen points:

he had no plan, no scheme, no constructive ideas whatever for clothing with the flesh of life the commandments which he had thundered from the White House. He could have preached a sermon on any one of them or addressed a stately prayer to the Almighty for their fulfil-ment; but he could not frame their concrete application to the actual state of Europe.[10]

He was neither statesman nor 'philosopher king'. He was, as Keynes so aptly put it, 'a man who had spent much of his life at a university'.[11]

For the first time in the present state system, a state which lost a war was branded with war guilt, and a massive reparations package was imposed. The Allied Powers wanted to dismantle German industry, cede some of her population and land to foreign control, seize not only German public assets but private assets of German nationals, both in Germany and abroad. The aim was a total subjugation of the German people. Keynes, a fervent critic of the settlement, believed that the treatment of Germany laid the seeds of future war.

> If we take the view that for at least a generation to come Germany cannot be trusted with even a modicum of prosperity, that while our recent allies are angels of light, all our recent enemies, Germans, Austrians, Hungar-ians, and the rest, are children of the devil, that year by year Germany must be kept impoverished and her children starved and crippled, and that she must be ringed by enemies. . . . if this view of nations and their relation to one another is adopted by the democracies of Western Eu-rope, and is financed by the United States, heaven help us all. If we aim deliberately at the impoverishment of Central Europe, vengeance, I dare predict, will not limp.[12]

Of course Keynes's fears were realised. Hilter's national socialism was an intensely nationalistic response to the humiliating treatment received at Versailles – a treatment born out of a belief in the moral inferiority of the vanquished in blind disregard of the dictates of reason of state.

The institution of the League of Nations reflected the same wave of moral idealism. It was established on the principles of 'open covenants openly arrived at' and collective security. But a collective security mechan-ism could never function in the system as it was (and is). There was no universal belief in the collective good. The USA did not join; the USSR joined only in 1934; France and Britain were more concerned with their individual state interests than with any notion of a community of like-minded nations. The Italian invasion of Abyssinia exposed the weaknesses of the League. Sanctions were mandatory under the Covenant, and Italy, the aggressor, was vulnerable to an economic blockade. It was believed in this instance that sanctions would be effective. So why were they not used? Britain and France, fearing a revival of German military power, felt it more prudent to have Italy as an ally. Britain was also worried that Japan might attack its possessions in the Far East. Italy's position on the communications route to the Far East reinforced Britain's prudential rejection of sanctions. These experiences of the inter-war years led liberal internationalists to conclude that 'power politics were the politics of not being overpowered'.[13]

ECONOMIC INTERVENTION

The damage that can be done by misplaced moralism in international affairs is demonstrated more recently by post-war US foreign policy. The US embarked on a world-wide crusade to stem the tide of communism and to promote democracy and capitalism. This of course has led to a whole series of interventions, most notably in Vietnam. Making the world safe for democracy is perceived by many Americans (not just hawkish ones) as an emancipating activity – even if its pursuance sometimes entails the support of governments with dubious claims to legitimacy.

However, the most pervasive interventionary aspect of American post-war foreign policy concerns economics, and it emanates both from the level of structure and of process. The US played the most formative role in the foundation of the post-war economic order, having the decisive voice in the choice of fundamental principles and in the day-to-day details of how the system should function.[14] With the growing interdependence of the capitalist world economy, the US as a major capitalist power plays an inherently interventionary role in the economic life of all states within the world economy. Capitalism is a force which pays no heed to territorial boundaries. The greatest problem here stems from a belief in a right of unrestricted access to materials and markets. The implications for intervention are clear in theory and practice. At the theoretical level, writers such as Edward Luttwak planned and pleaded for the takeover of the Gulf oilfields if the Gulf states for any reason should impose an embargo on sales. Interestingly, Luttwak tries to justify intervention in the oilfields on humanitarian grounds. Using self-serving utilitarian arguments, he claims that more people in the world would benefit from such an action than would suffer. At the level of practice, the US government's response to the efforts of its Bangladeshi counterpart to ban the import of drugs already proscribed in the US is instructive. It provides evidence of the interventionary policies which the US government is prepared to use to safeguard the interests of multinationals and hence the free movement of goods and capital. The rights and profits of those companies, and their influence on the domestic political scene in the US, was of greater concern to the US government than the health of the people in Bangladesh. Thus, at the behest of the US Pharmaceutical Manufacturer's Association, the US government successfully put pressure on the Bangladeshi government to convince it to reverse its policy of limiting pharmaceutical imports.[15]

Well-worn yet very important examples of economic intervention are provided by the policies of the IMF and World Bank.[16] These institutions are pillars of the post-war economic order, and they are dominated in their policy-making by the US. The weighted voting at the IMF effectively excludes most member states from any real influence there, and the US is the only state to have veto power over major decisions. The economic packages devised by the IMF reflect the preferred ideology of the leading western powers, that of the free market.[17] The imposition of conditionality in the IMF's structural adjustment packages subverts sovereignty and reinforces an already skewed distribution of wealth with massive social and political implications for the countries involved.[18] Even stable democracies can be rocked by the resultant strains, witness the riots in February and March 1989 in Venezuela.[19]

US domestic economic policies, such as changes in the interest rates, can have a direct and devastating effect on the economies of less developed countries (LDC)s. Such actions directly increase the repayments on foreign debt, undermine foreign reserves, reinforce trade barriers and affect the value of currencies. In the twelve months up to March 1989, the London interbank rate, to which most Latin American loans are pegged, rose from 7% to 10.5%, adding over US$3 billion in annual interest costs to Mexico's debt service alone.[20] Pursuing an autonomous national economic policy in such circumstance is impossible. It is hardly surprising that Third World countries unite to chastise the USA on the issue of economic intervention.

While we may be critical of physical atrocities carried out by certain Third World governments against their own people, it is worth bearing in mind that much – possibly more – harm results in *all* Third World countries due to the nature and function of international capitalism, and we in the North play a role in this. The majority of the world's people live within the constraints imposed by the poverty trap, lacking access and entitlement to basic needs. The structure of international trade is completely biased against Third World states.[21] In addition to unstable commodity prices and the frequently declining terms of trade, the ever-increasing debt burden means that Third World states must produce more and more simply to stand still domestically and to service debts. Indeed, since 1982 we have witnessed an amazing and absurd net financial flow, from South to North. This reached US$30 billion in 1988 alone.[22] While the Latin American states are the biggest debtors, the African states are also crippled. The amount owed by the latter is of little significance to the creditors, yet even so, western governments have argued that aid was a disincentive to reform and have urged the adoption of IMF medicine. Thus African currencies have been devalued, government spending has been cut and subsidies removed. The effect on the majority of people has been devastating. In some states, notably Morocco and the Sudan, there have been food riots popularly linked to the IMF austerity measures. It can be argued that an indirect result of the £120 billion owed by Africa to the industrialised world is the death of millions by hunger and disease through the diversion of potential funds away from basic needs.[23] More particularist western economic policies, such as the Common Agricultural Policy, have led to food mountains in the developed world while starvation continues in the developed world. This policy has also resulted in decreased opportunities for trade in the developing states. The problem of lack of entitlement and access to food occurs at several levels, both national and international. While the unwillingness of domestic governments to implement land reform and pursue distributive policies is crucial, all too often domestic shortcomings are highlighted to remove external responsibility. Indeed the standard IMF analysis sees domestic mismanagement as the key variable in the economic position of Third World states. The shocking images of famine portrayed by the media may trigger the idea of a need for humanitarian intervention in the Third World. However, we should realise that genuine humanitarian assistance for those starving in the Third World would entail structural transformations in our own economies and political processes.

NEW STATES, NEW MORAL CONCLUSIONS

The realisation of statehood throughout most of the Third World over the last forty years stands in great contrast to the experience of the Northern industrialised states, particularly those of Western Europe which are generally regarded as providing the model for statehood.[24] The latter have had long and bloody histories. They developed over several centuries in a conflictual and competitive international environment in which the majority of states disappeared.[25] The hostile nature of the geopolitical environment meant that arms and men were necessary to defend or extend a ruler's territory, and these had to be financed by ever-increasing taxation.[26] Thus the goal of survival provided rulers with an imperative to promote development and to mobilise and integrate their populations.[27] Hence the states which survived came to be characterised by a high degree of social homogeneity, the monopolisation of coercion by a single centre, and economic development.

In contrast to this pattern, nation-building and state-building is only just underway in many countries in the Third World.[28] Moreover, it is occurring in the context of a comparatively benign international environment. International law protects the arbitrary colonial boundaries and legitimises former colonies as sovereign states. Thus the contemporary international system freezes into place artificial political constructs which lack domestic legitimacy whilst enjoying international legitimacy.[29] The relative lack of geopolitical pressure means that many of these new states have not been forced to interact with their societies in the way that the European states did; it also means that the *domestic strife* which characterises the majority of conflicts in the world today can be expected to continue unabated.[30] Attempts are underway forcibly to engineer nation-state building at high speed in a 'hothouse' environment.

It is inevitable that ethnic conflict will persist, and this can be seen today throughout much of Africa and Asia. If Third World states are to become stable and autonomous actors in world affairs, then first they must become stronger states with a higher degree of domestic legitimacy. This may well mean authoritarian forms of government, one party states and so on along the way – things which are an anathema to many in the West. Yet the developed states did not emerge with their copybooks unblotted, and it is naive to think that artificial new Third World states can. As long as strong governments with domestic legitimacy are absent from the Third World, predatory interventions by external powers will persist.[31]

In conclusion, the hierarchical nature of the present state system endangers weak states and the majority of these are Third World states. If weak states are not to be the victims of self-seeking humanitarianism propounded by stronger powers, be they of the North or the South, then the value of sovereignty must be promoted. Non-intervention as a corollary of state sovereignty is one of the central norms in establishing and maintaining independent decision-making in the modern international system. In addition, it values and maintains the heterogeneity of an ideologically, economically, ethnically and religiously diverse world. In this respect the state has a moral force to it.

Sovereignty and non-intervention are unique features of our system and are not something to be dismissed lightly at the first onset of internationalist moral fervour. For all their flaws, they enable a kind of heterogeneity and autonomy in the system of states which is quite special. While they may impede the realisation of self-determination by smaller or different groups, they also provide some protection against the swallowing up of existing political units by the most powerful states. The most moral position that can be adopted within the constraints imposed by present configurations of power and ideology in our world is therefore strict adherence to the principle of non-intervention.

Notes

* With the exception of a few details on the debt crisis added in 1989, this chapter remains unchanged since it was first drafted in 1986. Hence it does not consider the momentous changes which have occurred in the international system since then. Nevertheless, many of the difficulties raised here remain relevant even in these changed circumstances.

1. M. Akehurst, 'Humanitarian Intervention' in H. Bull (ed.), *Intervention in World Politics* (Oxford, 1985) p. 118.
2. For an analysis of this action, see C. Thomas, *New States, Sovereignty and Intervention* (Aldershot, 1983) ch. 4.
3. See C. Thomas, 'Challenges of Nation-Building: A Case-study of Uganda', *India Quarterly* (July-December 1985) pp. 320–49.
4. For the debate on human rights in Uganda under Obote, see *Africa Contemporary Record*, 17 (1984/5) pp. B403–5.
5. For an account of the effects of diplomatic isolation on Kampuchea, see E. Mysliwiec, *Punishing the Poor: The International Isolation of Kampuchea* (Oxford, 1988). For an understanding of the Vietnamese intervention in Kampuchea and its ramifications, see J. van der Krof, 'Kampuchea: the diplomatic labyrinth', *Asian Survey* (October 1982); L. Dutter and R. Kania, 'Explaining Recent Vietnamese Behaviour', *Asian Survey* (September 1980); D. Pike, 'A Voyage into Unchartered Waters', *Far Eastern Economic Review* (11 June 1982); A. Wood, 'Nationalism and Poverty in the Breakdown of Sino-Vietnamese Relations', *Pacific Affairs* (Vol. 52, 1979); M. Leighton, 'Perspectives on the Vietnamese-Cambodia Border Conflict', *Asian Survey* (October 1978); N. M. Hung, 'The Sino-Vietnamese Conflict – Power Play Among Communist Neighbours', *Asian Survey* (October 1979); C. Thayer, 'Vietnamese Perspectives on International Security: Three Revolutionary Currents' in D. H. McMillen (ed.), *Asian Perspectives on International Security* (London, 1984); and J. Blodgett, 'Vietnam: Soviet Pawn or Regional Power?' in R. W. Jones and S. A. Hildreth (eds), *Emerging Powers: Defence and Security in the Third World* (New York, 1986).

6.   For discussions of the Indian intervention in Pakistan which led to the creation of Bangladesh, see L. Kuper, *On the Prevention of Genocide* (Harmondsworth, 1979). On the question of Indian sub-imperialism, see S. Dutt, *India and the Third World: Altruism or Hegemony?* (London, 1984).
7.   M. Walzer, *Just and Unjust Wars* (Harmondsworth, 1981) p. 101.
8.   See C. Thomas, *New States, Sovereignty and Intervention*, ch. 2.
9.   See *Yearbook of the UN, 1974* (New York, 1975), or *Keesings Contemporary Archives, 1974* (Bristol, 1974).
10.   J. M. Keynes, *The Economic Consequences of the Peace* (London, 1922) p. 27.
11.   Ibid., p. 26.
12.   Ibid.
13.   N. Angell, *After All* (London, 1951) p. 137.
14.   See C. F. Bergston, R. O. Keohane and J. S. Nye, 'International Economics and International Politics: A Framework for Analysis', *International Organization* (Winter, 1975) pp. 3–36, and R. Gilpin, *The Political Economy of International Relations* (Princeton, 1987).
15.   See 'Report to the Expert Committee for Drugs: Bangladesh', *World Development*, Vol. 11, No. 3 (1987) pp. 251–8. Also see C. Thomas, *In Search of Security: The Third World in International Relations* (Brighton, 1985) ch. 5.
16.   On the IMF, see C. Payer, *The Debt Trap* (Harmondsworth, 1986). On the World Bank, see C. Payer, *The World Bank* (New York, 1982).
17.   See C. Thomas, *In Search of Security*.
18.   See G. A. Cornia, R. Jolly and F. Stewart, *Adjustment with a Human Face* (Oxford, 1988).
19.   See P. Riddell, *Financial Times*, 13 March 1989.
20.   See *Wall Street Journal* (Europe) 22 March 1989.
21.   See, for example, S. Amin, *Imperialism and Unequal Development* (Brighton, 1977) or F. Cardosa and E. Faletto, *Dependency and Development in Latin America* (Berkeley, CA, 1979).
22.   See *Financial Times*, 15 March 1989.
23.   See *Independent*, 18 March 1989.
24.   See A. F. Mullins, *Born Arming: Development and Military Power in New States* (Stanford, CA, 1987).
25.   C. Tilly (ed.), *The Formation of National States in Western Europe* (Princeton, 1975).
26.   See M. Mann, *The Sources of Social Power: From the Beginning to AD 1700* (Cambridge, 1986).
27.   See J. Hall, *Powers and Liberties: The Causes and Consequences of the Rise of the West* (Oxford, 1985).
28.   See A. D. Smith, *Nation and State-Building in the Third World* (Brighton, 1984).
29.   For further details of the problem in the African context, see R. Jackson and C. Rosberg, 'Why Africa's Weak States Persist: The Empirical and the Juridical in Statehood', *World Politics*, Vol. 35, No. 1 (1982–3) pp. 1–24; and R. Jackson and C. Rosberg, 'Sovereignty and Underdevelopment: Juridical Statehood in the African Case', *The Journal of Modern African Studies*, Vol. 24, No. 1 (1986) pp. 1–31.
30.   On the question of the propensity for domestic as opposed to interstate

conflicts within the contemporary international political system, and the implications for intervention, see I. Kende, 'Twenty-Five Years of Local Wars', *Journal of Peace Research*, No. 8 (1971) pp. 5–22; and I. Kende, 'Wars of Ten Years', *Journal of Peace Research*, No. 3 (1978) pp. 227–41.

31. See P. Williams, 'Intervention in the Developing World: A View from the North', and, for a contrary opinion, M. Zuberi, 'Intervention in Developing Countries: A View from the South' both in C. Thomas and P. Saravanamuttu (eds), *Conflict and Consensus in South/North Security* (Cambridge, 1989).

8 The Justifications for Intervention: Needs before Contexts

Raymond Plant

INTERPRETING CONTEXTS

If we are to justify intervention there is the problem of whose values we employ: our values or those of the society in which we are proposing to intervene? One important way of thinking about politics, called 'interpretivism' or 'contextualism', is well employed by Michael Walzer in his book *Spheres of Justice*. It is based on the idea that we should abandon the search for transcultural moral foundations for thinking about politics at all. Rather, we should fix our attention on the values of the community that we are thinking about, whether it is our own or another. This does not mean that we are committed to some kind of unthinking conservatism. It does mean that the only basis for criticism in either our own society or another society is the existence of inconsistency between the basic values of that society and the way those values are realised in its social and political arrangements. In Walzer's view we can develop a strong theory critical of many Western societies. Their background and entrenched ideals about moral equality are not practically realised in their political and social culture. One can pursue similar arguments with other societies. This kind of view is anti-foundationalist. As such, it explicitly rejects the transcultural basis of theories of rights, which tries to provide universal criteria for political morality, responsibility, and action. Contextualism argues that there are no such transcultural foundations. We have to look to the way of life of particular societies and develop a critical perspective from that.

On Walzer's view there can be no way of avoiding the question of whether we should intervene in terms of our values or theirs because there are no transcultural values which could be the basis for justification. The answer has to be in terms of *their* values. Only when *their* values are critically understood can we have grounds for intervening in the life of another society. We could argue that the background values of that society are not being properly realised in its political and cultural arrangements.

There can be no other possibility of criticism or justification because there can be no objective moral foundations. Contextualism becomes the only effective form of social and practical criticism. If there is a moral defence of intervention at all it has to be based upon intervening in terms of the values which are professed but not realised in the way of life of that society. If the values exist and are being realised, then, however abhorrent we may find them, there is no justification for intervention at all.

However, within the contextualist position there is no answer to the question of whether those background values are just or unjust, right or wrong. They just have to be accepted as cultural givens. What we really want is some critical view of our own society from someone who is standing close to it, who understands it.

A NEED FOR RIGHTS

A more congenial starting point for dealing with the question of intervention would be a rights-based theory which argues that we need not choose between societies and their value systems. What human rights theories are trying to do, for good or ill, cogently or not, is to say that they are not ethnocentric. I mean, they are foundational, rational and objective irrespective of culture, irrespective of creed, irrespective of circumstance. In that sense, a theory of rights provides a way out of the problem of justifying intervention in terms of the values of a particular society. Moreover, in practical politics issues of rights have raised questions of intervention most clearly. For example, the Food Assistance Act and the Foreign Assistance Acts of the 1960s in the US empowered a President to withhold military aid or food if a state had a poor record of human rights. So it is fairly natural to turn to the idea of human rights when thinking of intervention. Intervention I take to be an action, or inaction, or failure to complete previous actions *with the intention of* influencing the domestic policy of a particular state. Intervention on the action side could be military force, to take the most extreme example. On the omission side, intervention would be a failure to do something which was in your power and which you would refrain from doing. On the failure to complete side, intervention would be stopping an action which you had previously done and which it was expected you would continue to do. All these have the intention and not just the consequence of influencing that state in relation to what are perceived by the active or inactive state as infringements of rights. We then want to know how far a rights-based theory can take us in providing defensible

grounds for intervention, answering questions such as, when are rights
infringed and who has the responsibility for rectifying such infringements?

However, before we can really answer that question we have to consider
what sort of formal requirements a theory of rights would have to satisfy. If
we are to have a properly developed theory of rights it has to be able to fit
into this kind of formula:

$$A \text{ has a right to } \phi \text{ in virtue of } X \text{ against } Y$$

Unless we can specify in detail all the elements in that formula we have
not got a coherent theory of rights. We have to identify the agent to whom
the right is ascribed; we have to characterise that to which the right is
asserted; we need some account of what it is about the agent that enables the
bearing of rights; and we have to say who has the duty or duties which
correspond to the agent's right to ϕ. For the purposes of this chapter, A is
not held to be problematic; we can take it that we are talking about adult
human agents.[1] In thinking about intervention therefore we have to concentrate on the other parts of this formula. They *are* problematic in the context
of rights and responsibilities in international relations.

The first problem is the 'in virtue of X' criterion. The strength of the
rights theory in the context of international relations is that such theories
claim that people have rights in virtue not of *our* values or *theirs*, not in
terms of culturally specific values, but in terms of their humanity. Humanity
refers to features which are not specific to culture, circumstance, race,
ethnic origin or any other culturally specific form. There are of course great
problems in specifying these transcultural values. Despite being extremely
abstract, these problems bear acutely on practical difficulties in trying to
assign responsibilities for the infringement of rights. Broadly speaking,
there are three answers given in the literature to the question in virtue of
what X is that makes us the bearer of rights. The first view is that what
makes human life distinctly worthwhile and that therefore ought to be
protected by rights is some idea of individual consciousness. The second
answer has tended to be in terms of human needs, that there are certain
distinctive human needs which all persons share irrespective of their culture
and context. Those needs underpin claims of various sorts which we could
call rights. A third strategy, a kind of Rawlsian position, defines a list of
rights in terms of the kinds of agreements that would have been arrived at
in a contractual situation between free and equal individuals.

Whatever the X is, it has to satisfy a number of constraints. It has to be
a universal quality and it must be morally relevant. It cannot be any old
feature of human life. Two features usually identified to satisfy these

conditions are the capacities for consciousness and agency. Consciousness alone, however, is not sufficient as a grounding, so must be understood in relation to needs. Similarly, agency requires certain kinds of necessary conditions which are created by the satisfaction of basic needs.

THE COMMON GROUNDING OF POSITIVE AND NEGATIVE RIGHTS

The next part of the formula I want to concentrate on is the ϕ to which a right is asserted and the duties that correspond to it. It is well known that there is a significant dispute in political theory about whether rights are to be understood positively or negatively. For example, does the right to life imply only the negative right not to be killed or a positive right to the means to life and the resources to sustain it? Without an answer to the question 'Are rights to be understood negatively or positively?', there is no means of answering the question of what is to count as an infringement of rights by Y, whether Y is a state or an individual. If we understand rights negatively, it is argued that the corresponding duties are duties of abstinence, so that my right to live is wholly satisfied if Y abstains from killing me. The fact that Y does not provide me with the resources to live does not actually infringe a negative right.

The argument in favour of negative rights is often defended by philosophers such as Cranston in terms of practicability. If we have a right to work or a right to education or other resources, then it may be that governments like that in India cannot in fact secure that right to individuals. Whereas in Cranston's view such states can secure the right not to be killed, they cannot ensure the right to life in the sense of the right to resources. They can ensure the right not to be killed since that right is always practical because it means *abstaining from action*. There is indeed an issue here – we can clearly run out of resources to satisfy positive rights and Cranston is right about that, whereas we do not seem to be able to run out of resources to satisfy negative rights. For example how can we *run out* of people not killing one another, not impairing one another's lives in various ways! These do not look like scarce resources.

However, it might be argued that the real distinction is not just in terms of practicability. If a right is a *positive* right to a resource then we have to get into utilitarian considerations because those rights cannot simultaneously be realised in relation to scarce resources. If we have an *absolute* or *basic* right that cannot be realised simultaneously by all right holders, in what sense can it be basic? If there are rights to scarce resources they clearly cannot always be simultaneously realised. There would have to be rationing, and this would involve utilitarian considerations. Hence if we are to talk at all plausibly about human rights they must be rights to negative resources; not to be killed, not to be interfered with. The corresponding duty is *not* to do certain things, rather than a duty to *provide* certain kinds of resources. On this view the only proper understanding of a right is that it is a right to a form of forbearance by other people, whether they be other individuals or the state.

If, in an international context, we are to say whose rights are being infringed in a particular set of circumstances, then clearly on this view an infringement of rights must be a positive interference in life and prosperity by the state rather than an infringement being the failure by the state to provide resources. For example, the fact that people are dying of starvation in a particular country would not be a ground for saying that their rights were being infringed and therefore a ground for possible intervention. On this account, people's rights are being infringed if they are being actively killed by the government because their right is *not* a right to resources; it is merely the right not to be killed. Negative rights are always practicable because they do not involve costs; the right in question is a right satisfied by the forbearance of government, and this is always practicable.

One standard counter-argument is that the right to life understood as the right not to be killed is not costless. Such rights need protecting by police forces, law courts and so forth, because the appropriate forms of forbearance are just not there.[2] It is possible to reply to this by arguing that while it may be that negative rights seem to involve resources, nevertheless there is still a categorical or conceptual difference between negative and positive rights. For example, we can imagine a world that is rather different from ours in which people did forbear and did not infringe one another's lives and property. In those circumstances rights would be costless. Although that is not the world in which we happen to live, it nevertheless shows there is a categorical or logical distinction between positive and negative rights.

This is an extraordinarily weak argument, since exactly the same counterfactual is available to the positive rights theorist, who could say, 'We could imagine a world in which there isn't scarcity and in those circumstances the right to the means to life would be costless'. What the argument shows in both cases is that arguments against the nature of scarcity are being used. In the first case the negative rights theorist claims that 'If there wasn't a scarcity of human motivation, that is, the motivation of forbearance, then negative rights would be costless'. Equally the positive rights theorist can claim, 'A world in which there was no scarcity of resources'. In both cases the argument is about scarcity and on that basis I do not therefore think that there is a categorical distinction between positive and negative rights.

THE BOUNDARIES OF DUTY

Whether we decide that we are dealing with a negative right to the forbearance of others or the positive right to the aid of others, we must address the question of who has the corresponding duty. The typical answer would be that it is the state which governs the territory within which the right holder lives. If *A* has a right to ϕ then it is the state that has the corresponding duty, whether it is a duty of forbearance or a duty of providing resources. Such an answer raises a very interesting question as to why the right should be held against the state, other than as a contingent matter of efficiency, rather than against all other human beings wherever they may be.[3] If we took the latter view, then the state is not the only *Y* against which the right to ϕ can be held. It could then be argued that all human beings have corresponding negative duty towards *A*, which could be easily discharged, namely by not infringing the right of *A* to ϕ. For example, if we think that *A*'s government is infringing a person's right, then our failure to intervene is not an additional infringement of *A*'s negative right to forbearance. *A* may be being killed by the government of that territory, but *A* is not being killed by you or me, hence the failure to intervene is not an additional infringement of that person's human rights. For example, in Kampuchea under Pol Pot, the West's failure to intervene in the slaughter that was going on meant that while the rights of Kampucheans were being infringed by Pol Pot, we, who could have done something, did not infringe the rights of those people. A negative view of rights severely limits the range of *responsibility* of others.

On the other hand, the positive view of rights changes everything. If *A* has a right to the means of life against all other human beings and we are not providing those means to life, then it could be argued that there is a responsibility and an infringement of rights if the appropriate duty of aid is not being fulfilled. If there is a positive right then the range of responsibilities for the infringement of rights becomes extremely large. This raises questions about action, omission and responsibility. If our government failed to provide aid for people who were starving in another country, then on the positive rights thesis, coupled with an account of acts and omissions, it would have to follow that this is the moral equivalent of killing. A theory of positive rights has the consequence of extending the boundaries of responsibility, even to the extent that we become responsible for the bad consequences that follow from all the good that we are not doing.

The justification for this is a kind of moral principle that would follow from the idea of positive rights. Let me take a micro-example to illustrate this: I walked down the street, there was no-one else available to help, I saw a baby face down in a gutter with water in it and I failed to pluck that baby out of the gutter. Given that the baby has a positive right to life, I have by my omission caused it to die and infringed its right. On the negative view of rights, that child has no right to my aid. If I choose to aid it I may be morally worthy but if I fail to do so I certainly have not infringed its rights. By analogy, if we fail to provide help for people in other countries who are dying of starvation we have not infringed their rights. On a positive view of rights we have. Taking the positive view of rights means that if we could aid somebody who has a positive right at no comparable cost to ourselves then we are responsible for the consequences of that failure to aid. We are *causing the deaths* of people whose lives we could have saved at no comparable cost to our own.[4] Our responsibility could be a basic justification for intervention if the government of the society in question is indifferent to those who are dying and who could be saved with our help. The fact that we would ourselves have a causal responsibility would provide us with grounds for intervention.

It does seem therefore that a positive right, implying a corresponding duty of aid, could ground a notion of responsibility and be used as a basis for arguing in favour of intervention. What a rights-based theory would need if it were to provide a basis for intervention is a hierarchical ordering of rights, where the rights gradually become more peripheral. Developing that kind of ordering relation is in fact extremely difficult. If there are human needs which would ground such a theory of rights, then we would have to derive the hierarchy of rights from an account of those needs which were related to the capacity for agency, however that agency was realised in different and culturally specific forms. Such a rationally defensible ordering of rights allows us to say that A's right to life is more fundamental than Y's right to non-intervention. That would be the only way of avoiding ethnocentrism or radical particularism.

What, then, is the moral significance of the state and its boundaries, assuming for the sake of argument that the state in question is failing to meet the basic needs of its inhabitants, but that it is also not prepared to allow other states to meet those needs? Could there be any moral justification for imposing a regime of distribution on such a state to save those lives?[5] I think that on a positive rights theory that answer must be yes; the reason for this is twofold. The first ground is in terms of our responsibility to people in other societies. This follows from the right to life coupled with a proper understanding of the acts and omissions. Second, on a rights-based political theory the justification of the state is after all the protection of rights. Therefore, if some fundamental rights, like the right to life, understood as the right to means to life, are not being secured by such a state, then that state can be regarded as losing some of its moral legitimacy. In those circumstances, given that it is failing in its basic duty, either intentionally or through omission, and given our responsibility to others, there is a strong justification for intervention.

THE NEED FOR INTERVENTION

This need follows fairly naturally from the understanding of a positive right. To ground a theory of positive rights we require a theory of needs. Human needs are those needs which are necessary to pursue any sort of human action. This view is consistent with an éxtreme degree of moral relativism. One can accept all the differences between cultures and argue that nevertheless there is some non-culturally specific account of basic needs. These are necessary for acting in accordance with the values of any culture, whatever its values might turn out to be. Those needs would be survival and autonomy. It is difficult to see how anyone could act within a specific culture without physical survival and the ability freely to deliberate and to choose between alternatives. Grounding a theory of rights in this way entails a right to resources as well as a right to forbearance. Two arguments support each other at this point. First, arguments about the costlessness of negative rights do not work, and both negative and positive rights imply costs and issues of practicability. Second, grounding rights in basic needs yields the theory of positive rights. A theory of positive rights produces a very strong theory of moral responsibility. If coupled with an account of acts and omissions, we have a very strong basis for intervention in societies which either are not able to respect positive rights out of their own resources or alternatively prefer not to respect them. The case for intervention would follow because the Y in question, against whom the rights are held, can be both the state and all other human beings, given that the *justification* of the state on a rights theory would be the protection that it affords to rights.

We want to be able to say that all questions of political theory are not just internal to existing values, that there has to be some possibility of the external critical assessment of those values, whether for the purposes of intervention or just for rational discussions. That kind of judgement must be rested on a foundational theory. The theory of positive rights outlined above provides a strong, defensible moral basis for intervention and for lessening the impact on our thought and practice of the moral significance of boundaries, frontiers and states.

Notes

1. *A* may be problematic for other cases, such as a foetus. If you take *A* to be some collective entity such as a people or a state, then, of course, none of the following argument goes through. Also, taking *A* as an individual might be problematic for international relations and its focus on the rights of states.
2. See, for example, D. D. Raphael, *Political Theory and the Rights of Man* (London, 1967).
3. Rights are held by individuals, and corresponding duties are also held by individuals. In most cases it is much more efficient for those duties to be organised within collectivities which we call states. I do not see any ultimate moral significance in that. This argument trades on the Lockean tradition regarding the relationship between the state and individual rights, wherein the state is the guarantor of rights, and its legitimacy and right to rule depend on satisfying the guarantee. I would not want to put the morality of states beyond the contingent efficient guarantors of individual rights. Thus the demands of Sikhs would more efficiently be directed to the Indian government, but in the case of South Africa, it is becoming more and more obvious that it is not just governments or governmental agencies, but groups of individuals, such as investors, that may be in a better position to effect changes in internal political arrangements.
4. The difficulty is that the comparable cost cannot be computed philosophically. It is a principle that would have to be filled in with some kind of detail and that task would be very complicated even within one's own society. But I do not think that this difficulty undermines the Gewirthian moral principle that someone has a duty to aid if that duty can be discharged without comparable cost.
5. If there was no state, or no recognisable state within a particular set of boundaries, then the grounds for intervention would be much more difficult. A rights-based theory of intervention is predicated on the defined state with a right to rule because within the theory of rights that right to rule depends on guaranteeing rights. If the state does not guarantee those rights, then it loses legitimacy and there is a ground for intervention. If there is no state at all, it becomes more problematic to discuss justified intervention.

9 Intervention and Virtue

Barrie Paskins

INTRODUCTION

Many modern approaches to the discussion of normative questions are guided and misguided by an over-emphasis on *rules*. It is often assumed that the range of possibilities can be derived from a basic contrast between absolutist ethics and consequentialism. The absolutist holds certain things to be completely forbidden, be it killing, torture, direct attacks on noncombatants or intervention. The consequentialist denies that there are any such absolutes, for the rightness of an action is determined by the totality of its consequences and there is no *a priori* guarantee that the consequences will never be such as to require killing, torture, intervention. Between the extremes of absolutism and consequentialism many rights-based theorists would like to find a middle position that somehow avoids both the absolutist's confidence that some things can be completely ruled out and the consequentialist's tendency to make every kind of iniquity a possibility for everyday calculation.

While the importance of studying the relative merits of absolutism, consequentialism and intermediate sets of rights cannot be denied, the exclusive preoccupation with rules that is encouraged by such study is grievously one-sided. Rules do not apply themselves but have to be applied by individuals and collective human entities. The quality of how the rules are applied is not itself reducible to rules. It derives from the skills and more especially from the virtues of human beings and human collectives. To be realistic, any normative theory must talk sense about these human qualities as well as about rules.

Such is the general belief underpinning this chapter, which seeks to illustrate and clarify the point by defining and discussing one specific feature of intervention, namely military intervention. This involves the attempt to do two things at once: to shed light on intervention by reference to the virtues; and to illumine the importance of the virtues for normative theory by showing one way (I suspect, one of many ways) in which sense can be talked about intervention only by invoking the virtues. This is a large task, and many necessary subtleties and qualifications will unavoidably be omitted in the course of this discussion.

113

THE NATURE OF VIRTUES

To begin, a short account of four virtues is needed.[1] They will be outlined as separate virtues, with an indication of the sense in which they might be regarded as sufficient for our present purpose. The four virtues in question shall be called humanity, justice, prudence and fortitude.

Humanity is the name that in other contexts might be called 'love', 'charity' or 'good will'. Humanity cherishes the wellbeing of one's neighbour whoever he or she may be. It does so without making any reward a precondition (though it assuredly need not involve indifference to the benefits of common interest and the joys of mutual esteem). Its workings can be marred by culture, as when the culture of slave ownership makes Huckleberry Finn think it a damnable sin to help black Jim. It can also carry a person beyond the de-humanising limits of his culture, and so it is that Huck decided to help Jim and be damned. Humanity is not confined to a narrow range of cultures. It is as well known in Buddhism and Islam as in Judaism and Christianity.

Justice is a virtue which is strictly subordinate to humanity. It is the virtue concerned with rules. The just person is the one who is good at inventing, discovering, following, sharing and enforcing the rules which humanity requires. The quality of humanity could not flourish without rules and the distinction between it and justice is strictly analytic; it is not to be looked for in a contrast between two types of person. But the distinction is necessary in human experience because humanity tends to carry us beyond even the best of existing rules, to set for us problems whose always-imperfect solution requires the special skills and temperament which make some people, such as law-givers, more especially embodiments of justice than other, equally virtuous people.

Prudence is the virtue of being alive to one's own particular opportunities and limitations. It is virtue because it is humanity by another name. The habits and rules which make up by far the greater part of our life are not sufficient for us to live well. The rules do not apply themselves but need the special quality of judgement called 'prudence'. Prudence can be made to sound dismal or amoral by one or both of two mistakes: its being in the service of humanity can be forgotten, often because of the mistaken assumption that self-interest is in conflict with humanity; and its concern with one's particular opportunities as well as one's particular limitations can make it sound defeatist, whereas it is in truth as keen for life as a lover in spring, and much less inconstant.

Fortitude includes courage to confront the enemies of humanity and the patience which prevents humanity from being broken by the tragic friction of human life.

VIRTUES AND INTERVENTION

The first virtue, humanity, obviously involves us in a very great problem concerning intervention. Humanity cherishes the wellbeing of one's neighbour, and there are many problematic ways in which this may lead to one's intervening in the life of one's neighbour. A parent must learn the painful discipline of severely curtailing his or her interventions in the child's life. When I am a wrongdoer you, my neighbour, must control humanity's kindness until I face up to the reality of what I have done. And so on. Humanity propels one into one's neighbour's life in all sorts of ways, yet humanity cherishes the real neighbour in his or her separateness. Humanity cannot but involve a problem, or a series of problems, about intervention. Such 'solutions' as are possible will probably require and lead us to, as humanity usually does, the virtues of justice, prudence and fortitude.

The humane life cannot be counted upon to consist of neatly packaged problems to which there are solutions that we can, or ought to be able to, derive from systems of principles. We find ourselves in the middle of a very complicated world. The best characterisation of some situations is extremely difficult, and in some cases there seems to be nothing to be done which can honestly be called 'right'. The best that can be done is to take the least awful line of action, and even this course of action might be seen as dangerously corrupting. In the face of such choices and dilemmas, the theorist of rights should not be allowed to persuade us with anything less than a surprisingly cogent argument that a clearcut set of principles of just intervention is possible when we know that life in general is so messy and that the business of intervention is especially so.

Another feature of the humane life is that concern for our neighbour involves us in complex concerns with collective entities and enterprises. If Jack and Jill are married, and Jilly and Jimmy are their children, then concern for these individuals may in fact be inseparable from concern with the parents' marriage – with the need to respect or salvage that marriage if at all possible, or perhaps persuade them that the marriage is finished. It would be surprising if our concern for the subjects or citizens of state X could be any more readily disentangled from concern with the preservation and flourishing, or the demise, of state X. Another kind of case: if Jenny and Joe are musicians, or have it in them to become good musicians, then concern for the individuals cannot safely be disentangled from concern with music – with its flourishing, and with its being cherished for its own sake as a blessing over and above the mere necessities of human nature.

These considerations demonstrate how easily humanity can mistakenly pare down its concerns to the bare essentials of life. Here, too, there may be complexities of intervention. If the lives of some or all of the subjects of state *X* are bound up with a noble and inspiring culture as Jenny and Joe are with music, then concern for the individuals may draw us into concern with the culture, and this can be an issue in intervention. The existence and wellbeing of collective entities (family, state) and enterprises (music, culture) as well as the wellbeing of individuals are inseparable objects of humane concern.

The complexity of the humane life is not a ground for scepticism but a reason for doubting that any exclusively rule-centred approach to a problem such as intervention can possibly be adequate. Preferably, systems of rules would at the most constitute partial representations of what is involved in justice and prudence – valuable for specialised purposes but not to be confused with the whole ethical substance of the problem.

Viewed in these terms, the humanitarian problem of when to intervene, if ever, in the life of our neighbour is not just *a* problem but *the* problem of intervention, of which the international relations cases are but a special set. Two rival formulations must suffice to indicate why humanitarian intervention can be judged to be *the* problem. One rival formulation might be termed consequentialist. It might go like this:

> *The consequences of international intervention are often grave and far-reaching for both states and individuals. The problem of intervention is that the consequences are liable to be so serious and unpredictable. That's the problem.*

We can all recognise a certain force in this formulation. But it is over-simple in that it omits the vital consideration that intervention is problematic not only because of the consequences but also because there is something intrinsically problematic about a parent's opening a child's letters, or a neighbour intruding upon the noisy disarray of the family next door. In the international case, one needs to know what that intrinsic consideration amounts to. One wants to know this because it is by humanity that we live, rather than by mere consequences.

A second formulation of the international relations problem might be:

> *As well as consequences, international intervention raises a deep issue of principle. Without sovereignty the state is nothing and intervention is a violation of sovereignty.*

This thought might be developed in either an absolutist way or through a rights-based theory lying somewhere between absolutism and consequentialism. As an absolute claim it is preposterous. It is so flagrantly contrary to humanity that one could hardly know where to begin discussing it. As part of an intermediate position, it would need to be put into a form which would enable us to see how, for example, the supposed sovereign right of states was to be reconciled with the rights of their subjects. This reconciliation between state rights and the rights of citizens can best be achieved by teasing the matter out in terms of the virtues.

JUST MILITARY INTERVENTION

So far intervention has been discussed without benefit of a definition. Specifically, the focus now concentrates on 'military intervention'. This is one of three principal subdivisions within the great range of activities which are governed by the so-called just war principles. Broadly speaking, war is between states; civil strife is between a state and some of its subjects or between conflicting claimants of political authority in a given state; and intervention is by state X in civil strife within the territory of state Y. In all of these cases, war-like activity is legitimate only if all of the just war principles are satisfied. There must be just cause and legitimate authority. All remedies short of military action must have been tried without success. Noncombatants must not be subject to direct attack. And so on. Military intervention in this sense resembles war between states to such an extent that the same just war principles apply for the same good if sometimes controverted reasons.

To this extent, the ethics of intervention is a matter of rules and as such subject to the usual controversies between absolutists and consequentialists. A means of seeing one way in which the virtues are relevant is provided by an examination of one of the (many) reasons that people have for being sceptical about the whole idea of just war, including the special case of just military intervention. The source of scepticism discussed here is the vague feeling, rarely stated with any precision, that the just war principles are applied too capriciously for anyone to believe in them as part of the real workings of genuine positive justice. The principles may have a sound and persuasive theoretical basis, but in practice they are not seen as part of the mechanism of such justice as there is in the real world. They are too abstract to be real.

This criticism can be made more precise. The sceptic is presumably not demanding that just war considerations *motivate* the just warrior, for motives are mixed and tangled without limit. What does shape the scepticism is the feeling that, to be real, these principles must play a regular and regulating part in the determination of action. It is certain that they play a regular part in the sense that the better states have legal departments who brief ministers on the legality of what they are proposing, but that is not sufficient. To see that it is not enough, consider how much more active than this are the institutions of criminal justice within a decent state. They are actively seeking to detect crime, to identify subjects, and to bring them to trial. If 'just intervention' is to be 'real justice', must it not have similarities to this reality of the domestic administration of justice?

One way *not* to pursue the analogy is by looking for a distribution of power internationally comparable to the domestic one. The institutions of domestic justice are backed by the state's having vastly greater power than any one of its subjects, or of any group of its subjects who are remotely likely to be under investigation for a particular offence or type of offence. Its autonomy is firmly backed by this ratio of power, whereas war, civil strife and intervention are often if not always characterised by relatively equal power among the belligerents acting in a system composed of a small number of great powers and a large number of small ones.

How are 'regular and regulative operations of justice' within such a distribution of power to be conceptualised? One possible approach is to consider how a single would-be just actor would have to behave to lend 'reality' to the just war principles. To be thought of as behaving justly in this respect, the single state would need to be intervening justly (where this lay within its power) and also be actively creating and strengthening rules for just intervention beyond its immediate sphere of influence. Notice that this latter requirement is more fundamental than it might first appear, for two reasons. First, rules of intervention are needed because the just person seeks good counsel rather than acting alone. Second, suspicion and resentment that the intervention is 'really' selfish will be the greater to the extent that it is unilateral; these charges will be deprived of credibility to the extent that action is preceded and guided by good counsel.

Another approach to the question of what 'reality' might attach to the just war principles is to consider what would be required for several or all of the great powers to be thought of as enacting this kind of justice. In a way this is still more demanding of empirical reality, for it requires something approaching virtue to be found in more powers than one. But in another way it is an occasion for less incredulity because, through reciprocity, this kind of justice might be easier. The benefits of relative virtue and the adverse costs of villainy might be the greater if we all go that way together.

There are, however, two objections to confining discussion to the great powers. First, the capacity for important intervention may lie within the scope of lesser powers, for example, the intervention in Liberia by the Economic Community of West African States (ECOWAS). Second, one of the many reasons why justice is such a central virtue is that the rules of justice bring with them new possibilities of action, over and above a mere ordered aggregation of those whose actions are coordinated by the rules. In practice, the possible importance of lesser powers and the potential for new opportunities emerging from the rules of justice are inter-connected in a way that can be seen best from a quick sketch of the United Nations system.

DEMOCRATIC CONTROL OF JUST INTERVENTIONS

Roughly speaking, the United Nations is a limited oligarchy. The oligarchy is manifest in the special powers of the permanent members of the Security Council. The limitation is embodied in the democratic membership of the General Assembly and non-permanent membership of the Security Council. (This is, of course, a democracy *of* states.) Within this limited oligarchy, an institution of the utmost importance for our present enquiry is the office of secretary-general. The system's constitution confers a measure of autonomy, a limited scope for independent action, upon the secretary-general. This can readily be imagined as being expanded to give substance to the idea of just intervention. All states have access to the secretary-general, who in turn has access to the Security Council. Individuals also could be given access to the secretary-general, perhaps most readily through nongovernmental organisations such as Amnesty International and the Minority Rights Group. The secretary-general's office could be empowered to draw possible cases for just intervention to the attention of the Security Council. This could be done in private or publicly. If a private approach was made, then a further step of reporting in public to the general assembly could be a strengthening of the quasi-accuser's office.

Such a development of the office of secretary-general would not make the United Nations into a world government. The identification of actual cases for just intervention would continue to be a matter which only political argument between states could settle. Military forces could remain entirely under the control of sovereign states. What would change would be the publicly visible process of the application of just war principles. Something very like the traditional distribution of power would be combined with a potentially far more uniform and effective administration of that part of justice which goes by the name of just war. It is commonly thought that talk of just war is too patchy and opportunistic to be taken seriously as an important part of how the world works. Even if justice is done in the particular cases, and this is a big if, scepticism remains. Reflection on the virtues shows good reason for such scepticism. The just person seeks for good counsel and the communal assurance of regular procedures. If patches of intervention that approximate what we think justice requires are promising, they are best called just only to the extent that we view them dynamically, as means to and early constituents of the emergence of a world order which is more just in the sense that the secretary-general's office is empowered to draw the Security Council's attention to possible cases of just intervention.

How does this suggestion measure up to the demands of humanity? Humanity prompts us to intervene in our neighbour's life in a great many ways at many levels, and sometimes it is military intervention that strikes one as being imperative. Military intervention of course requires prudence but there is also the question of principle: does military intervention sufficiently respect the separateness of our neighbour? This brief discussion of the United Nations system suggests that it can do so. To the extent that our neighbour's identity is that of state or aspirant to control a state, there could hardly be a more systematic guarantee of respect than action through the United Nations system of states.

CONCLUSION

To what practical effect might these thoughts be put? One of the main fears of those who are opposed to countenancing intervention is that any concession is liable to be exploited. Some say, for example, that any legitimation of humanitarian intervention lends itself to misuse by sectional interests whose real aims are far from virtuous. How are we to regard this objection? Much depends on the level at which it is advanced. What some objectors seem to want is to exclude legitimate intervention from the vocabulary of interstate discourse, a form of interchange in which precedents are fraught with danger and goodwill cannot be counted on. If this is all that the objection amounts to then it may be compatible with the legitimate thinking of interventionist thoughts at other levels. Above all, in conversations among friends who know one another to be persons of humanity and justice, the fear of exploitation may be misplaced. In such discussions, which constitute a vital and fundamental part of the formation of domestic and international public opinion, plain talking about *prima facie* cases of just intervention sets no dangerous precedents.

Can we trust ourselves sufficiently to draw such a clear cut distinction between private discourse among the virtuous and the dangerous discourse of interstate relations? There are both external and internal reasons for unease. Externally, our 'private' words may be monitored by our enemies and used against us, drawing us into the very precedent-setting we thought to avoid. Internally, our own capabilities for self-deception, ethnocentric blindness and so on may make us hesitate to regard ourselves as capable of virtuous practical thought.

The external threat is the more easily countered. A reasonable degree of rationality should be capable of recognising misuses of our own terminology and thus of continuing to draw the truly necessary distinctions between different cases. What is more insidious is the thought that our own thinking is itself more or less subtly corrupt. If we believe this, the feasibility of straight thinking about just intervention is open to doubt. But notice that this presumption threatens also to corrupt every other kind of thinking. For example, our deliberations about the balance of power are just as likely adversely to affect our thoughts about justice, and it is hard to see how we could expect to carry through any decent argument about the need for intervention or non-intervention on any basis whatever if we believed that our thought is so radically unsatisfactory that we cannot recognise virtue for what it is and cannot think straight about humanity and justice. If reason can be brought to bear on political issues, there is no special obstacle in the way of its guiding our thoughts about humanity and justice.

Perhaps the most important thrust of this discussion of intervention is concerned with the legitimate concerns of international public opinion. The most honest thinking about intervention is likely to occur when individuals with no special axe to grind deliberate together in ways that are structured by humanity, justice, prudence and fortitude. It seems unlikely that they will be able to construct simple rules to distinguish just from unjust interventions, especially if what we want are rules robust enough to resist abuse in the inhumane realm of interstate discourse. Perhaps the best we can hope for is an increasingly rich, systematic and incisively reasoned catalogue of cases whereby the next case can be compared with what has gone before. Individuals deliberating together cannot but recognise their limitations in both power and access to information. Their thinking will be the better if the United Nations system is so organised that some such office as that of the secretary-general exercises the quasi-inquisitorial role suggested above.

Note

1. Clearly much might be said about these definitions. I have myself written a book about them (*Goodwill in Ethics and Politics*, forthcoming) which is a quarter-of-a-million words long without by any means exhausting the subject. Here I can do no more than try to make them a little clearer and more persuasive by considering one of their connections with intervention.

10 Beyond Non-Intervention[1]

R. J. Vincent and Peter Wilson

In his chapter Raymond Plant, with the gentle trailing of the cloak, writes: 'It seems fairly obvious that a rights-based theory would be most congenial for someone who wanted to think about intervention'.[2] Other chapters have invited us to think of alternative starting places for an analysis of the ethics of intervention: realism offers us interest or prudence; the morality of states offers us rights, not of individuals but of states; and the Aristotelian position offers us virtues, in particular the virtue of humanity. These are rival and perfectly legitimate starting points for a theory justifying intervention, or non-intervention. Nevertheless, as will be seen below, the rights thesis is the most challenging one and the one to which the strongest antithesis should be offered.

Just to remind us of Plant's formula and grounding thesis, which is found originally in Alan Gewirth's work[3], a right is best conceived of as:

$$A \text{ has a right to } \phi \text{ in virtue of } X \text{ against } Y$$

An exploration of each element in this formula produces a coherent set of problems, if not answers to those problems. A discussion of who or what is A provides several possibilities: A is an individual, a group, a tribe, a nation, or a class. The question then arises: how do we establish a hierarchy among the claimants to the status of A? Should, for example, the rights of the individual take precedence over the rights of the nation? Always or only in certain circumstances? We then turn to X and what it is 'in virtue of' that we claim the existence of a human right. Plant advanced a basic human needs thesis, but there are other groundings such as human consciousness, human rationality or human dignity.[4] There is also the natural law position which relies upon a thick theory of rights; that is, a theory which posits that human rights should not only seek to protect human dignity but also to provide those basic goods necessary for human flourishing.[5]

This brings us to the question of ϕ. This could be the right to life, in its positive or negative forms, liberty, freedom of expression, freedom of association, the collective right to development or ecological well-being, or some other agreed set of rights. If, for instance, human rights find their foundations in the natural law position, then any list of rights would have to include not only the right of life but perhaps also the right to such things as knowledge, play, aesthetic experience, sociability, and religion.[6] In this tradition human rights are concerned with more than just the survival of individual human beings.

But a theory of rights also entails a theory of obligations. This brings us to the Y of the formula. If rights violations are taking place in a particular state, then there are at least three different levels at which obligation might lie towards the individuals in that state. The first is the vertical notion of obligation: individuals have rights which correlate with the obligation of their own state to look after them. But the government itself may be offending against the rights of these individuals. What then are the obligations of outsiders? This leads to the second level of obligations correlative to these rights. We could say that there is an obligation on an outside government derived from the traditional doctrine of humanitarian intervention.[7] If this is the case, then it is the duty of outside governments to react to these violations.

It might be argued that the point about basic human rights is that they impose obligations on everyone, not just on other governments: everyone has obligations in virtue of the rights of these individuals. In that case we would want something broader than the traditional doctrine of humanitarian intervention in international law. This points us in the direction of the third and perhaps the most interesting level of obligations: the obligations that all individuals have towards all other individuals by virtue of being a part of a cosmopolitan community of humankind. This approach produces a theory of international distributive justice erected on the basis of these universal rights and duties. However, if we are serious about this view, then we have to think about the nature of the political institutions which could organise it and make it practicable.[8] It is not enough to assert that universal rights exist and that everyone has an obligation to uphold them. We also need to think about the means by which they can be implemented.

The beauty of the rights thesis is that it provides a clear set of questions to ask. The difficulty is whether it faces up to the kind of world in which we live. Do outsiders recognise that rights of individuals or groups or tribes or classes within other states trigger meaningful obligations in the international community as a whole? In *Duties Beyond Borders*[9], Stanley Hoffmann argues that the point about rights and rights talk is that they set obligations which are ahead of current practice. Part of the purpose is to establish norms and if these were not at least to some degree ahead of current practice there would be little point in establishing them in the first place. We are not simply collecting in some positivist way what states happen to have done, we are trying to point out directions in which they ought to go. The objection to this is that obligations will be set that are too far ahead of what can conceivably be achieved in the current international community. Hence the need to consider the question of implementation. It may be true that the world we inhabit in some respects resembles a world society rather than an international society; a world of individuals rather than a world of states. But the latter still has the upper hand, and given the nature and structure of international society, the question of human rights implementation is a question of fundamental, rather than of secondary importance. It would be irresponsible to ignore the means of implementing the rights that are being asserted.

The consequentialist and realist critiques argue that the only universal value in the contemporary international community is sovereignty. We are confronted with the rather gloomy domain of power politics, of cultural pluralism, of power determining right rather than right determining power. Given this, it is very difficult to achieve some singular moral vision. The ethical defence of the international system of sovereign states may produce a second-rate morality but, say its defenders, it is all we have got. And, after all, there is something moral to be said about the claim that order precedes justice. In her contribution, Caroline Thomas, however, focuses on justice rather than order.[10] Exploring the doctrine of state sovereignty and the consequent notion of non-intervention, she notes that these at least provide a buttress or means of protest for weak states against the intervention of the strong. It should be emphasised in this context that the doctrine of non-intervention encourages and seeks to legitimate a preoccupation with the affairs of one's own state. Implied is the argument that people work out their own destiny: rebels serious about their cause will demonstrate their attachment to self-evident principles of justice. The non-intervention principle in this respect works as a buttress against imperialism.

In effect this is a weak moral defence because it turns out to be no more than a rationalisation of the existing international order without any interest in its transformation. To think purely in terms of the existing order is to work within the paradigm of the legal positivists; a paradigm which expresses itself in the form of the morality of states. This rationalises not the practice of states but the notions on which the practice of states are supposed to be based: the principles of state sovereignty, the sovereign equality of states and non-intervention. International legitimacy is based upon sovereignty and its recognition by the international community. Endorsing this particular notion of international legitimacy overlooks the problem of international legitimacy. This is, in effect, Walzer's argument: we have to act *as if* other sovereign states are legitimate, not because they *are* legitimate but because to do otherwise would lead to chaos.[11] To do this, however, is to ignore the difference between the morality of states and the morality of *the* state. The moral status and appeal of existing states are taken for granted rather than questioned. No attention is paid to whether states ought to be nation-states, or self-determining states, or whether states ought to satisfy certain basic requirements of decency before they qualify for the protection which the principle of non-intervention provides.

This 'moral standing of states' position is less an ethical defence than a prudential defence of non-intervention. It might be better characterised as a sociological defence of non-intervention given the fact that states themselves have tended to defend the principle in terms of prudence. However, if this weak moral defence is to become fully-fledged it needs to be based on a theory of the good state, not just on an account of relations among separate sovereign states in whose goodness we have no great interest. On this view the principle of non-intervention would protect goods states from outside interference, but not others. A generalised notion of what is prudent in international society consequently could not be used in defence of those states guilty of gross misconduct. This would be the strong antithesis to Plant's rights thesis: rights violations would not automatically justify intervention; everything would depend on the nature and extent of those violations and the definition we give to the concept of the 'good state'.

In his contribution, Barrie Paskins offers the notion of virtues as the basis for a comprehensive theory of intervention.[12] One difficulty with this position is the tendency to move between an idea of the good life in terms of the individual within the state and an idea of the good life in terms of the state within international society. It assumes that what is virtuous for the individual is also virtuous for the state and *vice versa*. However, this may not be the case. As Carr classically demonstrated, such virtues as generosity and honesty, whilst laudable among individuals, can be seen, in certain contexts, to be acts of irresponsibility when practised by large group entities such as states.[13] Being generous in arms control negotiations may detract from, rather than augment international security. Similarly, a policy of complete frankness in diplomacy may diminish rather than enhance friendly relations among states. On this latter point it may be argued that the same applies among individuals; the notion of 'brutal frankness' is a familiar one and it suggests that the virtue of honesty may be compromised in certain circumstances. However, such compromises are likely to be much amplified in international relations. If correct this may give rise to a set of virtues in international society incommensurable with the virtues relating to the individual within domestic society.

A second difficulty in starting with virtues is that they are not strong enough to trigger the duty of intervention. The problem with the virtues is that they cannot be claimed. Therefore no obligation is entailed. They only create *expectations* of behaviour. When observing that a famine is taking place or massive oppression is occurring we would not want to respond simply by depending on the humanity, justice, prudence and/or fortitude of others. That is theoretically and practically inadequate.

A third and perhaps equally substantial objection to Paskins' thesis is that his eloquent critique of legal rights and obligations is followed by his own scholastic set of rules to justify intervention. This set of rules is derived from a just war tradition that many have criticised for its rule boundedness. Others have argued that just war rules are insufficiently impregnated with practice.

By way of synthesis, there are several points to be made. A rights thesis may still be a congenial place to start thinking about intervention, but we must start with a special conception of rights. Henry Shue's minimalist account of basic rights satisfies the criterion for rights which combine the need for internal with external legitimacy.[14] These rights are sufficiently extensive to ensure that their universal realisation would safeguard a basic level of decency in all societies; and they are sufficiently restricted to ensure that they do not upset national and cultural sensibilities. However, it may be claimed that there is a difficulty with taking this account of basic rights as a programme for international relations. Shue's minimalist position very rapidly becomes a maximalist one. Taking rights seriously leads us, for example, from the first level of obligation (that is, one's own state) to the second level (that is, other states in international society), but this necessarily impels us on to the third level (that is, the community of humankind) where global political institutions are necessary. This is clearly the case with the right to subsistence, since consumption patterns in the West may have an indirect but nonetheless profound effect on entitlements in some Third World regions. It may also become increasingly the case with the right to life, if the disturbing estimates of the future warming of the planet and depletion of the ozone layer turn out to be true. These ecological problems are of course impeccably global, as opposed to national or international, problems. And again the implication is that the future satisfaction of basic rights in all parts of the world, and not merely in this state or that region, may become more and more dependent on the willingness of societies in the West (but not only in the West) to change their consumption habits. In general terms the satisfaction of certain basic rights may increasingly come to depend on the third level of obligations.

However, the argument can be made, as it was in *Human Rights and International Relations*[15], that changes in the international system are not producing some kind of cosmopolitan advance on the society of states. Rather there has developed within sovereign states a realm that may now be legitimately scrutinised by other sovereign states. This is not something new, but a return to the medieval tradition of *ius gentium intra se*, that part of the law of nations which is common to all nations in the sense of being common to their domestic life. Henry Shue's basic rights constitute that part of the law common to all. International law, therefore, is not just concerned with the relations between states but also with what goes on within states in certain narrowly defined respects.

BACK TO NON-INTERVENTION?

Many discussions on intervention quickly dissolve into a defence of non-intervention on the grounds that recourse to any inclusive principles are likely to undermine our precarious international order. But if we are unable to be any more constructive, then we have to think again about the definition of intervention. There are different understandings of the term. Some take intervention to be coercive interference that starts and stops, with a beginning and an end. It is seen as a periodic if persistent visitor in international society, not something resident in international society in the same way it might be in an imperial society. Others prefer a view of intervention as structural interference, which is somehow built into the structure of world society as a permanent feature. If this is so, then the concept of intervention in the first place is intrinsically problematic. Intervention becomes synonymous with international relations itself. Consequently both the notion and the principle of non-intervention become devoid of meaning. In any event if we are going to have a principle of non-intervention we need to know exactly what it is that the principle protects. A simple notion of domestic jurisdiction or political space is hardly adequate. The argument, if it is to be morally convincing, needs to be about the precise nature and content of that space.

The difficulty with the principle of non-intervention in this regard relates to the initial allocation of that political space we now call the state. Was it allocated according to some just principle? As Andrew Linklater reminds us in *Men and Citizens in the Theory of International Relations*,[16] the prior questions remain: Why did we decide to play sovereign states in the first place? On what principle was the world divided up into this or that sovereign state? Consequentialist and realist proponents of international order prefer such questions to remain unasked. This is because the attempt to specify the legitimate actors in international society raises difficult questions about self-determination, which logically require us to examine self-determination in other contexts. However, the meaning of legitimacy and self-determination needs to be examined. It seems no longer adequate to define legitimacy in terms of a narrow conception of self-determination. For example, the standard interpretation of the famous General Assembly Resolution 1514,[17] that self-determination applies to 'colonial peoples' subject to colonial (that is, principally European) domination, no longer seems relevant in an age that has witnessed the disintegration of the European colonial empires. Moreover, it no longer seems relevant in an age in which several 'self-determining' and therefore 'legitimate' states have nevertheless committed, and in certain cases continued to commit, gross violations of the basic rights of their citizens. In what sense, except in the formal sense of legal positivism, can such states be considered to be self-determining? It might be said that what needs to be done is to challenge the traditional meaning of self-determination, or at least to complement it with other meanings.

BEYOND NON-INTERVENTION

In the face of the various difficulties outlined above, we have to engage with an emerging notion of international legitimacy: 'emerging' since it can now be argued that the international law of human rights is recognised as part of the *ius gentium intra se*, especially with respect to those rules prohibiting racial discrimination.[18] This opens up the state to scrutiny from outsiders and propels us beyond non-intervention.

We are confronted with a new order of things and a new order of thoughts. The new order of things is the interdependent, interconnected world that is persistently nudging international society in the direction of a world society. The nature of interdependence in the twentieth-century is different from, and more complex than the mythical proportions of the nineteenth-century international order. The distinction between low politics and high politics has been much eroded. Moreover, the technological revolution in instant communications now gives practical meaning to Kant's idea that a wrong done anywhere should be felt everywhere.

Part of the task of international relations is to come to terms with this new order of things, to recognise, in Charles Beitz's phrase, that the sovereign state's boundaries no longer mark the outer limit of social co-operation.[19] It may have been that state boundaries never did mark the limits of social co-operation, but there can be no doubt that the extent to which the state is capable of doing this has radically diminished. The fact that major economic transactions are now conducted by telephone and fax is a striking example of this development. And it may be concluded that there is a need to go beyond non-intervention for the reason that the autonomous system of sovereign states, which had the principle of non-intervention at its heart, has now been replaced by a much more complex world.

The key to the new order of thought is the attempt to enrich international relations thinking – which has tended to be unphilosophical, untheoretical and unreflective – with political theory – which has been all those things but has not dealt with the question 'How do these universalistic notions apply in the context of international politics?' When a conversation has occurred, there has been an airing of differences rather than the generation of a common discourse. International relations theorists point out to political theorists the differences of the international system. The starting places of political theory, it is claimed, do not advance thinking about international relations very far. International political analysis starts from somewhere else and tries to make sense of international politics in its own terms. On the other hand, there are those engaging in political theory who are, consciously or not, doing world politics. The assumption is not that political theory should apply only to this party or to that state, but that it should apply to any decent, civilised social organisation. If we are to take rights seriously, then we should take rights seriously for the whole of humankind and not merely for this or that part of it.

Bearing in mind this new order of things and a new order of thoughts, how does this affect the questions implicit in Plant's formula of rights? How, most importantly, do we find an answer to the practical question of what Y is in the formula: A has a right to ϕ in virtue of X against Y. It was suggested above that there were at least three different levels where obligations might rest. However, more specifically, it is conceivable that Y could be one or more than one of the following six possibilities: individuals in one's own state; one's own state; individuals in other states; other states; non-state actors; or the community of humankind as a whole. The difficulty with the list is that we do not recognise in these disembodied phrases any accountable political institution. What we need, therefore, is a more highly developed theory of the external relations of the state which recognises that the principle of non-intervention no longer sums up the morality of states. This, in turn, requires the development of the notion of international legitimacy, a neglected idea in international relations thought. In developing this area, we may continue to insist upon the principle and corollaries of non-intervention, but we open them up to inspection and exception.

Notes

1. This chapter is based on two presentations and various comments made by John Vincent during the course of the workshops and conferences. He was in the process of rewriting it for publication at the time of his death. It, therefore, represents 'work in progress' and this should be taken into account when reading the chapter. However, it is illuminating to compare the train of thought which John Vincent was developing in these contributions with his more fully and carefully developed arguments in 'Grotius, Human Rights and Intervention' in H. Bull, B. Kingsbury and A. Roberts (eds), *Hugo Grotius and International Relations* (Oxford, 1990) pp. 248–52. The final version has been edited and revised for publication by Peter Wilson.
2. See the contribution in this volume by R. Plant.
3. See A. Gewirth, 'The Epistemology of Human Rights', in E. F. Paul, F. D. Miller, Jr., and J. Paul (eds), *Human Rights* (Oxford, 1984).
4. See J. Donnelly, *The Concept of Human Rights* (New York, 1985); R. Dworkin, *Taking Rights Seriously* (London, 1977); and H. Shue, *Basic Rights: Subsistence, Affluence, and US Foreign Policy* (Princeton, 1980).
5. See J. Finnis, *Natural Law and Natural Rights* (Oxford, 1980) pp. 34–75.
6. See R. J. Vincent, *Human Rights and International Relations* (Cambridge, 1986) pp. 32–3.
7. See R. J. Vincent, 'Grotius, Human Rights, and Intervention'.
8. Implicit in the Kantian position discussed in P. Johnson's contribution to this volume is the argument that it is possible to have some notion of an international community, based on a notion of international distributive justice, which does not require the whole paraphernalia of a judiciary, a government, or other institutions in order to protect the rights of individuals in different groups.
9. S. Hoffmann, *Duties Beyond Borders* (New York, 1977).
10. See the contribution by C. Thomas in this volume.
11. See M. Walzer, *Just and Unjust Wars* (Harmondsworth, 1980).
12. See the contribution in this volume by B. Paskins.
13. See E. H. Carr, *The Twenty Years' Crisis, 1919–1939* (London, 1939), especially pp. 186–215.
14. See H. Shue, *Basic Rights*.
15. R. J. Vincent, *Human Rights and International Relations*, ch. 7.
16. A. Linklater, *Men and Citizens in the Theory of International Relations* (London, 1980).
17. 'Declaration on the Granting of Independence to Colonial Countries and Peoples', 14 December 1960. Text in I. Brownlie (ed.), *Basic Documents in International Law*, 2nd edn (Oxford, 1972) pp. 187–89.
18. R. J. Vincent, 'Grotius, Human Rights, and Intervention', pp. 252–6.
19. See C. Beitz, *Political Theory and International Relations* (Princeton, 1979).

Part III

Hard Cases

11 Confronting Moral Dilemmas in an Amoral World: The Non-State of Lebanon and Israeli Interventionism

Ali Sadeghi

This chapter explores the nature and character of both intervening and target states. Israeli intervention in Lebanon since 1982 provides a focus for analysis and discussion. Three interrelated questions are dealt with: What, in Israeli terms, was the justification for their intervention? Did the status of the Lebanese state trigger circumstances likely to provoke intervention? Does the Israeli justification gain its force and relevance from its own perspective, or from a universal moral framework?

The possibility of justified intervention presupposes an account of morality. Chronologically speaking the first post-Greek, Western definition of morality is provided by Christianity. Within this religious framework of order, state intervention was a meaningless term, since God's authority in the person of the Pope clearly crossed territorial boundaries. Order refers to meaning and significance in the universe of thought and action. Christianity, by assuming a transcendent, provides authoritative answers to all moral and political questions.

Order stems from a belief in the notion of a coherent, intelligent and rational cosmic order. The characters in Dante belong, for example, to a teleologically ordered universe, a world whose laws do not change. They know these laws and are morally bound by them.[1] These laws are static before the transcendent which is itself timeless and is also immanent. Hence, the state becomes a republic in which the individuals are morally responsible for their actions. 'The state provides the framework of moral choice and the law the framework of action.'[2] In the republic, the citizens are individually responsible for their actions. It implies the idea of democratic choice. The inheritors of this tradition may be broadly grouped into two factions: one emphasises the sovereignty of the state and has excluded or severely restricted the right of one state to interfere in the internal affairs of another; the second group supported the idea of intervention based on the eternal laws of order. The latter group includes those who believed in natural rights, a concept closely associated with and largely based upon the idea of natural law. The modern successors of this group are those who believe in the idea of human rights.

The first group, whom we would recognise as realists, are perhaps best represented by Hobbes. Hobbes based his theory of the state on two major assumptions: natural law and the theory of social contract. In Hobbes, realism is based upon the notion of an intelligible natural law, an order that is already potentially present but has to be actualised. This actualisation takes place by means of the social contract. In Morgenthau, on the other hand, realism is based upon human nature. In either form, therefore, realism requires a belief in something that transcends the 'reality' of the empiricist. If one takes a realist position, one can reject intervention in the internal affairs of another state. However, one should be aware that one has done so by accepting two contradictory positions at the same time. This is reflected in the argument that sovereignty has two aspects: internal and external. Internally, the supremacy of the state is based on the eternal yet immanent transcendence of natural law. Externally, Locke's theory of ideas and its political correspondent, namely, the theory of tolerance, has restricted the power of the transcendent within the national borders.

It is with regard to a teleologically organised *order* that realism contradicts itself. Realism banishes the transcendent in explanations of the development of the secular state. In order to stop contradicting itself, realism may wish to abandon its claim for a connection to the transcendence. It may, for example, reject the notion that it is based upon natural law or human nature. In that case, it can become purely empiricist and talk not about order but about *system*. System refers to a set of laws that enables the members of the system to interact with each other on an orderly basis. These laws are, of course, positive laws. The laws have nothing to do with the laws of the universe, be they natural laws or religious precepts or rationalist assumptions. Order is hence about morally accepted practice, while system refers to expected practice. Non-intervention can be upheld as a principle of the system but as a law of the cosmic order it becomes absurdly self-contradictory.

In a sense, the internal and external aspects of sovereignty are essential for the creation and maintenance of a European order. Without tolerance, the European civil wars of the seventeenth century would have continued for a great deal longer. The transcendent was thus banished from the state. The nationalisation of God, a process that was largely initiated by

Henry VIII, was to have a profound impact on international relations. Indeed, it made possible the existence of international relations. The idea of the state as a republic in which individuals had moral choice, and the necessity of choice, could not be carried forward once the laws of the state had no relation to the laws of the universe. The republic could no longer be an arena of moral choice, despite its claims to the contrary. The state in the West has lost its connection to the transcendent but has at the same time increased its claim to moral authority. The principle of non-intervention, itself the product of an uneasy alliance between tolerance and transcendence, has come to be challenged by a self-righteous claim to moral authority by the states that have lost their connection with the moral transcendent. The United States is the best example of this.[3]

The second group of inheritors of the Western Christian tradition, the proponents of natural law, natural rights, and more recently human rights, have long tried to undermine the tradition of non-intervention. Here I am of course referring to a wide variety of different schools of thought and I realise that these different groups cannot be treated as if they were one. Broadly speaking, however, advocates of these ideas can be said to uphold that there are some rights inherent in the essence of all human beings, a fixed *a priori* attribute. There are difficulties in pointing out exactly what these rights are, the greatest of which stems from the lack of agreement between different cultures and different periods of history over what constitutes human essence.

The problem is compounded by the attempt to apply rights-based theories to the state. Three major problems are evident. First, the question of whether the state can be considered a moral agent with rights and duties is still hotly debated. Second, rights-based theories are often theories concerned with duties. How else could one talk about animal rights except by saying that animals have certain interests and that these create a duty *for us*? The third problem occurs because rights are historically contingent.

One can only go beyond the principle of non-intervention if we question some of the prevalent assumptions about the nature of international society and the role of the state. As noted above, human rights cannot be a fixed attribute of human beings. This doesn't mean that one cannot talk about human rights. Human rights, being historically determined, reflect a growing self-consciousness of and by the human race. Human rights become rights through a constant rethinking of old values, beliefs and ideas about what constitutes a human being. This requires not a paradigm, but a discourse. It is only through such a discourse that the species being can produce a definition of human rights, albeit a definition that has to be constantly re-evaluated. For example, the principle of national self-determination is a right only established in the twentieth century and would have been completely incomprehensible in an earlier era.

To sum up what I have argued so far: if one believes in common humanity as a *fixed* feature of the human condition, one may be able to justify intervention when certain criteria are met. If one takes a realist position, a position that has been historically closely associated with the idea of Natural Law but has also emphasised state sovereignty, one rejects intervention in the internal affairs of the state. But if realism is self-contradictory and the belief in common humanity requires a leap of faith, what then is left of a teleological order within which one can discuss the nature of a moral choice? Perhaps nothing. On the other hand, the historical contingency of rights, of rights that have developed through history, may provide a convenient starting point for an exploration of the intervention in Lebanon. This must be seen in the wider context of the Arab–Israeli conflict, particularly in respect of the way the Israelis look at the Palestinians and the Palestinians look at the Israelis. The question of right has always been at the centre of their dispute.[4]

ISRAEL'S INTERVENTION IN LEBANON

On the basis of the available modes of explanation outlined above, the invasion of Lebanon can be interpreted in quite different ways. The major distinctions arise over the characterisation of the intervention. There are several possibilities linked to the distinction between order and system: the realist account; doubts about the existence of the Lebanese state; and the nature of the state of Israel.

The realist perspective casts all interventions in terms of the primacy of state interests. Middle Eastern politics on the whole seems to be an exercise in power politics. Prior to 1982, for example, Lebanon was subject to Syrian intervention. Syria wanted to see a Lebanon supportive of its policy and under its influence. The Israeli intervention of June 1982 was claimed by the government to have been concerned with improving the security of the state of Israel. The purpose of the intervention was to change the political identity of the nominal state of Lebanon. The object was to shape the political order and remake the political map of the Middle East so that there would be a developing set of relationships similar to that established with Egypt in the Camp David Accords.[5] In that way the security of the state of Israel would be consolidated. For the realist, both the Israelis and the Syrians closely calculated their 'national interest'. Both viewed the situation in terms of power and influence.[6] Both Israel and Syria wanted to re-establish the authority of the Lebanese state, but on their own terms. However, contrary to popular opinion, Arab politics is not based on the immanence of the Islamic God. There seem to be some accepted rules of practice among most of the Arab statesmen. This is not based on a liberal view of morality. 'Accepted' practice does not mean morally agreed principles but simply refers to 'expected practice'. This then may be said to provide the system within which local states interact, even if no teleological order is present.

While a discussion of the intervention at the level of the security of the state of Israel makes self-contained sense, it ignores a more interesting, complex and problematic explanation based on an understanding of the nature of the state itself. This is a problem for both Israel and Lebanon. In the case of Israel, the problem of the state consists in the relationship between Zionism and the legitimacy of the state of Israel itself and its peculiarity in comparison with the rest of international society. As soon as we start to discuss the security of the state of Israel externally, then we have to talk about it internally and about the nature of the state of Israel.[7] Some of these things hold true for Lebanon as well, but the major factor is the difficulty of characterising such a fractured society as a state.

LEBANON: THE ABSENCE OF STATEHOOD?

It has often been said that Lebanon is a country at war with itself. Factional rivalry has led to a more or less continuous civil war in the country since 1975. There is a sense in which external involvement in internal Lebanese affairs could be said to have been a permanent feature of its relations with other states over the past two decades. Internal Lebanese factors have often associated themselves with one or more foreign powers. It is through these groups that outside states sometimes fight their proxy wars. Factionalism and the lack of civic responsibility 'have frequently transformed Lebanon into a battlefield where Lebanese factions, often unknowingly, have fought the undeclared wars of other nations by proxy'.[8] At the time of the Israeli intervention, there was no effective state of Lebanon beyond the Presidential palace.[9]

It seems logical to ask whether Lebanon still exists as a state. It could be argued that Lebanon had ceased to be a proper state in the 1980s. If sovereignty partly relates to the state's supreme authority to make and enforce laws within its territory, then Lebanon could hardly be called a sovereign state. Both Israel and Syria have attempted with varying degrees of success (or rather failure) to exploit the situation in Lebanon. They have also usually tried to prevent the complete disintegration of Lebanon. In other words, at different times, both Israel and Syria have tried to preserve Lebanon as a state – albeit one which would be supportive of their policies.

The view that Lebanon is not a state significantly affects our judgement of the intervention and its possible justifications. If there is no state, this makes the relationship between sovereignty and power even more problematic. Internal sovereignty usually means supremacy. The inability of the Lebanese government to govern and protect effectively its population and to control the actions of outside forces, such as the PLO in the southern regions, may provide a justification for Israeli intervention. On the other hand, if there is no state, then the Hobbesian realist could argue that there is no moral dilemma at all, as Lebanon is in a state of nature, irrespective of any legal attributes of the state that may remain. There is no real act of intervention. Are we going to talk about sovereignty only in a purely legal framework? At an abstract philosophical level this may be adequate, but at the empirical level this is unhelpful. There is obviously something there: land, people, and so on. The impact of what the Syrians and Israelis did had real consequences for those people. Both the legalist approach and the philosophical, Hobbesian view of intervention and non-intervention thus become irrelevant in the reality of the situation.

Paradoxically, it can be argued that if sovereignty was the issue, then it was Israeli and not Lebanese sovereignty that was at stake. Lebanon could be seen as an example of an 'inward intervention' in which aspects of the nature of the state of Israel required intervention in Lebanon. The intervention was not directed against the people, government or state of Lebanon. It was directed against the PLO, whose presence in southern Lebanon threatened the legitimacy of the state of Israel. This situation in southern Lebanon was not merely a security problem but had a moral dimension concerning the nature of the state of Israel.

THE NATURE OF THE STATE OF ISRAEL

The initial justification for the Israeli invasion on 6 June 1982 drew attention to the PLO bombing of Jewish settlements in northern Israel and the Israeli desire to push the PLO guns back beyond a 25-mile zone. However, the limited military objective was quickly abandoned. Within a matter of four days, the Israeli army had crossed the 25-mile barrier. It stopped only when it had established itself in Beirut. This action required further justification. Justificationary claims were made by the government in terms of the security of the state of Israel. A number of people, both outside and inside Israel, accepted these claims. This raises the questions: What is the security of the state of Israel? Does it create a moral framework for action?

To answer these questions we need to discuss Zionism, which is central to the idea of the security of the state of Israel. The reason for focusing on Zionism is that the Israeli intervention in Lebanon was a rather peculiar one. It was peculiar partly because the primary justification for Israel's intervention was not to help anyone in Lebanon or even to affect the internal Lebanese political climate or balance of power. The major Israeli reason for going into Lebanon was claimed to be the protection of Jews in Israel. It was based upon internal, domestic reasons. In the case of Israel the debate over whether foreign policy is ideology or national interest does not make sense at all. Each provides the framework for defining the other. Zionism provides the framework within which one defines the interests of the state of Israel. Those interests cannot be defined without reference to Zionism. Without the state of Israel, Zionism would be an unfulfilled ideal. Therefore, we cannot really separate the two, especially when Zionism became official state ideology after 1948.

The development of Zionism in the late nineteenth century reflected political crises in Europe. The first large-scale Jewish immigration to the Middle East occurred after 1881 when all hopes of a labour reform programme in Russia were dashed. The second wave started in 1905 with the failure of revolution in Russia. The third started after the beginning of the Russian Revolution and civil war, which created ghastly conditions for Jews in Russia, and the end of the First World War. The early Zionism was a socialist-humanist and utopian ideology. It borrowed its humanism from the Enlightenment, its love of land from the German Romantics and its extreme egalitarianism from the Russian Populists, from whom it also received its introduction to the means of terrorism. This original Zionism is often used as a vindication for most of what Israel does.

This raises the interesting question: Why Israel? In the history of the Zionist movement a number of alternative locations for asylum were discussed, including Kenya. Alternatives to Palestine were rejected by reference to the theological base of Zionism, albeit a base which has become secularised. Nevertheless, even the essence of secularised Zionism draws on the covenant between God and Abraham. The efforts at historical justification therefore refer to a time that has a distinct religious dimension. This leads to a tension within secular Zionism. It wants to use history to strengthen its claims, but that history is religious. The notion of a secular state of Israel is thus a contradiction in terms for Zionism. But how far does Zionism and the experience from which Zionism emanated provide a moral framework?

The war in Lebanon provoked an intensive debate between the Right and the Left, and the younger and the older generations within Israel. This debate was not conducted in the form of international law, neither was it conducted in terms of the precepts of the Old Testament. What was the framework that was used to talk about the invasion in a moral sense? The framework for the Israelis was provided by the experience of diaspora and, much more particularly, by the experience of the Holocaust. It is almost impossible to exaggerate the significance of the Holocaust in the making of Israel and in the way the Israelis think. The question for me is, do these experiences amount to or allow us to create a moral framework within which we can talk about the morality of Israel from 1948 onwards? Or do they only amount to personal beliefs, prejudices and grief that do not move beyond personal considerations of morality?

Post-1948 Israel is a very complex society. It is based partly upon the ideals of the late nineteenth and early twentieth centuries, but also partly upon the ghastly horrors of the concentration camps. The dual interplay between these two factors is constantly challenging Israel – more so than the hostility of the Arabs. If we look at some of the ideas of the post-1948 generation we can see this. We can see it in one line from a poem of that period: 'We came to build the land and to be rebuilt by it'. What is important is the idea of 'rebuilding' and what it means for a generation which had just experienced the Holocaust. It did not mean a kind of Hegelian attempt to create human beings, or what Marx would call species being, through labour. It was the opposite of that. It was the attempt to assert that one already was a human being in the sense of the Jews being *the* chosen people. This was the assertion of an old idea, namely a work ethos which was part of the Romantic imagination.

It is also through the experiences of the Holocaust that the post-1948 generation relates to the previous generation. The focal point of the inter-generational relationship is the passivity of the Jews in the Holocaust. Passivity has come to be regarded as complicity and guilt. If one accepts this kind of argument, as Hannah Arendt did in her book on the Eichmann trial, then the passivity of the Jews in the Holocaust means that they were partly responsible for what happened. This created in post-1948 Israel a strong sense of guilt. Indeed, so strong was the sense of guilt for having been passive, that the younger generation refer to the older generation as 'soap'. To 'soap' someone up means to ruin them without them being able to do anything about it. It came to mean cowardice.

The response to this guilt is that future threats to the existence of the Jewish people will not meet with such passivity. The result is the attempt to show that the Jews are no longer frightened – indeed, that the Jewish nation can itself become frightening. This resolute attitude not to show the weakness characteristic of the Jewish experience in the Holocaust is central to Israeli action in Suez in 1956, in the 1967 and 1973 wars, and in its response to the PLO. It is also a central point in accounting for the rising religious Right which is often explained in terms of Sephardic Jews constituting 54 per cent of the population in Israel. This explanation is partly true, but partly misleading. Roughly 60 per cent of the Israelis are native born. This, along with other factors, seems to suggest that there is an Israeli identity coming into being which is separate from the Jewish national identity emanating from the diaspora. This accounts for the hostility towards Jews who immigrate to Israel and try to tell the native born what to do. There is definitely the feeling that they have made the country and it is theirs. In that sense the state is more Israeli than Jewish.[10]

Therefore, one has to look at the slow development of a separate Israeli identity. Israel is fascinating because it constantly has to go back to its own origins as no other country in the world. It ceaselessly questions its own existence and the reason for its own existence. There is a continual intellectual challenge to justify its existence. Within that, one has to take into account that Israel is composed of people who emigrated from more than 100 different countries. In this sense, it is an incredible endeavour. But there is also a sense in which this creates a divided and unsettled society – between the old and the young, between the Left and Right, the religious and the secular, between the European and Sephardic Jews. Some very disturbing questions are coming to be asked: for example, who is a Jew or – more to the point – who says who is a Jew? These internal divisions are externalised by the Israeli intervention in Lebanon.

If there is an Israeli identity which is separate from Zionism, it is not that separate. All Israelis are bound up in something that is inescapably religious in that they are all struggling with the religious content of the state. This is true even for those who want to make it secular. This tension in their identity endures. This provides some content in explaining some of the reaction to Israeli intervention in Lebanon or their policies in the West Bank when some Israelis stop and think, 'We are beginning to behave like the people who gave us the deepest sense that we can never escape from being Jewish'. This cuts to the heart of what we can say about the state of Israel in a way that it cannot be said of any other state. All states derive their legitimacy from their historical experience. But no other state rests its legitimacy on the historical experience of its people having been victims. Other states developed precisely *because* they had made others victims, so there would be no crisis of legitimacy if they were to engage in such acts. But for Israel it runs counter to the basic justifications for the state. The problem for Israelis is, given their historical experience, how do they justify their unjust actions?

CONTINGENCY RIGHTS, NATIONAL SELF-DETERMINATION AND PALESTINE

If we turn back to the question of rights, it is clear that the Jews felt they had the right to establish a state in 1948. This right was not based on historical documents but very much on what was happening in Europe and what was happening to the Jews. The major justification for the state is this development of a self-conscious nationalism, of a separate people. But the principle of self-determination, derived from the Enlightenment, is a universalist notion which operates between states *and* within states. What gives each state the right to self-determination is that all citizens of that state are equally able to take part in determining the destiny of that state. That is where the notion of Israel as a Zionist state faces problems. It is implicitly saying that there is not a universalism but rather a concept of Jews as absolutely separate from everyone else. This creates a tension in 'humanistic Zionism'. The humanist view is 'I am a Jew because I am a human being'. But the Zionist view is 'I am a human being because I am a Jew'. The universalist succumbs to the particularist. To this extent, the state of Israel is an anomaly in terms of late-twentieth-century understandings of the state and national self-determination.

The self-determination argument can be applied to the Palestinians at the moment. The growing sense of national self-identity makes it quite legitimate to talk about the need for a Palestinian state.[11] In the context of an historically derived right of national self-determination, the Israeli intervention in Lebanon, which was largely aimed at suppressing the legitimate rights of the Palestinians, cannot be considered legitimate.

CONCLUSION

At the beginning of this chapter I made a distinction between system and order. A system is characterised by certain rules and conventions from which one can draw certain conclusions based upon these rules and conventions, such as are found in international law. It is a system within which judgements can be made. It is not, however, a teleologically organised order within which one can discuss the morality of the judgement. To assess the morality of the judgement requires a leap from the level of the system to the level of order. Realism claims to have such an order. So it is in terms of the argument that it has an order that it is self-contradictory. Realism may prefer to talk in terms not of *accepted* practice but *expected* practice. If so the focus shifts to the system. To claim that this is a system is possible, but not very satisfactory. One cannot make moral decisions *within* that Realist system. If one wants to make moral decisions then one must stay with the question of order. With the demise of a Christian world order, this is not available to us. As an alternative I offered the idea of historically contingent rights. This may not be a wholly satisfactory position, but it does allow us to talk about moral choice even if we do not have an order within which to discuss it. International relations then becomes an attempt to set up an agenda for discourse rather than a search for the 'correct' paradigm.

Notes

1. P. Windsor, 'The Justification of the State', in M. Donelan (ed.), *The Reason of States: a study in international political theory* (London, 1978) p. 171.
2. Ibid.
3. Ibid.
4. To give a brief example, both Israelis and Palestinians have consistently used historical argument to substantiate their claims to territory. The Israelis say, 'We were here 2000 years ago'. To which the Palestinians reply, 'We were here as long as we can remember'. Both sides have made recourse to historical documents in order to sustain their case. This kind of argument is meaningless and unproductive. Neither can say 'We were a nation 2000 years ago', since the very idea of the nation is relatively modern. The question of whether the Jews or the Palestinians are a nation is a recent twentieth-century question. To argue in those terms may be good propaganda, but it is bad history.
5. It is also possible to argue that there was no clear understanding of what the intervention was meant to achieve. It was a rolling intervention with the plans being changed according to the degree of success of the operation. It is possible to account for the intervention in terms of a bureaucratic-political process. While not wholly incompatible with realism, this explanation does cut across rational reductionist theses.
6. Begin's notion of 'Biblical Borders' seems to have added a religious aspect to this, but one that does not seem to be wholly inconsistent with realist thinking.
7. It is an interesting question whether this problem is peculiar to Israel and its questioning of its own justifications for existence. At one level this is true. At another it could be argued that what we are looking at is a peculiar manifestation of something entailed in the nature of most or all states that engage in interventionary activity: what sort of state against what sort of state? What are the implications for the legitimacy of the intervening state?

8. M. Kirswani, 'Foreign Interference and Religious Animosity in Lebanon', *Journal of Contemporary History*, Vol. 15, No. 4 (1980) p. 685.
9. Lebanon did not exist as a single state, but as a series of potential states within itself. And there were several states, not just Israel, whose interests were affected by this 'broken state'.
10. Despite the identity of Israel being separate from diaspora, it is interesting that the links between the two are stronger from the Israeli side than the diaspora. This results from a growing recognition within Israel of its own vulnerability, that it cannot be self-sufficient. It needs a continual infusion from the diaspora.
11. The parallelism between the formation of the state of Israel and the formation of the embryonic state of Palestine is limited, however, by the fact that the Palestinians are not claiming to be a chosen people.

12 Vietnam's Intervention in Kampuchea: The Rights of State v. the Rights of People

Michael Leifer

It is notoriously difficult to formulate a precise definition of intervention which can fit all cases. Intervention is best understood as an act that can be placed along a continuum of state practice which may include such diverse undertakings as economic sanctions and radio broadcasts. The particular example of Vietnam's intervention in Kampuchea[1] is straightforward, however. On 25 December 1978, the Vietnamese Army carried a new government into Kampuchea almost literally in their saddlebags. They displaced an established government which enjoyed international recognition, including a seat at the United Nations, and installed a new government of their own choosing.

The formal agency for intervention was a so-called National Salvation Front for National Liberation,[2] made up in the main of dissident Khmer Rouge; that is, dissidents from the ruling revolutionary party in the so-called Democratic Kampuchea. Vietnam acted in support of this National Salvation Front through the deployment of 'volunteers', in the same way as China had conducted its intervention in Korea at the end of 1950.

Vietnam's public justification was the need to remove a genocidal regime. Clearly, in light of what we now know went on inside Kampuchea between April 1975 and December 1978, that justification carries a high degree of validity. On 18 February 1979, Vietnam entered into a Treaty of Friendship with the government of the new People's Republic of Kampuchea, which had been set up in early January. That Treaty of Friendship served as the legal basis for the acknowledged presence of Vietnamese troops inside the country until their declared withdrawal in September 1989.

PUBLIC v. PRIVATE JUSTIFICATIONS

There is a fundamental difference between the public justification for inter-

145

vention and the private and informal positions which the Vietnamese have been willing to reveal. In discussions in Hanoi and outside the country, it has been made quite clear that human rights violations in Kampuchea were not the pressing priority. Indeed, the whole process of human rights violations of the most gruesome kind, beginning with the invasion of Phnom Penh by the Khmer Rouge in April 1975 and the forcible despatch of its population to the countryside, failed to attract Vietnamese condemnation – until it was politically convenient. For the Vietnamese, the requirement in December 1978 to remove the government in Phnom Penh and replace it with one of their own choosing was a matter of strategic imperative rooted in geopolitical doctrine.[3] That doctrine contemplated Indochina as a natural entity in strategic terms which had to be maintained. Otherwise the integrity and political identity of the Vietnamese state might be placed at risk. This was a view which had been adopted partly from a long-standing proprietary attitude of pre-colonial vintage, and also importantly from Vietnamese Communist experience of fighting both the French and the Americans during the First and Second Indochina Wars. The lesser countries of Laos and Kampuchea were regarded as platforms from which Vietnam could be threatened (partly because of its vulnerable geographic shape). Such platforms had been used to military purpose by both the French and the Americans. It was deemed necessary therefore to establish a close structure of special political relationships in the interests of Vietnamese security. That strategic outlook corresponds closely to the general terms of the now-defunct Brezhnev Doctrine: namely, that the lesser states of Indochina constituted a security zone within which Vietnam had a licence to intervene in the interests of Indochinese Socialist solidarity.[4]

PUBLIC CONDEMNATION AND PRIVATE INTERESTS

International recognition and acceptability of the new Kampuchean regime was crucial to validate Vietnam's action. The public explanation offered, that it was justifiable to remove a genocidal regime, related to that purpose. In the declaratory position of the Vietnamese government, the ethical dimension was integral to the legitimacy of Vietnamese support through 'volunteers' for the agency of intervention. When Phan Van Dong went to Phnom Penh to sign a Treaty of Friendship on 18 February 1979, he stated:

> In the atmosphere of this friendly meeting our delegation warmly welcomes the fraternal Kampuchean peoples' historic victory. A victory which has smashed the tyranny of the Pol Pot clique, eliminated for good

the genocide and slavery imposed by this clique. . . . The victory of the Kampuchean revolution is a victory of the indomitable struggle of the people, who for independence and national sovereignty and for the right to live, oppose the treacherous scheme of expansion and hegemony of the Peking rulers and the fascists' regime of the Pol Pot clique, unprecedented in human history.

The Vietnamese represented themselves as supporting an act of liberation and self-determination. The declaratory position adopted indicated the way in which public justification was sought for action in support of the agency of intervention. In other words, the National Salvation Front which they had promoted had been engaged in legitimate acts. Moreover, the Vietnamese never admitted direct intervention at the outset. What they did admit was a measure of retaliation against the Pol Pot regime to defend their frontiers and preserve their national integrity.[5] The actual troop presence was only admitted and justified in retrospect under Article 2 of the Treaty of Friendship. That article states that '[o]n the principle that national defence and construction are the cause of each people, the two parties undertake to whole-heartedly support and assist each other in all domains and in all necessary forms in order to strengthen the capacity to defend their independent sovereignty and unity'. This was cited as an act of consent by the People's Republic of Kampuchea (PRK) to the presence of 'fraternal' Vietnamese troops in Kampuchea.

These pronouncements were seen by the Vietnamese, at least in principle, as functional in international debate, and as a way of trying to rally diplomatic support for their position (though with limited success). They also had relevance to domestic control. To the extent that the spectre of the return of a genocidal regime was the only alternative, then clearly a temporary alien presence in Kampuchea would be less objectionable than the terrorism of Pol Pot. However, informal communication made it explicit that the intervention had been a matter of strategic necessity. It was put in terms of *realpolitik* rather than of ideology. The different justifications might be explained with reference to the practice of price discrimination in different markets. Where the market is the formal arena of the General Assembly of the United Nations and the aim is to secure legitimisation, then arguments with reference to the publicly accepted norms of that organisation have been advanced. In the corridors, other appeals to governments with differing interests have been made, albeit in conflict with public positions.

There were a number of other related issues at stake in the public discourse about the Kampuchean conflict. First, there was the question of the nature of the ousted government of Democratic Kampuchea, changing in form to become the Coalition Government of Democratic Kampuchea from the middle of 1982. Clearly ethical considerations were relevant to this change. The demonic side of the ousted government had been played up by Vietnam and its supporters. Correspondingly, that aspect had been played down and diluted by the Association of South-East Asian Nations (ASEAN), primarily concerned about the sanctity of national sovereignty. It went out of its way to promote that dilution by encouraging a coalition through the addition of the two non-communist factions. Second, there was the question of representation in the United Nations. If, for example, the PRK could displace the Coalition of Democratic Kampuchea from its United Nations seat, then other important consequences could follow. It would reinforce the legitimacy of the government in Phnom Penh and make it more difficult to continue diplomatic and other support to the Khmer resistance. It would also give the PRK government access to avenues of economic support previously denied it, while Vietnam would be released from a pariah diplomatic position.

To sum up, then, the Vietnamese employed a public justification for intervention based on appeal to the humanitarian norms of the international community. Private or informal justification was couched, however, in terms of perception of the strategic requirements in Indochina, made up of three separate states. On both counts they were unable to overcome a critical objection: namely, the violation of the cardinal rule of the society of states to respect the sanctity of national sovereignty.

INTERVENTION AND THE CONSEQUENCES FOR LEGITIMACY

The main argument against the Vietnamese relates to their propping up the PRK government which was established through a military initiative. This role distinguished the situation from some other interventions such as India in Pakistan and Tanzania in Uganda, which were limited operations, not a prelude to externally contrived political reconstruction. That argument animated public debate in the United Nations. When the Vietnamese complained that they had done no more than other governments who had not been put in the dock, the reply was that the government of the PRK existed only because Vietnamese armed forces were in the country and that the removal of those forces would mean the disappearance of that government. The ability of the government in Phnom Penh to sustain itself independently without Vietnamese military support had regularly been an issue in UN debates. For example, Singapore's one-time Ambassador to the UN, Tommy

Koh, speaking on behalf of the ASEAN group, said that, 'The government of the PRK is nothing more than a puppet regime installed by Vietnam and kept in office by more than 200 000 troops in Kampuchea'. A fundamental question had been the legitimacy of that regime. ASEAN regarded it as illegitimate because, it was claimed, the PRK could only sustain itself with the support of an external agency.

This raises the question of whether it is possible to determine the legitimacy or illegitimacy of a particular regime with reference to ethical considerations. The debate over Kampuchea suggests a presumption that regimes are illegitimate if they are put in place by another country by force of arms, even if they continue in power. Indeed, the solution to the conflict over Cambodia worked out by the permanent members of the UN Security Council turns on 'free and fair elections' to determine the political future of the country. If there could be clearly specified criteria for the legitimate existence of a regime, then ethical considerations might inform judgement about intervention. However, the fundamental problem for international society is that an act of military intervention is deemed, in principle, to threaten the independence of the state, which if tolerated threatens the independence of all states. Therefore, all governments have, in principle at least, a general and equal interest in opposing all interventions, even if justified on ethical grounds.

THE SUPERPOWERS AND COUNTER-INTERVENTION

In practice, in the society of states, some governments are more interested than others in opposing intervention. The experience of Kampuchea provides a clear-cut case of intervention, but the situation and argument had been complicated considerably by superpower rivalry over Vietnam's action. It should be noted that the post-intervention diplomacy occurred within the context of what had been called the Second Cold War. That dimension of the conflict arose from the revision of the structure of global alignments which had been set in train from 1971–2. The rapprochement between the US and the People's Republic of China (PRC), the deteriorating relationship between the US and the Soviet Union and also between the Soviet Union and China, together with the decision by the United States to make the management of the central balance with the Soviet Union its main strategic priority, determined that revision. As far as the Soviet Union was concerned, the deteriorating relationship between Vietnam and Kampuchea and China provided an opportunity to promote an alternative containment of the People's Republic. During the whole period of the Second Indochina War from 1960 (when the National Liberation Front of South Vietnam was set up) to its conclusion in 1975, it had never been thought necessary in Hanoi to enter into an exclusive Treaty of Friendship with the Soviet Union. That Treaty was concluded in November 1978. The Vietnamese were obliged to display dependence because the Soviet Union had became a natural geopolitical partner and a source of countervailing power against China.

The United States viewed Vietnam's intervention in terms of its central adversarial relationship with the Soviet Union as well as in light of its own ignominious exit from Indochina. Vietnam's intervention was interpreted as an extension of Soviet influence; the US stood with those countries opposed to Vietnam and its Soviet patron.

Moreover, the onset of the Kampuchean conflict corresponded with the formal restoration of diplomatic relations between the US and the PRC joined in suspicion of the Soviet Union. In the regional context, the US lent its support to Thailand and its ASEAN partners. When the Thai Prime Minister travelled to Washington in January 1979 in the wake of the invasion, the US disinterred its obligations under the Manila Pact of 1954. For its part, China came to an agreement with Thailand on the supply of military assistance to the surviving echelons of the Khmer Rouge army.

Soviet support for Vietnam did not reflect its government's private justification for military domination of its national security zone in Indochina. The Soviet Union stressed humanitarian arguments initially and later put forward legal arguments based on conventional criteria for statehood. An official statement pointed out: 'The Kampuchean people regard the government of the Republic as a sovereign authority, that this government controls the entire area of Kampuchea and exercises real power in that territory in keeping with the principle of effectiveness upon which representation at the United Nations is based'. Irrespective of the public position of the Soviet Union and Vietnam, the former provided considerable military and other material assistance to underpin the occupation of Kampuchea. Major power intervention distinguished the conflict from the outset but its form was *indirect*. The Soviet Union made it possible for the Vietnamese to sustain their expeditionary force in Kampuchea until Mikhail Gorbachev revised that policy during the late 1980s. Correspondingly, the US, although not providing military material for the Khmer Rouge, was lax in monitoring the distribution of food and medical supplies, a proportion of which was filtered off to the Khmer Rouge. Indeed, the international relief programme for Kampuchean refugees played a major part in rehabilitating the Khmer Rouge, allowing them to revive as a fighting force. The PRC have been the main direct benefactors of the Khmer Rouge who have also enjoyed sanctuary and logistical support from Thailand.

REGIONAL INTERESTS AND COUNTER-INTERVENTION

One reason why the conflict over Kampuchea was sustained in protracted stalemate during the 1980s is that multiple interventions fuelled the furnaces. Such engagement had taken place at an acceptable cost to all the external parties at least until Soviet policy made it increasingly difficult for Vietnam to carry the burden of intervention. This was true of the other regional actors involved, such as the member-states of the Association of South East Asian Nations (ASEAN). ASEAN has not been a direct party to the conflict but has taken a corporate position on the basis of the cardinal rule of the society of states. That position has been incorporated in public argument, especially within the United Nations. ASEAN has also been involved in promoting the legitimacy of the ousted Kampuchean government and reconstituting it in a form which would sustain international voting support. The governments of ASEAN played the primary role in putting together the so-called Coalition Government of Democratic Kampuchea in June 1982. The attempt to dilute the bestial identity of the Khmer Rouge through the addition of non-Communist factions was designed to prevent seepage from the constituency which supported its claim to representation in the United Nations. To some extent, this can be seen as a backhanded acknowledgement of ethical considerations. It was also a way of widening the basis for counter-intervention. The five governments of ASEAN (increased to six with Brunei's membership in 1984) were all very conservative and anti-Communist. It would have been difficult for them to lend support to a communist insurgency, even against another Communist government. To the extent that they were able to promote a coalition that included non-communist components then it could be seen as legitimate to provide them with arms and military training. Malaysia, Singapore and Thailand, with US assistance, engaged in such an undertaking.

The ASEAN governments have continually argued that Vietnam's invasion and occupation of Kampuchea was intolerable because it violated a cardinal rule of the society of sovereign states: namely, the sanctity of national sovereignty. National sovereignty has been put forward time and time again as the primary basis for a minimal structure of regional order within South-East Asia between states who are not necessarily of the same ideological persuasion. The ASEAN governments' position over Kampuchea had been informed also by a counter-interventionist disposition. Failure to take counter-measures, if only diplomatic, was judged to be tolerant by default of a disturbing precedent. If the line were not drawn against Vietnam's act of intervention, then it might be deployed in future circumstances against an ASEAN state, without any redress. The 'domino' concept, resurrected from the 1950s, joined the interests and responses of the ASEAN governments at this time.

More fundamental for ASEAN than the principle of national sovereignty was the danger that independent Thai responses might pose to the cohesion and viability of the Association. The invasion of Kampuchea had not only diminished that country's national sovereignty, it had also violated Thailand's strategic environment. It had done so by raising the prospect of an unprecedented historical development: namely, the establishment of a new centre of power in Indochina dominated by Vietnam. Such a fundamental revision of the regional balance of power would place the Thai state in a subordinate position. In other circumstances, its government might have been obliged to accommodate, but the Chinese made it clear that they were adamantly opposed to the Vietnamese invasion and occupation. Their opposition, expressed in a physical attack on Vietnam in February 1979, allowed Thailand to take up the challenge. Lack of support from other ASEAN states in these circumstances would have put the cohesion of the Association at risk. The Thai access to external countervailing power with which to challenge the Vietnamese threat encouraged the other ASEAN governments to close ranks despite mixed feelings. If they had not stood by their 'front line state', then Thailand might well have pursued a unilateral course with serious consequences for the Association, then in existence for over twelve years.

ETHICS AND SOVEREIGNTY

The ethical factor in the Kampuchean conflict had been a utilitarian one, employed by one side. The terms of public debate about the merits and demerits of intervention were set by international norms. These norms are enshrined in the United Nations Charter and have informed the vocabulary of international discourse. To the extent that states see themselves as beneficiaries of these norms, then they are willing to support them in principle. But the issue of ethics has entered this conflict primarily by way of trying to secure justification or international legitimacy for adverse positions adopted. The Vietnamese used the argument of necessity with reference to the removal of a genocidal regime. That was not effective and was blocked by the far more well-established cardinal rule of the society of states.

The arguments that have been made against the Vietnamese and which have prevailed as arguments are best regarded as prudential rather than ethical. They hold that the nature of the state and its government cannot really be regarded as a criterion for membership or exclusion from membership of international society. Notwithstanding the way that members of international society share ideals and norms, a state which appears to have transgressed certain ethical values is not deemed to be void of legitimacy. Traditionally, therefore, a state's record in human rights is not one of the criteria by which to approve or reject the credentials of a delegation to the UN. Were it introduced into the necessary qualifications for membership of the UN, then at least half the governments would be excluded.

Two other arguments were put forward within the General Assembly. First, accepting the validity of Vietnam's action would set an extremely dangerous precedent. Second, the key issue was the sanctity of national sovereignty and its violation. All member governments have a general interest in upholding that sanctity. A convergence of separate realist interests occurred which served to sustain that general interest. To that extent, the issue of the sanctity of sovereignty has been upheld against arguments based upon ethical considerations of human rights. The rights of state took priority over the rights of people. This prevailing reasoning may be set against the Vietnamese private justification for their presence in and hold on Kampuchea until their declared unilateral withdrawal in September 1989. That position is that the Kampuchean state, in light of its experience of civil war, has been so debilitated in its physical and personal infrastructure that it cannot be an independent entity. It cannot sustain itself as a buffer state, which would serve the security interests of Vietnam, without external protection. To the extent that it is believed that Kampuchea can only be a satellite of another country, the Vietnamese have been determined on geopolitical grounds, as far as their resources have allowed, that it should be their satellite.

Before Vietnam's intervention there was no full public debate on the merits of intervention in Kampuchea on ethical grounds. In part this was because of an absence of full information until well after the event. The internationally condemned intervention by Vietnam suggests a terrible irony. Its direct effect was to halt the process of slaughter in Kampuchea. That was not its prime purpose. Vietnam was unable to use the effect of its intervention to justify its purpose.

CONCLUSION

Vietnam's intervention was the culmination of a process of conflict involving China in particular. The Politburo in Hanoi came to the view during 1978 that there was no other way of dealing with a hostile and ferocious government in Phnom Penh, whose unhygienic political relationship with China seemed designed to place Vietnam in a strategic trap. That government had conducted deep penetration raids into southern Vietnam employing Chinese artillery to shell population centres. Nevertheless, the cardinal rule of the society of states, namely respect for the sanctity of national sovereignty, prevailed as a basis for judging Vietnam because most states share a vested interest in upholding that sanctity. ASEAN resolutions in the General Assembly of the UN calling for the withdrawal of Vietnamese forces from Kampuchea drew progressively increasing majorities during the course of the 1980s, with only lip service paid at the end of the decade to a concern over human rights violations.

In response to international pressure and its own economic distress, Vietnam repeatedly expressed its willingness to withdraw troops from Kampuchea. Nominal withdrawals began in 1982, while a finite date of 1990 was set in the mid-1980s. The transformation in major power relations and an international conference on Cambodia, albeit abortive, prompted a declared accelerated withdrawal in September 1989. However, an attendant upsurge in Khmer Rouge military pressure made it necessary to return 'advisers' to stiffen the resistance of the Phnom Penh government. At issue as far as international response was concerned was the absence of any authoritative monitoring of withdrawal. Provision for the United Nations to undertake this role in the context of a comprehensive political settlement was accepted by Vietnam. National security has been Vietnam's abiding priority in the diplomacy over a settlement; its object has been to uphold the tenure of the incumbent government in Phnom Penh and correspondingly to deny political success to the Khmer Rouge. Condemnation of the Khmer Rouge's bestial record has not been sufficient to overcome international pressure for a settlement designed to deny the legitimacy of Vietnam's intervention and its political outcome through an electoral process. United Nations' management of that process cannot provide a guarantee that Cambodia will be freed of the scourge of the Khmer Rouge, whose military strength has made them, of necessity, a party to a political settlement.

In considering the experience of Kampuchea between 1975 and 1978, the motivation for intervention should ideally have been humanitarian. In the event, intervention was governed by strategic priorities and the interna-

so much in blood and treasure. This is certainly at the root of the Vietnamese attitude.

5.   When discussing the justifications offered privately in terms of national security, the Vietnamese might subsequently have had recourse to a self-defence claim in relation to Kampuchean deep-raids and shelling. Vietnam was very careful to assess the weak points in the possible case against them and to defend them, but they did have a *prima facie* right of self-defence under the UN Charter if they were being attacked. They could have intervened in a legitimate way, with due observance of the principle of proportionality. There had been a previous intervention into Kampuchea in December 1977, with the object of imposing a sanction in the hope that it would deter the Khmer Rouge. Instead, it had just the opposite effect.

13 Legitimate Intervention and Illegitimate States: Sanctions Against South Africa

John Hoffman

It has been argued that questions of intervention involve both utilitarian considerations as well as wider philosophical questions about the nature of the state and the international order. It is suggested here that there is an important link between the two. Responses to the utility and practicality of sanctions against South Africa, for example, inevitably relate to the view taken concerning the nature of the South African state and its international standing.

It is argued that the case for sanctions against South Africa arose from the fact that it is a country governed by a radically illegitimate state. Those who raised what are ostensibly utilitarian objections to sanctions invariably support a more favourable characterisation of the South African state than the one asserted here.

Comparing President Reagan's approval of sanctions against Nicaragua, for example, with his stiff opposition to sanctions against South Africa, does not demonstrate that sanctions were 'practical' in one case but not in the other. Utilitarian considerations in this as in other instances are coloured by a wider philosophical stance, and it seems clear that for the US President at least, the Nicaraguan state (with its democratic socialist policies) was illegitimate in a way in which the South African (with its commitment to free enterprise) is not. It would seem naive therefore to take utilitarian arguments for and against intervention at face value.

THE UTILITARIAN CASE AGAINST SANCTIONS

It may be argued, however, that the link between utilitarian arguments and philosophical stances has been unduly exaggerated in the above example. Even though South Africa might have been described as a radically illegit- imate state, a policy of sanctions against apartheid was not necessarily the appropriate policy response. The utilitarian objections are such that they override any wide philosophical characterisations that can be presented.

Scepticism about this position can be met, first by considering the utilitarian objections to sanctions as an argument in its own right. It can be shown that these utilitarian objections are weak and untenable – even when they are taken in isolation from those philosophical considerations which in the past provided a decisive argument for intervention against South Africa.

There are two key objections raised against intervention. The first might be characterised as the 'limitation' argument. How could sanctions against South Africa be limited and thereby prevent an escalation into a destructive assault on the society as a whole? The second (in some logical tension, it would seem, with the first) might be called the 'efficacy' argument: why should it be supposed that sanctions can serve to hasten the end of apartheid anyway?

Each of these objections will be taken in turn. Talk of limiting sanctions should not confuse the comprehensive scope of the sanctions (as demanded by most of the international community) with the question of targeting these sanctions around a precise and focused set of objectives. Sanctions can be comprehensive and yet at the same time have the clear and 'limited' objective of requiring the target state to negotiate with the representatives of the people in order to bring about the desired change – in South Africa's case the dismantling of apartheid.

Indeed after the dramatic developments in February 1990 when the liberation movements were unbanned and Nelson Mandela and other leaders released, this process is *beginning* slowly and painfully to get under way. If anything, these developments enable us to see even more clearly than before why the case for comprehensive sanctions can be 'limited' to specific objectives. The African National Congress wanted the international community to continue with sanctions until a post-apartheid legislative framework has been negotiated and transitional arrangements agreed. There is an analogy here with the sanctions policy on Rhodesia. Once it was clear that Zimbabwe was to become an independent sovereign state, sanctions were lifted. They had a specific objective and when this was achieved, retraction occurred. Why should the same process not take place in relation to South Africa?

But what of the 'efficacy argument' sometimes raised as a utilitarian objection to sanctions policy – that sanctions would not actually work to bring about the desired ends? There can surely be little doubt that sanctions make an impact. The Washington-based Institute for International Economics has studied 103 cases of economic intervention, and claims that such an impact can be pin-pointed with an almost mathematical precision. Imposing a cost 4 per cent of GNP on the target state can cause destabilisation: raising this to 5.9 per cent brings about more far reaching consequences.[1]

These general observations about the efficacy of sanctions are underlined by the experience of states in the southern African region. It seems clear, for example, that without sanctions, civil war would have continued for much longer in the struggle for Zimbabwe's independence, and that with more *effective* sanctions, independence would have come sooner. In this regard the conduct of the South African state itself is illuminating. By sabotaging international sanctions against the Smith regime, the South African government succeeded in prolonging the life of colonial Rhodesia. However, when South Africa decided that settlement of the Rhodesian crisis was imperative following the collapse of the Portuguese empire, they threatened sanctions of their own in order to force the Rhodesians to go along with the Kissinger plan for majority rule in two years. South African sanctions in 1979 were also decisive in bringing about a military coup in Lesotho. The objection therefore that 'sanctions don't work' is called into question both by international experience in general and by the impact in particular which South Africa's own regional policies have had on its neighbours.

However, it might be said that the point of the 'efficacy argument' is not to deny that sanctions can make an impact on South Africa. It is rather to assert that such an impact would not serve to hasten the complete end of apartheid. This point can be answered by simply posing two questions. Would P. W. Botha's limited reform programme have occurred without international pressure? Would President De Klerk have unbanned the liberation movements in 1990 unless his party and government feared that the modest sanctions already imposed on his country would inevitably be followed by more comprehensive sanctions in the future?

Since the ruling National Party itself has repeatedly alluded (for example during the general election in September 1989) to the problems which these pressures have posed, it seems clear that sanctions (and the threat of their escalation) have played a significant role. First, they pushed the government into a limited reform strategy under P. W. Botha. Then, they forced the Pretoria government to the negotiating table under F. W. De Klerk. If it is now possible to see a post-apartheid South Africa emerging in the next few years, this is surely because the international community has insisted (with varying degrees of rigour) that sanctions could and should make a practical and constructive contribution to the development of a democratic South Africa.

Utilitarian arguments against sanctions have always been weak. Recent events have demolished them altogether. The South African government itself now acknowledges the sanctions played a significant role in compelling its policy makers to change tack. The utilitarian objection to sanctions against South Africa can thus be rebutted as an argument in its own right. However, those who oppose sanctions often do so on philosophical rather than practical grounds. The case against sanctions against South Africa is really made by those who are not persuaded of the radically illegitimate nature of the apartheid state.

COLONIALISM AND THE PROBLEM OF THE STATE

One critic of sanctions has noted that South Africa is unique in the way it has institutionalised racial discrimination.[2] He argues persuasively that in the post-war world racism has been found particularly offensive because of the experience of the Holocaust. But if South Africa is unique in its institutionalised racism, why not characterise it then as a radically illegitimate state against which the international community ought to act? Here it is worth recalling Alexis de Tocqueville's comment in his *Democracy in America*. Discussing the impact made by the new world on blacks and native Americans, he writes: 'The European is to men of other races what man is to the animals. He makes them serve his convenience and when he cannot bend them to his will, he destroys them'.[3]

De Tocqueville's comment deserves attention for two reasons. The first is that it stands out in the nineteenth century as an unusually sensitive denunciation of racism. Today such a revulsion towards racism has become part of an international consensus. But secondly, it is important to see that what de Tocqueville is condemning is not simply racism and the violation of human rights. He is condemning *colonialism*. What makes South Africa uniquely illegitimate in the post-war world is not simply that it practises racial discrimination. The point is that it has done so as a state which has yet to shed its colonial character.

The condemnation of colonialism, however, should not be tantamount to an idealisation of the liberal democratic state. It is not just colonialism which is problematic – it is the state itself; it is both the source of oppression and the vehicle for allowing us to transcend this oppression. The state has been characterised as a 'pathological paradox' on the grounds that it has an absurd and contradictory character. It is an institution which claims (in the celebrated phrase of Max Weber) a 'monopoly of legitimate force'.[4]

Herein arises the absurdity. To ask *why* the state claims this monopoly is to discover that it does not (and cannot) actually have one. Every state

claims a monopoly of legitimate force which is of necessity continually
challenged by those who exercise a rival force and with a rival legitimacy
as criminals, rebels, dissidents, and so on. In other words, the state claims
something in theory which it cannot possibly achieve in practice. The state
which *really* did enjoy a monopoly of legitimate force would necessarily
render itself redundant as a state. Rousseau puts the matter exquisitely when
he says that laws only exist because people break them.[5]

The truth is that despite its moralistic and logical pretensions, the sovereign is a majestically hypocritical institution. This hypocrisy is not however
without positive consequences; for by asserting the need for a community
and common order, the state itself confesses to its own paradoxical character. In this way it highlights the fact that for all its unifying aspirations, it
reflects and entrenches *division*. The liberal state is particularly contradictory in this regard because it is premised on the autonomy of the individual
while asserting at the same time the need (however regrettable) for a
monopoly of legitimate force. Unlike ancient and medieval polities which
accepted hierarchy as natural, the liberal state poses self-government as an
ideal. Although this is a theoretical right which cannot actually be concretised
(while the state itself exists), it is a right nevertheless, leading conservatives
to denounce liberals as 'democrats' and even 'communists' from time to
time!

The 'legitimate' state as it has come to be known in the modern world
is really the liberal state. It has its logical problems but at least it does offer
political citizenship and a somewhat abstract right to self-government.
Colonialism, on the other hand, rejects even this abstract right by asserting
that the people to be governed are subjects but not citizens. When Mill
contends in *On Liberty* that 'despotism is a legitimate mode of government
in dealing with barbarians',[6] he reverts to what is essentially the pre-liberal
notion of the state as a paternal institution governing those who are destined
to live perpetually as children. It is a comment in tension with the rights he
prescribes for his own countrymen and women, and in South Africa it is a
hierarchical judgement which has prevailed for over 300 years.

THE COLONIAL CHARACTER OF THE SOUTH AFRICAN STATE

The US Declaration of Independence might be described as a supremely
liberal and (therefore) superbly hypocritical document. All men have the
right to life, liberty and happiness – all adults, that is, except for women,
650 000 slaves, 250 000 indentured labourers and 300 000 native Americans who were around at the time of the Declaration. It confirmed slavery
in practice but at least it promised freedom in theory.

Compare this with the arguments of the Cape Patriots at the turn of the eighteenth-century in their revolt against the Dutch East India Company. Revolutionary change was in the air but in South Africa it took a decisively 'particularistic' form. The Patriots protested in 1789 that the company was preventing them from flogging their servants without restraint. In the subsequent rebellion of 1795 they duly enshrined their version of human rights: 'Every bushman and hottentot [that is, San and Khoi Khoi] shall be the lawful property of such burgers as may possess them'.[7] A few years later they protested bitterly at the emancipation of the slaves. When the great trek northwards occurs, the complaint boils down to the fact that the Boers are oppressed because others have been allowed to be free. Enshrined of course in the Boer constitutions in the Transvaal and Orange Free State are explicit provisions for the inequality of black and white.

Throughout the nineteenth and twentieth centuries South Africa underwent considerable constitutional evolution: it moved through the forms of crown colony, responsible government, representative government and in 1961 became a republic. But although these changes bring greater autonomy for the *whites*, the colonial character of the state does not change. This becomes strikingly clear after an examination of the wording of Article 147 of the 1910 Union Act. It states that 'control and administration of native affairs shall be vested in the Governor General in Council who shall exercise all special powers in regard to native administration hitherto invested in the Governors of the colonies'. As far as the indigenous population is concerned, in other words, the continuity with the past remains. In the same way, Section 8.4 of the Republic Constitution of 1961 vests in the State President the powers which had earlier been exercised by the Governor General. The office may have changed but the subject status of the African population continues.

It is true that after 1948 explicit references to the colonial character of white rule began to disappear. Africans were referred to less and less often in statutes and official documents as 'natives'. In the same way the whites ceased to be 'Europeans' and the National Party moved away from the United Party's concept of trusteeship – the idea that whites would rule over blacks until some threshold of 'civilisation' was reached. But despite these linguistic and conceptual changes, a profound continuity with the past still remains.

Indeed, when the Afrikaner nationalists came to office in 1948, they asserted vigorously that apartheid was simply an Afrikaans word for 'segregation'. They could be trusted to continue the tradition of white supremacist rule. By the 1950s, however, it became clear that colonial rule was no longer acceptable in a post-war world. If colonialism was to continue, it would have to be *disguised* – and this in essence is what apartheid as a system and an ideology sought to do. Segregationist policies were not only 'tightened up' and implemented more systematically. They were also dressed up as a kind of a democratic revolution.

Discrimination as such became a thing of the past. The African population were to enjoy full political rights. They were to determine their own lives, but as arbitrarily concocted tribal 'nations' in impoverished home-lands allocated to them by apartheid planners. Dr Verwoerd himself made it clear that the homelands policy represented a form of fragmentation that the white government would have preferred to avoid. However, international and domestic pressures made this impossible. An attempt had to be made to accommodate the 'winds of change'. Old fashioned colonialism was reborn as 'multi-national' apartheid.

In the 1970s even the term apartheid was dropped and the South African authorities declared their new found enthusiasm for policies of 'pluralism'. When P. W. Botha introduced his Tri-Cameral parliament in 1983 he told the world that at last South Africa had shed its colonial past. But since this parliament continued to entrench white political control, it is not surprising that it proved totally unacceptable to the black population. Now the government of F. W. De Klerk seeks to negotiate a settlement which will realise 'democracy' (so we are told) but not majority rule.

It is clear that until South Africa emerges as a non-racial democracy (of a serious rather than a De Klerkian kind), the continuity of the South African state with its colonial origins will remain. Africans will be correct to argue that the 300-year-old occupation of their country has yet to end.

CONTEXTUAL CONSIDERATIONS

It has been argued that until the apartheid system is finally dismantled, South Africa remains a colonial state which treats its indigenous population as subjects without citizenship. As a state which denies even a theoretical right to self-government, it can be characterised as pre-liberal. It might even be said that for this reason South Africa is also pre-Weberian, since no state can plausibly claim to exercise a monopoly of *legitimate* force when those who are expected to obey the law have no right to participate in making it.

As a colonial state, the South African regime is a radically illegitimate one – hence the case for sanctions against its policies. But it might be objected that this is a somewhat 'absolute' position which sets up an ethical view of the state and then calls for intervention against those states which do not conform to these 'timeless' criteria. Surely the case for intervention has to take into account contextual considerations – the way in which the view of what constitutes a legitimate state *changes* from one historical situation to another.

This is a fair point. Democracy in ancient Greece was a highly discriminatory system (and yet it was admirable when compared to its autocratic rivals). Colonialism and racism have only really become illegitimate since the time of the Enlightenment when the notion of self-determination and autonomy has been asserted. Even here it could be said that colonial and paternalistic government are only embryonically illegitimate until agents arise who actually challenge it. Britain, for example, denied economic and political rights to the mass of its population for centuries but this only became an *issue* and a problem when the mass of the population began to agitate for those rights which had been denied to them.

'Universal rights' necessarily come to the fore in particular 'contexts'. Up to and even during the Second World War, South Africa's prime minister Jan Smuts was regarded as an international statesman of great repute even though he defended white supremacy in trusteeship terms. Colonialism had yet to become a burning issue, at least in international politics. On the other hand, colonialism would never become a burning issue unless there was a body of argument gathering credibility which asserted human rights in universal terms.

The question of context must not therefore be expressed at the expense of the ethical absolute. The 'universal' expresses itself through the contingent. It emerges as an unfolding historical reality. Take away the case for human rights as such – in general – and all that remains is a paralysing relativism. As a consequence, there would be no basis to criticise any regime at all. Democracy and autocracy, freedom and paternalism would confront us as alternative and competing values which everyone is free to choose according to their subjective whims.

Context, therefore, is important but only as the medium through which developing universal 'truths' express themselves. On the one hand, it would be fatuous to argue on the basis of what we now believe about colonialism that the international community should have imposed sanctions against Holland in the seventeenth-century because of the Dutch settlements in the Cape. After all, anti-colonialism had yet to establish itself as a compelling international norm. On the other hand, it is important nevertheless to record that it was with these Dutch settlements that illegitimate and repressive rule began.

Today South Africans who support the Freedom Charter look to their country becoming a 'fully independent state, which accepts the rights and sovereignty of all nations'. The implication of this clause of the charter is clear. South Africa is not *yet* a 'fully independent state'. It can only become one – a normal state enjoying rights and duties in terms of international law – when it sheds its colonial heritage. The nation is yet to be fully constituted. The people are yet to exercise their rights to self-determination. A common citizenship has yet to be established. Only when these conditions have been satisfied can South Africa become a legitimate state – a 'legal' state – able to invoke the international norms of non-intervention in its defence.

When this demand was first articled in 1955, most of Africa was under colonial rule. Today only South Africa remains with its colonialism of a 'special type'. The 'universality' of this demand for independent statehood has been rendered even more compelling by the changing historical context.

INTERVENTION AND SELF-DETERMINATION

Intervention against South Africa is sometimes presented as a form of 'interference' from the outside. But if this were true, why is it that sanctions have been demanded for over thirty years by the liberation movements themselves? The fact that the South African government is prepared to negotiate with the oldest and most significant of these movements, the ANC, underscores the point. The intervention by the international community in imposing sanctions on the country has been an intervention to assist the transition to self-government and democracy – to help South Africa shed its colonial heritage and join the world community as a legitimate state.

In this case, intervention has clearly been justified and successful. The demand for sanctions has always been tied to the 'limited' objective of bringing South Africa to a democratic legitimacy. F. W. De Klerk asked the international community to lift sanctions, arguing that the unbanning of the ANC and the other liberation movements and the negotiations to dismantle apartheid was sufficient justification for ceasing interventionary activity.

It is a plea (as his right-wing critics angrily point out) which devastates the case against sanctions. For the implication of such an argument can only be that the international community was right to have applied sanctions, that those sanctions were effective, and so need not continue any longer. The international community, however, has exhibited some caution. It is only when promises become realities and stated intentions are reflected in statutory changes, that the case for relaxing sanctions will have been properly established. In other words, external interventionary activity should only cease when South Africa has become an independent state with a legitimate government, and can take its place in international society.

Of course this will by no means signal the end of its problems. To the extent that it remains a state at all, a gulf will exist between the theoretical rights it offers its citizens and the concrete powers they actually enjoy – between the state as a monopoly of legitimate force and the reality of self-government. But South Africa will at least have become a 'pathological paradox' of the normal variety. It will no longer exist as a colonial relic buttressed by concepts from a pre-liberal age.

Notes

1. See on this W. Minter, 'South Africa: Straight Talk on Sanctions', *Foreign Affairs* 65 (Winter 1986–7).
2. J. E. Spence, 'The most popular corpse in history', *Optima* 43:1 (1986). See also my debate with Professor Spence, 'Should Britain impose sanctions against South Africa?', *Social Studies Review* (November 1989).
3. A. de Tocqueville, *Democracy in America*, vol. 2 (London 1965) p. 392.
4. See J. Hoffman, *State, Power and Democracy* (Brighton, 1988) pp. 33–38.
5. J. J. Rousseau, *The Social Contract and Discourses*, rev. edn (London, 1973) p. 99.
6. J. S. Mill, *On Liberty* (Harmondsworth, 1982) p. 69.
7. H. J. and R. E. Simons, *Class and Colour in South Africa, 1850–1950* (Harmondsworth, 1983) p. 12.

14 Non-Intervention, Self-Determination and the New World Order

James Mayall

INTRODUCTION

In 1867 J. S. Mill wrote: 'There seems to be no little need that the whole doctrine of non-interference with foreign nations should be reconsidered, if it can be said to have as yet been considered as a really moral question at all'.[1] His statement neatly encapsulates the liberal dream and dilemma of a reformed international society. According to this vision, states are to be protected from aggression by a working and workable system of collective security, and the democratic and human rights of their citizens guaranteed by the evolution of a genuine (and preferably self-policing) international civil society.[2] For most of the period since 1945, liberal values were championed by one side in the Cold War, but in reality the international system was both defined and maintained by the rivalry of the two superpowers and their respective alliances. Throughout this period, the role of the balance of terror – whether in maintaining or threatening international peace and security – remained the dominant and most fiercely argued question in world politics.

Ostensibly, the most consistent public support for the ideal of liberal international society came from the Third World. A large group of non-aligned, mostly ex-colonial, states asserted the continuing relevance of the principle of non-interference in the domestic affairs of other states. Since many of their governments were despotic tyrannies, their public commitment to the liberal vision failed to impress any but the most gullible of their Western supporters. The activities of the major powers were consequently not seriously constrained. Non-alignment was undoubtedly a sensible foreign policy stance for some countries, but it was not a viable means of transcending power politics in general.

The end of the Cold War has reopened the question of how domestic and international politics should be related. So long as the two superpowers could co-operate in facilitating political settlements in Third World conflicts – as in southern Africa – it was possible to believe that the established principles of liberal international society were finally being upheld and reinforced. After all, what was essentially involved was the negotiated withdrawal of foreign interference in civil conflicts, and support for the efforts of local protagonists in reaching political settlements based on constitutional principles. Moreover, at the centre of the great transformation in the former Soviet Union and Eastern Europe, the commitment to liberalise and democratise society was in the first instance a response to internal demands for reform, rather than external harassment or pressure. Once Gorbachev had made it clear that he would not intervene to save East European governments from their democratic opponents, the way was opened for a much more liberal interpretation of the Helsinki Final Act than his predecessors had been willing to contemplate after 1975. Self-determination and human rights could now be honoured in the same way as in the West, without risk from interference from Moscow. At the same time there was no sentiment, on either side of the old East-West divide, in favour of revising those parts of the Helsinki accord which entrenched the principles of inviolability of frontiers and territorial integrity.[3]

Externally, the co-operation between the five permanent members of the Security Council, which began during the closing stages of the Iran/Iraq war, had at last established the preconditions for a working collective security system, broadly along the lines envisaged in the UN Charter. The coalition assembled under American leadership following Saddam Hussein's invasion of Kuwait in August 1990 held together, despite internal strains, throughout the recent Gulf crisis. That it was able to do so was partly because its mandate was defined by the Security Council strictly in terms of Chapter VII of the Charter: coalition forces were empowered to force Iraq out of Kuwait, not to overthrow the Iraqi regime. There were those who interpreted the Security Council resolutions more broadly, but the general view appears to have been that Saddam Hussein's government was protected by Article 2(7) of the Charter, like any other member of the United Nations (with the possible exception until recently of South Africa). Even so, the worldwide resurgence of constitutionalism could not but affect this first major test of the 'New World Order'. There was something deeply anomalous about the mobilisation of so awesome a force to protect the independence of a small patrimonial state whose hereditary rulers had recently suspended the democratic rights of their own subjects.

In his essay on non-intervention, Mill wrote that:

> a people the most attracted to freedom, the most capable of defending and making good use of free institutions, may be unable to contend successfully for them against the military strength of another nation

much more powerful. To assist a people thus kept down is not to disturb the balance of forces on which the permanent maintenance of freedom in a country depends, but to redress that balance when it is already unfairly and violently disturbed.[4]

It is not immediately obvious that this famous defense of liberal intervention fits the Kuwaiti case, although – under pressure – the ruling family has now committed itself to elections once the immediate tasks of postwar recovery have been accomplished. The Iraqi government has also pledged itself to introduce a democratic, multi-party constitution,[5] presumably in an effort to secure the lifting of economic sanctions.

It is too early to say whether the aftermath of the war will include a genuine liberalisation of society in Kuwait, let alone Iraq, but a measure of scepticism is probably justified. In neither country has the population previously demonstrated spirited determination to defend (or even create) the free institutions of a genuine civil society. There may be good and sufficient reasons for this, deeply embedded in the structure of Arab society and Islam,[6] but it remains as inherently unlikely that a people can be made 'free' against its own inclinations as it was when Mill distinguished (rather complacently for modern taste) between the appropriate rules governing relations between civilised states and those between these states and barbarians. If true, this observation may have implications for international society beyond the present crisis in the Middle East. For example, it should introduce a note of caution into the optimistic discovery by the World Bank and the IMF that structural adjustment and economic recovery in many Third World countries can only be achieved with good (that is, democratic) governance.

Mill was untroubled by the relativist doubts which cloud the vision of his intellectual heirs. Independence and nationality, he believed, were among the greatest blessings of civilisation, but only if society had evolved to a point where these attributes would support, rather than subvert, the development of free institutions. Elsewhere, he makes it clear that, ideally, cultural assimilation should have been accomplished under autocracy.[7] The reason is instantly recognisable today, in the former Soviet Union and Europe as much as in Africa and Asia. Wherever powerful, unassimilated, national communities must coexist within a single polity, they are likely to use the institutions of democracy to gain preferential access to state power (and the patronage that goes with it) at the expense of their ethnic rivals. The competition to establish their respective national rights is likely to prove sufficiently ferocious to ensure that any commitment to uphold the merely human rights of all citizens will remain theoretical.

Mill may have correctly forseen the predicament of many contemporary states, but his implied solution – the maintenance of liberal empire – is no longer available. It is in this context that it is worth reflecting on the wider implications of the international response to the post-Gulf War Kurdish crisis. Is there an international obligation to assist the Kurds? If there is, must we acknowledge a similar obligation to protect other national groups which are similarly oppressed by their own governments? Indeed, will international action to enforce respect for fundamental human rights become an established feature of the 'new international order'?

Before addressing these questions directly, it may be useful to recall the present status that the principle of national self-determination enjoys within international society. Its elevation to the apex of political values at the Versailles Peace Conference notoriously created as many problems as it solved. The League of Nations Covenant provided for the protection of national minorities, in an effort to deal with the awkward fact that the national and political maps of the new Europe could not be made to coincide. However, the concept of minority rights was a casualty of the fascist era and did not survive in the 1945 UN Charter. In its place, the right of self-determination of all peoples was acknowledged as an inalienable human right, while the members of the United Nations all signed the Universal Declaration of Human Rights. The sovereign state and the self-determining individual triumphed in the new formulation; the idea that a minority group could possess rights was eclipsed.

If we take state practice as our guide, it is clear that the international community subscribes to a highly conventional interpretation of the principle of national self-determination. It has been accepted as a synonym for west European decolonisation in Asia, Africa, the Caribbean and the Pacific, and the transition to majority rule in South Africa. It cannot be invoked – at least with any hope of securing widespread support by dissatisfied minorities within existing states. The fiction that these states, the majority of which are in fact multinational, have exercised their right to self-determination at some point in the past, is vigorously upheld by the sovereign governments of great and small powers alike. It is also reflected in the preference for territorial, over social, classifications in contemporary political language as, for example, in the repeated but inaccurate references to 'the Iraqi people' by British and American politicians during the Gulf War.

It should be said, that there are compelling practical, even moral, reasons in favour of the conventional interpretation. In a 1991 speech, the British Foreign Secretary, Douglas Hurd, explained the conventional view in a way which illustrates both its attraction and its vulnerability, from a moral point of view:

> There are occasions, as today, when the world calls out in anger and shared sorrow against cruelty and suffering within states and we, the diplomatic profession, have to work out what should that response be. It does not mean, in my view, choosing, imposing, sustaining governments from outside their country. . . . Nor does that response mean, in my view again, redrawing boundaries. We all know that boundaries can be artificial, they can be inconvenient, but those of us who have studied these matters know that when the countries of Africa became independent they laid down in the Organisation of African Unity the wise principle that despite the artificiality, despite the inconvenience of the boundaries between nations states in Africa, those boundaries should be respected for the common good. That is a principle which we in Europe have laid down again in recent times as we have reflected on and acted on the needs and anxieties of central and eastern Europe, and now also even more recently in the Middle East although there are many disputes and differences, there is common ground that the boundaries between nation states should be respected unless even greater chaos were to come upon us. One can conceive that *well-defined entities* like the Baltic Republics could reach independence through negotiations, but we have all learned enough, perhaps particularly between the two great wars of this century, about the dangers of trying to right wrongs by meddling with boundaries.[8]

There are two features of this statement worth noting. The first is the frank, if tacit, admission that public opinion can force governments into actions which are possibly against their own instincts and in dubious accord with the established rules of international relations. The question then becomes whether such departures from traditional practice will lead to a change in the rules, or on the contrary, will be treated as exceptions which uphold their general validity. I will return to this question shortly in connection with the international plan to provide a safe-haven for the Kurds within Iraq.

The second noteworthy feature is the way in which the Foreign Secretary relaxes the commitment to territorial integrity to allow for the possibility that the Baltic Republics may negotiate their way to independence. It is possible to conceive of several criteria which might be invoked to justify treating the Baltics differently from other would-be secessionist groups.

Perhaps the Foreign Secretary had in mind the brief period of independence and international recognition between the wars, before their forceful incorporation into the Soviet Union by Stalin. Alternatively, it may be said that the status of limitations, which effectively upholds the principle of *uti possidetis*[9] in international law, does not hold for land-grabs carried out since 1919. Perhaps the Baltics are singled out for purely practical reasons, reflecting a judgement by Western governments that to allow them a special status would check, rather than accelerate, the disintegration of the Soviet Union and the right-wing backlash against *perestroika* and *glasnost*.

The list could easily be extended. However, the point is that the Foreign Secretary did not give his reasons for treating the Baltic republics differently from other well-defined secessionist groups. It is true that he referred to negotiation, but then not only would the Baltics have no chance at all of securing independence by any other route, but there is nothing in international law to suggest that the international community could have any legitimate objection to a negotiated settlement of other secessionist conflicts. If the Ethiopian government agreed to the independence of Eritrea, or the Sudanese agreed to partition the country between North and South, this would clearly fall within their sovereign competence. The possibility of legitimate secession, therefore, cannot be confined to the Baltic Republics. It follows that we have to ask whether, in general, there are circumstances in which foreign powers should take a stand on civil conflicts, despite their commitment to uphold Article 2(7) of the UN Charter.

To return to the questions raised earlier. First, is there an international obligation to assist the Kurds? When President Bush suspended Operation Desert Storm at midnight on 27 February 1991, the official view was that the mission – to clear Iraq out of Kuwait – had been accomplished. Western leaders made no secret of their hope that the Iraqi people would exact their own revenge on Saddam Hussein, but they were adamant that the coalition would not attempt to impose a political settlement within Iraq. Indeed, when Shiites in the south and Kurds in the north rebelled against the central government, the US administration decided not to intervene to prevent Baghdad using combat helicopters against the insurgents.[10] Coalition forces thus stood by while Saddam Hussein re-established control of the rebel areas. This was predictably followed by a mass exodus of refugees towards Turkey and Iran. The official answer to the first question was initially unequivocal, namely that the international obligation did not extend beyond repelling aggression.

At the beginning of April 1991, this position changed – not because of a reassessment of international obligations towards those who have had their fundamental rights systematically abused, but because the attention devoted by the Western media to the plight of the Kurds along the Turkish border threatened the political dividends that Western governments had secured from their conduct of the war itself. It seems that the official answer to the second question – will action to protect the Kurds create a precedent for similar action on behalf of other oppressed national minorities? – is also likely to be negative. Despite the intervention by ECOWAS (the Economic Community of West African States) in the Liberian civil war from August to December 1990, no one has suggested a major international effort to create safe-havens which would allow those driven into precarious exile in Guinea and Sierra Leone to return to their homes in safety.

In his address to Congress, on 6 March 1991, President Bush spoke enthusiastically about the prospect for a New World Order in the aftermath of the Gulf War. He quoted Winston Churchill in describing this order as one in which 'the principles of justice and fair play . . . protect the weak against the strong', adding that it would be 'a world where the United Nations, freed from Cold War stalemate, is poised to fulfil the historic vision of its founders. A world in which freedom and respect for human rights find a home among all nations.'[11] In reality, there is little evidence to suggest that human rights law has begun to impose significant limitations on the exercise of sovereign power. On the other hand, regardless of the motives which eventually compelled Western governments to act in the Kurdish case, a strong argument can be advanced supporting the proposition that this action was indeed an international obligation, that it should have been extended earlier, and that if, but only if, a similar set of circumstances was to arise in the future, the Kurdish safe-haven plan should be accepted as a precedent.

It is Mill, once again, who provides the basic sketch of this case. His own argument was addressed to the relationship between the British Raj and the Indian Princely States, about which he writes as follows:

A civilised government cannot help having barbarous neighbours: when it has, it cannot always content itself with a defensive position, one of mere resistance to aggression. After a longer, or shorter interval of forbearance, it either finds itself obliged to conquer them, or to assert so much authority over them, and so break their spirit that they gradually sink into a state of dependence upon itself; and when that time arrives, they are indeed no longer formidable to it, but it has had so much to do with setting up and putting down their governments, and they have grown so accustomed to lean on it, that it has become morally responsible for all evil it allows them to do.[12]

More pointedly still, he defended the conquest of Oude by insisting that:

> The act by which the Government of British India at last . . . assumed the power of fulfilling the obligation it has so long before incurred, of giving to the people of Oude a tolerable government, far from being the political crime it is so often ignorantly called, was a criminally tardy discharge of an imperative duty.[13]

The parallel is, of course, not exact. Empire is no longer an acceptable political form, although we may note that some of those who opposed the United Nations operation in the Gulf, for example the former British Prime Minister, Edward Heath, did so partly on the grounds that it represented a new form of collective imperialism. It is also the case that the former Soviet Union must share with the Western democracies the responsibility for propping up (and arming to the teeth) the Ba'thist tyranny in Iraq during the Cold War. But the parallel is close enough nonetheless.

If therefore an international obligation to assist the Kurds exists, it arose essentially because the coalition had inflicted such devastation on Iraq as to reduce the country to chaos, making rebellion all but inevitable. Moreover, after the war, Western leaders encouraged the Iraqi people to overthrow Hussein.[14] It is true that they did not explicitly promise coalition support to any rebellion and that, in appealing to the Iraqi people to do the job themselves, they chose to ignore the communal and ethnic divisions of Iraqi society. But they cannot have expected the Kurds, with their long history of national revolts, and virtually hopeless diplomatic prospects, to have exercised restraint.[15] To have done so, at a time when 'Iraqis' were being encouraged from Washington to overthrow their government, would have been tantamount to admitting publicly what the rest of the world has apparently long believed, namely that the Kurds have no chance at all of achieving their national aspirations. In the mid-1970s, when there was no talk of a new international order, a Kurdish insurgency had been supported manipulatively by the Americans and the Shah of Iran for reasons of *realpolitik*.[16] The initial willingness of the major coalition partners to abandon the Kurds to their fate seems to have been motivated by a similarly cynical refusal to accept moral responsibility for an evil which, in Mill's terms, they had done much to bring about.

What then are the wider implications of the Kurdish revolt for the new order? Two points are perhaps worth making in conclusion. First, it would be imprudent in practice, and wrong in theory, to generalise from the international obligations towards the Kurds in favour of an international enforcement mechanism for human rights, wherever they are abused. It would be imprudent because, however desirable such enforcement might be, the system would be unlikely to attract either the degree of public support, or the resources, to make it credible. It would be wrong in theory because the obligation towards the Kurds does not arise merely from a general principle of human solidarity. Nor can it be derived from stretching the analogy with Mill's argument to a point where the West as a whole stands in the same relation to the Third World as the British Raj to the Indian Princely States. It arises as a result of the attribution of responsibility for the consequences of specific acts.

Secondly, extreme care will be required in handing over responsibility for Kurdish security to the United Nations. This is clearly desirable, particularly if the dangers of an anti-American backlash are to be avoided in the Middle East, and if the Gulf episode, as a whole, is to mark the opening of a period of international co-operation, albeit on a more modest scale than President Bush's inflated rhetoric suggested. But the Kurds are unlikely to feel secure in their traditional homeland, whatever deals necessity forces on them, so long as the ruling group (itself a minority) in Iraq is not deterred militarily from tearing them up whenever circumstances permit. A lightly armed UN police force would be unlikely to provide this security.[17] It is worth recalling that in Europe, the Helsinki process, once it was allowed to develop, was greatly facilitated, not merely by confidence-building measures in the military sphere, but by the signature on the final act of all the major Western powers and the former Soviet Union. In this way, the internal conditions of European states were placed on the international agenda by common agreement. The prospects for achieving a credible Middle East settlement along the same lines are virtually non-existent. But nothing short of it will allow the full disengagement of coalition forces from Iraq without putting Iraqi Kurds and Shiites at grave risk.

Notes

1. J. S. Mill, 'A Few Words on Non-Intervention', *Dissertations and Discussions* (London, 1867) pp. 153–78.
2. This elusive idea was felicitously described by Adam Roberts in his Martin Wight memorial lecture, delivered at Chatham House on 8 May 1991. Referring to developments in Europe, he spoke of 'a civil society of civil societies with sovereignty fraying at the edges'.
3. Articles III and IV. For text, see J. Mayall and C. Navari (eds), *The End of the Post-War Era: Documents on Great-Power Relations, 1968–75* (Cambridge, 1980) pp. 293–344.
4. J. S. Mill, 'A Few Words on Non-Intervention', p. 176.

5.   *The Times*, 5 May 1991.
6.   E. Gellner, 'Islam and Marxism: Some Comparisons', *International Affairs*, Vol. 67, No. 1 (January 1991) pp. 1–6.
7.   J. S. Mill, *Considerations on Representative Government* (London, 1861) ch. 16.
8.   Speech given by the Rt Hon. Douglas Hurd CBE, MP at the Lord Mayor's Banquet, London, 10 April 1991. *Verbatim Service*, VS008/91. Emphasis added.
9.   *Uti possidetis* ('As you now possess') is a doctrine formulated in Central and South America but now applied by the International Court to Africa, and thought to be of general application. The doctrine provides that states will not change the boundaries they succeed to at the moment of their independence from colonial rule.
10. *International Herald Tribune*, 28 March 1991. There seems to be some doubt as to whether Washington first warned the Iraqi government against using helicopters as well as fixed-wing aircraft and then decided against acting on this warning; or, as seems more likely, failed to proscribe their use in the first place.
11. Official text, United States Information Service (US Embassy, London) 7 May 1991.
12. J. S. Mill, 'A Few Words on Non-Intervention', pp. 168–9.
13. Ibid., p. 170.
14. 'But there's another way for the bloodshed to stop, and that is for the Iraqi military and the Iraqi people to take matters into their own hands to force Saddam Hussein the dictator to step aside and to comply with the UN and then rejoin the family of peace-loving nations.' Remarks made by President Bush to the American Academy for the Advancement of Science, 15 February 1991, *Financial Times*, 16–17 February 1991.
15. See D. Bradshaw, 'After the Gulf War: the Kurds', *The World Today*, Vol. 47, No. 5 (May 1991) pp. 78–80.
16. See L. C. Buchheit, *Secession: The Legitimacy of Self-Determination* (New Haven, 1978) p. 119.
17. See, for example, the letter to *The Times* from Major-General H. M. Tillotson, 1 May 1991. 'In a chaotic situation such as persists in parts of Lebanon and now appears in Iraq, lightly armed soldiers in blue berets, or policemen, are incapable of protecting civilians against regular or irregular troops with tank and artillery support. Worse still, they are vulnerable as objects of political coercion, by either of the factions they are supposed to keep apart, against the Security Council or any of the nations providing elements of the force. On the ground, UN troops can be humiliated and even murdered at will.'

Part IV

Theoretical Departures

15 Contextuality, Interdependence and the Ethics of Intervention

N. J. Rengger

INTRODUCTION

For 350 years, intervention has been the 'sweet enemy' of the European states system, as it now is of the wider international system. A system of states based upon territorial integrity and political sovereignty must view the possibility of legitimate intervention as, at least potentially, one of the most fundamental challenges possible to its ruling feature. Yet in the modern history of the theory and practice of international relations the twin notions of sovereignty and legitimate intervention are, like England and France in the sixteenth century, bound together in mutual dependence and reciprocity even as they sit, precariously, on opposite sides of a conceptual chasm. In this chapter, the question, 'When is it legitimate for one state to intervene in the affairs of another?' will be approached from a perspective which tries to formulate and revitalise certain aspects of the classical traditions of international relations discourse. In the process a different light will be cast on the nature of the relationship between the twin pillars of the contemporary international system: sovereignty and intervention.

INTERVENTION AND CONVENTION

Although discussions of intervention are a permanent feature of the evolution and development of the contemporary international system, the phenomenon has been receiving more than usual attention in recent reflective literature.[1] One of the hallmarks of this corpus of work is the recognition of the problematic status of the concept of 'legitimate intervention' itself. Intervention as a legitimate tool of state policy, a common enough position in the eighteenth and nineteenth century, is no longer deemed acceptable. Given the current state of the international system, Hedley Bull argues, intervention would be easier to justify if it were, in some sense, collective intervention. This view of intervention explicitly draws upon a 'Grotian' tradition in international theory. Christian Wolff, writing in the seventeenth century, remarked that intervention is acceptable only when it is carried out by the *civitas maxima*. Similarly, Bull argues that:

> Ultimately we have a rule of non-intervention because unilateral intervention threatens the harmony and concord of the society of sovereign states. If, however, an intervention expresses the collective will of the society of states, it may be carried out without bringing that harmony and concord into jeopardy.[2]

Despite the long pedigree of this view, the general position of modern international law is that intervention can only be justified in the most specialised and narrowly defined circumstances. Coercive military intervention, for example, is forbidden under Articles 2 and 51 of the United Nations Charter. This prohibition was elaborated in the Declaration on Friendly Relations Between Nations of 1970.[3] However, aspects of the contemporary international system make a clear position on intervention very difficult. Of particular significance are contemporary notions of interdependence. In this context, expanding the definition of intervention to include economic, cultural and political measures makes the general position even less clear.

INTERESTS AND CONSEQUENCES

In the light of these developments, it is interesting to examine two opposing kinds of answers to the question, 'When is one state justified in intervening in the affairs of another?'[4] The first answer is that intervention of any kind is not ethically justifiable. There are, of course, a large number of variants of this position. An interesting example is provided in the present volume by Caroline Thomas.[5] The argument she explores is predicated on three assumptions about the contemporary states system: the primacy of the state: heterogeneity within that system; and the hierarchical nature of the system. On these foundations, she erects a case against 'intervention to promote human causes'. Developing the argument by means of a series of case studies, she concludes that if small states are not to be the victims of self-seeking humanitarianism by stronger powers then the value of sovereignty must be protected through promoting the rule of non-intervention.

The main thrust of this argument is a consequentialist one, based upon an ethics generated primarily by a narrow conception of 'interests'.[6] These interests are the promotion of state sovereignty as the guarantor of the political, economic and cultural integrity of a particular community. However, a strict pursuance of the logic of this position would lead to an almost inhuman passivity in international affairs. Given the complexity of contemporary notions of interdependence, anything which challenged the three basic assumptions that govern the model that Thomas explores would have to be seen as 'intervention'. It is, to say the least, open to doubt that in an even partially interdependent world such rigid distinctions are either possible or desirable.

Even if one grants the ethical premises of the argument examined by Thomas, it does not follow that a hard and fast prohibition on intervention could be maintained. The reason is that this consequentialist approach depends on a view of the ethical which is strangely attenuated. It ignores the well-documented fact that political actors feel committed towards or against certain policy choices, that these commitments tend to be ethical in nature and that often they conflict, giving rise to what is usually referred to as the problem of 'dirty hands'.[7] As a result, such an appeal to interests and consequences proves not to be a suitable basis for '*ethical*' arguments against intervention, even on its own quasi-utilitarian grounds.

THE WRONGS OF RIGHT-BASED APPROACHES

The obverse of the case developed by Thomas is put by strong versions of the rights-based approach to intervention. Of all the arguments favouring intervention on humanitarian grounds, the rights-based approach has the widest appeal and is often the most powerfully made. In this volume it is Raymond Plant who puts it in its strongest form.[8] Plant expresses his argument, formally, in the following way:

$$A \text{ has a right to } \phi \text{ in virtue of } X \text{ against } Y$$

The phrase that carries the weight in this formula is 'in virtue of X', where X is translated as the referent of subject A's rights. In Plant's version this reference is the idea of human needs. The focus on needs has the advantage of being consistent with an extreme degree of moral relativism. This, Plant claims, sidesteps the cultural relativist critique of the rights thesis: however the notion of rights is deployed, the content of such rights will always be culturally (and therefore morally) relative. First, even the cultural relativist has to admit that humans do have needs. Second, there are a series of basic needs about which there can be no argument as they form a common baseline for the idea and the possibility of human life. These basic needs are: food, some degree of shelter, and freedom from arbitrary harm caused by other humans.[9]

In order to make clear precisely what is at stake in this version of the rights thesis, I want to dwell on the implications for the problem of intervention as they emerge in a debate between two rights theorists: David Luban and Michael Walzer.[10] The essential premise of Walzer's argument is a derivation of the rights of political communities from the rights of individuals: 'the duties and rights of states are nothing more than the duties and rights of the men who compose them'.[11] For Walzer, the process by which such a derivation takes place is a very complex one and is best understood in terms of social contract theory. This implies that instances of states' rights, for example territorial integrity, derive from this same complex process involving individual rights. Therefore they are subject to the vicissitudes of the common life. This form of argumentation leads Walzer to see the international order as equivalent in important respects to the domestic order. Walzer adopts, in short, the 'domestic analogy'. Alongside this, he asserts what he calls the 'legalist paradigm'.[12]

This combination of the domestic analogy and the legalist paradigm leads Walzer to adopt a strict principle of non-intervention which nevertheless can be vitiated in circumstances, 'where the ban on boundary crossings . . . does not serve the purposes for which it was established'.[13] There are three such circumstances: secession, counter-intervention in the context of civil war, and in cases of massacre and genocide. Thus, for Walzer, intervention is justified ethically if it represents the spirit of the ban on boundary crossings enshrined in international law as the principle of sovereignty even though it appears to violate that principle. Obviously, this position puts Walzer quite close to Hedley Bull and the 'Grotian' view. Less obvious is the extent to which Walzer's conception is governed by a view of ethics deeply grounded in historical experience. Walzer argues that:

> The moral understanding on which the community is founded takes shape over a long period of time, but the idea of communal integrity derives its moral and political force from the rights of contemporary men and women to live as members of an historic community and to express their inherited culture in forms worked out among themselves.[14]

This serves radically to separate Walzer both from rights-based approach articulated by Plant and from the consequentialists approach explored by Thomas.

For David Luban, rights are not separable, even by a complex derivation,

from social relations; they are always claims on other people. Like Plant
and Vincent, he adopts Shue's notion of socially basic human rights and
identifies them as 'those rights whose satisfaction is necessary to the enjoy-
ment of other rights . . . everyone's minimum reasonable demands on the
rest of humanity'.[15] This leads Luban to put forward a much more ambitious
principle of intervention. For Luban:

> A state (or government) established against the will of its own people,
> ruling violently, may well forfeit its right . . . even against a foreign
> invasion . . . [thus] it would appear that in such a case intervention is
> justified even in the absence of massacre or slavery.[16]

Elsewhere he is even more explicit:

> Human rights accrue to people no matter what country they live in and
> regardless of history or tradition. If human rights exist at all they set a
> moral limit to pluralism . . . moreover [rights] are crucial to us – as
> Walzer points out they are deeply connected with our notions of person-
> ality and moral agency.[17]

In other words, on this view, intervention is not merely a right; under certain
circumstances it is a duty. It is not simply extreme cases, such as genocide
and massacre, but *any* violation of socially basic human rights which
justifies, perhaps necessitates, intervention. Luban suggests that the 'romance of the nation state' vitiates the real force of Walzer's commitment to
intervention on humanitarian grounds. It is Walzer's subscription to the
'morality of states' which leads him into a pluralistic relativism that defeats
the ends for which it is brought into being, namely the existence of the
common life and the possibility of moral agency.

It is clear from the foregoing that, whatever else might separate them,
Luban and Walzer have a fundamental disagreement over the nature of our
ethical life. For Luban, it is universalistic and absolute, for Walzer, historically generated and, in that sense, contingent. This disagreement is reflected in the different approaches each adopts to the question of legitimacy,
both of the state itself and, as a consequence, of possible interference with
the state. Walzer claims, in fact, not to be dealing with the state at all but
rather with the community that underlies it. This community, he believes,
rests on the Burkean contract between the dead, the living and the unborn
and thereby creates the moral understanding of that community.[18] Walzer
claims that:

> foreigners don't know enough about [a state's] history and they have
> no direct experience, and can form no concrete judgements, of the
> conflicts and harmonies, the historical choices and cultural affinities, the
> loyalties and resentments that underlie it.[19]

As a result, judgements affecting that community ought only to be made by
the members of that community, without outside interference except under
special and extreme circumstances.

Luban, on the other hand, argues that Walzer's view is too simplistic.
Mistaking a 'Lockean' contract for a 'Hobbesian' one, Walzer confuses and
conflates two ways in which the contract metaphor might be used in discussing the modern state. The former consists of a contract by which people
bind themselves into a community prior to the existence of a state, the latter
a contract by which people set a sovereign authority over themselves. The
former can give rise to a nation, Luban argues, but only the latter can
legitimate a state.[20] The legitimacy of the modern state is predicated on both
forms of contract. As far as the ethics of intervention is concerned, the
significance of this dual contract arises out of the rights and duties that are
created:

> aggression violates a state's rights only when the state possesses these
> rights. According to contract theory this entails that the state has been
> legitimated by the consent of its citizens. An illegitimate state, that is,
> one governing without the consent of the governed is, therefore, morally,
> if not legally, stopped from asserting a right against aggression. The
> nation possesses such a right, to be sure, but the state does not.[21]

This debate over what constitutes legitimacy is continued by Jeff
McMahan, who diverges from both Walzer's and Luban's position.[22] For
McMahan, 'there are cases where intervention against a legitimate state
might be permissible'.[23] McMahan argues that the state is best seen as
instantiated in the government of the day and its apparatus. The crucial
question is how consent to the state is to be determined. He rejects Walzer's
criterion explicitly and Luban's effectively by concluding that the difficult
cases are not where states are clearly legitimate or illegitimate, but where
legitimacy is disputed. In such cases, the question of intervention may not
have a yes or no answer. In the case of clearly illegitimate states, there is no
presumption against intervention. Normally, in such circumstances, intervention may be justified. 'If the moral reasons favouring intervention are
very strong, then intervention may even be morally required.'[24] However,
even in such cases, caution should be exercised in respect of the importance

of self-determination. In the difficult cases of disputed legitimacy, McMahan suggests that there is no formula for right action. Nor is a 'neutral' response available. 'We must consult our own values' and ask a series of questions concerning the overall level of violence in the target country and whether the cause of social justice would be served by intervention.[25]

The above, then, shows three versions of a rights-based approach and the extent to which, even within a broadly sympathetic account of the right of intervention, they can differ from one another. Walzer, Luban and McMahan all wish to argue that, however rights are defined, and on whatever they are based, there are rights for the protection of which it may be necessary for one state to intervene in the internal affairs of another. Of the three only Luban's would really suffer at the hands of the moral or cultural relativity argument; it is the argument which insists most strongly on certain specific moral principles as guidelines to action. McMahan, although his terminology is different, stands rather close to the kind of conclusions offered by Plant: a belief that a rights-based approach is essential and that it is important to develop it in ways that can overcome reliance on norms that are specific to a certain culture. Walzer's argument, while wishing to retain the rights terminology and, of course, the moral force of a rights-based case, develops an ethical underpinning that runs the risk of making such rights as are derivable from it virtually redundant – the argument that is levelled at him by Luban and McMahan as well as by critics such as Doppelt and Beitz.[26]

The key difficulty with the rights-based interventionists is not simply cultural or moral relativity, but that any rights-based argument must adopt, at some level, foundationalist premises. Virtually all such positions rest upon two fundamental premises: first, that the contemporary states system is still principally a system of states *in the traditional sense*; and second, that the most appropriate type of ethical discourse is expressed in the language of rights and interests, however defined. Neither of these two premises hold unambiguously. For this reason, alternatives to such strong foundationalist arguments need to be developed in order to deal with the complexities of intervention.

VIRTUES BEFORE DUTIES

It might be thought that Paskins' argument in the current volume satisfies this criterion. Paskins suggests that a virtue-based approach steers a middle way between the rights-based interventionist and the consequentialist. In some respects Paskins remains close to Walzer, but is determined to avoid using rights-based language to express a position which he feels is not assimilable to a rights-based case. Walzer argues that ethical consciousness must be sensitive to historical nuance and complexity. However, he does not wish to abandon rights terminology altogether, partly because he wants to be able to justify intervention in certain restricted circumstances, and partly because of his reliance on the theory of the social contract.

By drawing on the notion of virtues, Paskins is freed from foundationalism of the rights-based approach. He realises that what we want to say about intervention cannot be captured in terms of principles or rules.[27] Nevertheless, he too wishes to provide grounds for recommending intervention in case *A* or under circumstances *X* but not in case *B* or under circumstances *Y*. He does not wish to challenge the view that there are unambiguous cases of justified intervention; it is precisely to decide on hard cases that the absolutists draw up the 'neat rules' that he does not believe are possible. Such cases also revolve around the notion of legitimacy. His deployment of a 'middle way' based on the idea of virtues is meant to point to an alternative view which stresses the contextuality of cases, without abandoning the ethical imperative.

However, Paskins deployment of the tradition of virtues in the context of just intervention attracts criticisms similar to those levelled at Alisdair MacIntyre's *After Virtue*.[28] The criticism is that any list of virtues cannot be context free; they are products of a particular cultural milieu. Exclusion and exclusivity were the hallmark both of Aristotle's own thought and its medieval descendants. However, the interpretations of the virtues offered by MacIntyre and Paskins are drawn up in the light of principles hammered out and established in the Enlightenment. These principles entail the abandonment of exclusion and exclusivity. This is particularly problematic for international relations.[29] The abandonment of exclusivity makes the attempt to 'recapture the just war for political theory' (Walzer's avowed aim in *Just and Unjust Wars*) virtually impossible. Equally, it casts serious doubt on Paskins' attempt to develop a reasoned account of virtues as they pertain to the international context.

The tradition of the virtues is predicated upon a cultural (or possibly evaluative) consensus, at least within certain parameters. But it is impossible to extend this tradition to cover contemporary international relations which is characterised by the fragmentation and erosion of such a consensus.[30] In the contemporary international system, there is no agreement on who might be said to be 'men of good will'; nor is there agreement on the norms and values that should govern international behaviour. This is not because all states are 'realist' in orientation. The difficulty is that the contemporary international system is unique in its attempt to cope with high

levels of cultural and evaluative differences while refusing to admit that
there are any intrinsic differences between members of the system in terms
of their legal and metaphorical status. It is not simply that the actors in the
contemporary system have this view; they have it in respect of a particular
set of historical circumstances, part of which are certain key beliefs about
the criteria of the ethical life and, therefore, the legitimacy of moral claims
within that life. There can be differences about the nature of the ethical
life. However, there are no beliefs which can be applied to vastly different societies at widely disparate times and yet still be true. For this reason,
Paskins' arguments remain interesting and suggestive but ultimately incapable of breaking the deadlock in any convincing fashion.

INTERVENTION IN CONTEXT

All the above authors adopt a state-centric view of the system. A state-
centric view is consistent with a rights terminology because it is in congruence with the evolution of the modern European state system, and the
development in the nineteenth and twentieth centuries of the ideology of
rights (and especially 'human rights').[31] However, it is a commonplace of
the theory of international relations that the state-centric view no longer
commands anything like universal acceptance. Leaving aside the more
radical critiques,[32] both within and without the general parameters of the
'inter-paradigm debate',[33] the best known elaboration of the critique is
probably that of Keohane and Nye.[34] Without necessarily accepting their
views of complex interdependence, it can be argued that the state-centric
view of international relations must, at the very least, be heavily qualified
under certain circumstances. This suggests that the domestic analogy and
the legalist paradigm cannot bear the weight put on them by both rights-
based interventionist and consequentialist arguments. They do not describe
the multi-faceted nature of the contemporary system and therefore cannot
be expected to account adequately for the totality of experience within it.

The problem, then, is how to characterize the view of the ethical required
by the new and evolving circumstances of the international system. The
answers offered by the various approaches outlined here are inadequate
because, whatever the differences that separate them, they all rely on a
certain form of minimal foundationalism.[35] The essentials of this minimal
foundationalist case are that, in principle, all ethical claims are commensurable. In other words, they are 'able to be brought under a set of rules which
will tell us how rational agreement can be reached on what would settle
the issue on every point where statements seem to conflict'.[36] This minimal

foundationalism does not hold that there is a specific content to a set of rules, only that such a set is possible. In the case of intervention, this could mean a set of rules based on the idea of minimal norms. This would still be compatible with a high degree of dispute about the content of such norms.

If one suggests, however, that the ethical state of the contemporary international system is a fragmented one, then it is possible under certain circumstances to make statements such as 'this is a justified intervention' but that no 'set of rules' with universal applicability could be drawn up to tell us what those circumstances might be. Thus Walzer, McMahan and Paskins are all in their different ways quite right to stress the importance of hard cases, but not because they highlight the real need for 'rules'. Rather, they demonstrate that all sets of rules are necessarily wrong. They must ignore the culture-specific elements of a particular instance of intervention and so cannot adequately account for, explain, justify or criticise it. This implies that we need to view ethical questions in the light of the assumption of both systemic and ethical fragmentation.[37]

This contextualist interpretation of intervention is predicated on a set of assumptions about the nature of the contemporary system, the status of knowledge claims, the appropriate conception of our ethical life and the propositions that can legitimately be made in each case. In each respect, there is a significant divergence from or development of the classical approach to these questions. Apart from the general ramifications of this view, there are specific implications regarding the question of intervention and how, consequently, our perspective about the associated ethical questions is to be altered.

First, the legal arrangements that the international community currently has in force to deal with putative instances of intervention recognise neither the practical nor the ethical effects of fragmentation and interdependence. As a result, they need substantial reform. Such reform would not, of course, be able to produce 'rules' for intervention. Rather, the attempt should be made to structure the fact of intervention and assess its consequences in the light of a reformulated idea of the notion of international society, though not necessarily along the lines suggested by Bull and others.[38] Judgements about a particular case of intervention should be sensitive to the competing levels of ethical discourse that may be at work in such instances, and it should be recognised that simple judgements will, in most cases, not be possible.

Second, the state system is itself undergoing considerable transformation. The variable conditions of complex interdependence increasingly entail multiple channels of communication between societies; an absence of hierarchy among issues; and a virtual abandonment of resort to force.[39] In such an evolving context, our understanding of what constitutes intervention will have to be broadened. In these circumstances, states will inevitably intervene in one another's 'domestic' concerns. Existing prohibitions on military intervention – however they might be defined – are clearly not appropriate to non-military intervention. The 'ethics of intervention' question would necessarily have to reflect other assumptions and values.

Third, the possibility of a predictive ethics of intervention is precluded. If one abandons the notion of a list of conditions for 'just' intervention and a list of prohibitions for its 'unjust' correlate, then one is beginning to ask a non-traditional set of questions about the ethics of intervention. These questions are premised on a recognition of the irreducible contextuality (though not necessarily incommensurability) of judgement. This contextuality, however, is not one that is wedded to the Realist tradition. The preconditions for such an argument may only be contingently present in the contemporary world and in many cases will not be present at all. Moreover, contextualism accommodates the sense of the fragmentation of traditional views of ethics. It holds simply that ethical discourse in the contemporary international system is fragmented in a way that makes traditional approaches to ethical judgement in international relations largely irrelevant. This is not, however, an abandonment of the notion of ethical judgement in international relations at all. On the contrary, it argues that it is only in realising that this is our contemporary situation that meaningful ethical judgements can be made. This recognition involves the abandonment of the ethical (and epistemological) foundationalism characteristic of contemporary ethical discourse.

The question, 'When is it legitimate for one state to intervene in the affairs of another?' thus becomes an investigation into the contextual setting of a particular instance of conflict, its relation to other instances and to our own understanding of the appropriate ethical response. This is very different from traditional attempts to establish limits to interstate conflict. Some fear that it opens the door to an international system whose key principle of order based upon sovereignty is largely ignored and that, as a result, both the possibility and the permissibility of conflict will be thereby increased. However, this fear is misconceived as the contemporary international system is best described in other terms.[40] An appropriate understanding of the conditions governing the ethics of intervention must recognise systemic and ethical fragmentation as an inescapable feature of the contemporary international system, and adapt its conversation accordingly.

In effect, the traditional approaches to the ethical and explanatory questions involved in assessing instances of intervention no longer work. The main reason is that they subscribe to certain types of foundationalist premises that are no longer warranted by a unity of cultural approaches in the international system. Moreover, they are in any case open to serious philosophical challenge. This leaves us with a view that accepts the importance of ethical judgements in international relations, but denies that they can take the form of a 'set of rules or norms' for the resolution of any dispute about their legitimacy or applicability. Some might find this depressing. I do not; I would in any case agree with Isaiah Berlin that 'to know the worst is not always to be liberated from its consequences; nevertheless it is preferable to ignorance'.[41]

Notes

1. H. Bull (ed.), *Intervention in World Politics* (Oxford, 1984); C. Beitz, M. Cohen, T. Scanlon and M. Simmons (eds), *International Ethics* (Princeton, 1985); M. Wright (ed.), *Rights and Obligations in North-South Relations* (London, 1986); A. Ellis (ed.), *Ethics and International Relations* (Manchester, 1986).

2. Bull's reference is to Wolff's *Ius Gentium* (Halle, 1754), the philosophical basis of which is to be found in his *Philosophia Practica Universalis*, 2 vols (Halle, 1736–9). The discussion is found in H. Bull, *Intervention in World Politics*.

3. For the full version of this prohibition, see the treaties concerned and the discussion in N. J. Rengger (ed.), *Treaties and Alliances of the World* (Harlow, 1990).

4. The Realist view is that it is nonsense to attempt an 'ethical' justification of actions that might be undertaken in defence of a state's legitimate interests. This is simply a matter of how the international system works; thus intervention is a fact but not, ethically speaking, a problem. States may be wrong about the perception of their interests but this, in itself, does not mean they are not right to act on this (mistaken) perception. Classic statements of the Realist view are H. J. Morgenthau, *Politics Among Nations* (New York, 1948 [and subsequent editions]), and E. H. Carr, *The Twenty Years' Crisis* (London, 1939). More recent versions are K. Waltz, *Theory of International Politics* (Reading, 1979), and R. Gilpin, *War and Change in World Politics* (Princeton, 1981).

5. See the contribution by C. Thomas in this volume. Other examples might be, for example, N. Chomsky – at least in some moods; perhaps in his essays on East Timor and Vietnam, though he has not, so far as I know, made a clear statement on this. For a representative selection see J. Peck (ed.), *The Chomsky Reader* (London, 1988).

6. For a fair spread of the well-known arguments against consequentialism, see S. J. Schleffer (ed.), *Consequentialism and Its Critics* (Oxford, 1988); S. J. Schleffer, *The Rejection of Consequentialism* (Oxford, 1982); B. Williams and J. J. C. Smart, *Utilitarianism: For and Against* (Cambridge, 1973); and D. Parfit, *Reasons and Persons* (Oxford, 1984).

7. See M. Walzer, 'Political Action: The Problem of Dirty Hands', *Philosophy and Public Affairs*, No. 2 (Winter 1973); and S. Hampshire (ed.), *Public and Private Morality* (Cambridge, 1978).

8. See the contribution by R. Plant in this volume.

9. These ideas are similar to those developed and deployed by Shue in the idea of socially basic human rights as a minimum common standard of rights. See H. Shue, *Basic Rights: Subsistence, Affluence and US Foreign Policy* (Princeton, 1980). The political consequences of such a common standard are developed in D. Luban, 'Just War and Human Rights' and 'The Romance of the Nation State', in C. Beitz, M. Cohen, T. Scanlon and M. Simmons (eds), *International Ethics* and also in A. J. M. Milne, 'Human Rights and the Diversity of Morals: A Philosophical Analysis of Rights and Obligations in the Global System' in M. Wright (ed.), *Rights and Obligations in North-South Relations* (London, 1986).

10. See M. Walzer, *Just and Unjust Wars* (Harmondsworth, 1977), and also D. Luban, 'The Romance of the Nation State'.

11. M. Walzer, *Just and Unjust War*, p. 53, quoting with approval J. Westlake.

12. Walzer's legalist paradigm consists of six propositions:
    1. There exists an international society of independent states.
    2. This international society has a law that establishes the rights of its members – above all the rights of territorial integrity and political sovereignty.
    3. Any use of force or imminent threat of force by one state against the political sovereignty or territorial integrity of another constitutes aggression and is a criminal act.
    4. Aggression justifies two kinds of violent response: a war of self defence by the victim; and a war of law enforcement by the victim and any other member of international society.
    5. Nothing but aggression can justify war.
    6. Once the aggressor state has been militarily repulsed, it can also be punished.

13. Ibid., p. 90.

14. M. Walzer, 'The Moral Standing of States: A Response to Four Critics', in C. Beitz *et al.* (eds), *International Ethics*, p. 219.

15. D. Luban, 'Just War and Human Rights', pp. 209–10.

16. Ibid., p. 215.

17. D. Luban, 'The Romance of the Nation State', p. 242.

18. M. Walzer, 'The Moral Standing of States', p. 220.

19. Ibid., p. 220.

20. D. Luban, 'The Romance of the Nation State', pp. 202–7.

21. Ibid., p. 204.

22. J. McMahan, 'The Ethics of International Intervention' in A. Ellis (ed.), *Ethics and International Relations*.

23. Ibid., p. 45.

24. Ibid.

25. Ibid., p. 48.

26. See C. Beitz, *Political Theory and International Relations* (Princeton, 1979), and G. Doppelt, 'Walzer's Theory of Morality in International Relations', *Philosophy and Public Affairs*, Vol. 8, No. 1 (1979).

27.   See the contribution by B. Paskins in this volume.

28.   A. MacIntyre, *After Virtue* (London, 1981). See also A. MacIntyre, *Whose Justice? Which Rationality?* (London, 1988), and A. MacIntyre, *The Relevance of Moral Enquiry* (London, 1990).

29.   On Aristotle and the principle of exclusion, see E. Barker, *Translation of The Politics* (Oxford, [1946] 1977). See specifically the selections dealing with the nature and role of the Greeks and the ideas about natural slavery, particularly Aristotle's ambiguity over allowing the enslavement of fellow Greeks. There are also good discussions of aspects of the problem in parts of J. Barnes, M. Schofield and R. Sorabji (eds), *Articles on Aristotle* (London, 1975–9). See also M. Wight, 'The States System of Hellas' and 'Hellas and Persia' in *Systems of States*, ed. by H. Bull (Leicester, 1977). For a modern treatment of Aristotle that also discusses some of the same issues, see A. MacIntyre, *After Virtue* and *Whose Justice? Which Rationality?*

      On Medieval and Renaissance treatments of sovereignty and of the Respublica Christiana and its significance, see the brilliant and influential interpretation in Q. Skinner, *The Foundations of Modern Political Thought*, 2 vols (Cambridge, 1978); and M. J. Wilks, *The Problem of Sovereignty in the Later Middle Ages* (Cambridge, 1963).

30.   I have treated this in more detail elsewhere. See N. J. Rengger, 'Incommensurability, International Theory and the Fragmentation of Political Culture' in J. Gibbins (ed.), *Contemporary Political Culture* (Beverly Hills, 1989). For a more general approach, see my 'The Fearful Sphere of International Relations', *Review of International Studies*, Vol. 15, No. 4 (October, 1990); and 'Context and Interpretation in International Theory' in N. J. Rengger and M. Hoffman (eds), *Critical Theory and International Relations: Beyond the Inter-Paradigm Debate* (Hemel Hempstead, 1993).

31.   See, for example, H. Bull, 'The Emergence of a Universal International Society' in H. Bull and A. Watson (eds), *The Expansion of International Society* (Oxford, 1985); and F. H. Hinsley, *Power and The Pursuit of Peace* (Cambridge, 1963).

32.   For a representative selection, see J. W. Burton, *World Society* (Cambridge, 1972); and R. Falk, *A Study of Future Worlds* (New York, 1975).

33.   See M. Banks, 'The Evolution of International Relations Theory' in M. Banks (ed.), *Conflict in World Society* (Brighton, 1984). See also M. Hoffman, 'Critical Theory and the Inter-Paradigm Debate', *Millennium: Journal of International Studies*, Vol. 16, No. 2 (Summer 1987).

34.   See R. O. Keohane and J. S. Nye, *Power and Interdependence*, 2nd rev. edn (Boston, 1991).

35.   See N. J. Rengger, 'Context and Interpretation'.

36.   R. Rorty, *Philosophy and The Mirror of Nature* (Oxford, 1980) p. 316.

37.   See N. J. Rengger, 'Incommensurability, International Theory and the Fragmentation of Western Political Culture' and 'Context and Interpretation in International Theory'.

38.   See H. Bull and A. Watson (eds), *The Expansion of International Society*; H. Bull, *The Anarchical Society* (London, 1977); and M. Donelan (ed.), *The Reason of States* (London, 1978).

39.   See R. O. Keohane and J. S. Nye, *Power and Interdependence*, pp. 24–9.

40. See N. J. Rengger, 'The Fearful Sphere of International Relations' and 'Context and Interpretation in International Theory'.
41. I. Berlin, 'The Originality of Machiavelli', in *Against the Current: Essays in the History of Ideas* (Oxford, 1981) p. 79.

16 Agency, Identity and Intervention

Mark Hoffman

INTRODUCTION

The contributions in this volume address a number of interconnected questions regarding the ethics of intervention (and non-intervention). What kind of problem is intervention? What moral dilemmas are raised by, and ethical justifications offered for, acts of (non)intervention? What are the practical implications and limitations of such justifications? Answers to these questions can be developed at a number of levels and from a number of perspectives. Intervention can be discussed in legal terms, in political terms, in anthropological or social psychological terms, in normative terms or, more likely, in some combination of these and other frameworks.

What is common to each of these perspectives are the problems being addressed: the nature of political space and the nature of responsibility and obligations between 'insiders' and 'outsiders'. These are usually characterised in terms of relations between states, between the state and citizens, either its own or those of other states, or between citizens of different states. What is at stake is not simply 'political space', or the agents by which that political space is transgressed, but how that political space is constructed and the nature of the identities which follow from it. The very act of intervention or non-intervention and the justification offered tells us a great deal – about how we conceive of ourselves, how we construct our identities and how we conceive of and construct the world in which we live.

Seen in the light of these concerns, intervention is a 'problem' because the nature of the act itself – its meaning, intentions, justifications and consequences – is ambiguous. Intervention (or non-intervention) can be construed as an act of transgression, affirmation or transformation of identities and the boundaries between them. It brings into play the tensions between constructions of self and other, of insider and outsider, and of particularism and universalism in both theory and practice.

Intervention is traditionally viewed as the reaffirmation or transgression of sovereignty. Indeed, the very act of intervention or non-intervention is central to the meaning of sovereignty: the former is seen as its violation; the latter as a corollary of its maintenance. Both views posit a sovereign state with a set of fixed territorial boundaries that can be transgressed. When the practices of such an entity are seen to undermine the meaning of 'sovereignty', the state is deemed to be aberrant, illegitimate and open to acts of intervention. When the practices of the state do not fall outside the accepted meaning of the term, then such interventionary activity is supposed to be condemned by the other members of the international community.

Thus, within international relations, intervention arises and is addressed from within the confines of a particular set of social practices and institutions. These practices and institutions define an international system constructed on the basis of a specific understanding of the possibilities and limits of order within an anarchical system. Traditionally within international theory, this system is characterised as either one of Hobbesian anarchy or Grotian international society. In the former, *realpolitik* concerns of state are seen as dominant. In the latter, the emphasis is placed on the cardinal rule of state sovereignty.

Both of these views of the international system over-emphasise the features of anarchy and sovereignty.[1] The international system is characterised less by these two traditionally identified features than it is by two sets of countervailing pressures: political fragmentation and internationalisation.[2] Political fragmentation is evident in the collapse of the former Soviet Union and the violent implosion of Yugoslavia, the continued role of nonstate actors and the rise of a broad range of sub-national social, economic, political, ethnic, gender and cultural forces, particularly in the oppositional forms of new social movements and increasingly virulent manifestations of nationalism. Internationalisation refers to longer-term phenomena, including the globalisation of trade and markets, technology, production and finance, transportation, communication, information, and knowledge, environmental and health issues, and the speed with which interactions within, between and across these areas take place.

The aggregate effect of these forces has been contradictory. On the one hand, these forces have arguably strengthened the centralising powers of the state and fostered particularist political and social forces in the form of ethnic and nationalist sentiments. On the other hand, they are disruptive of pre-existing social and political practices and institutions. The tensions between formal claims to state sovereignty and the fluidity and acceleration of global processes which served to constrain or undermine state autonomy challenge and call into question the constructions of identities, of conceptions of self and other, that are predicated on the sovereign, territorial state and the notion of international society.

The combination of these diffuse features produces an international system characterised by an amorphous and elusive heterogeneity in which individuals, groups, states and societies impinge on each other, directly and indirectly, to an ever greater degree than they did in the past. The result is a network of complex yet uneven interdependencies – some harmonious, some discordant – which create competing, complementary and contradictory systems of inclusion and exclusion.[3] It is within the context of these systems of inclusion/exclusion, rather than the more limited confines of the state-system, that the normative, political and practical questions concerning intervention need to be addressed.

Traditional approaches within the international relations and political theory disciplines are too limited in scope adequately to address the theoretical and practical questions regarding intervention within the context of the contending forces of political fragmentation and globalisation. These limitations are rooted in the intellectual division of labour, deriving from the manner in which the central concerns and concepts of the two disciplines are constructed. Each is premised on a sharp demarcation from the other, producing different tradition of discourse and practice. And these intellectual boundaries are located in the 'reality' of the boundaries between political communities in the form of sovereign states. Internally, the sovereign state provides a context for the possible realisation of a discourse and practice of universal rights and justice. Conversely, this same sovereign status places a limitation on the external realisation of such possibilities in the form of an anarchical international society and its 'cardinal rule' of non-intervention.

Such approaches are forms of what Cox has called 'problem-solving theory'.[4] This is an ahistorical form of theorising which takes the prevailing social and power relationships, and the institutions into which they are organised, as the given framework for action. Its goal is conservative in that it seeks to make an existing political order – its relationships, its institutions and its practices – function smoothly. It achieves this by the fragmentation of theory and practice into separate, specialised areas of activity. Each autonomous area of investigation is seen as having its own set of particular issues and problems. Solutions to particular problems are developed within a given set of boundaries by assuming stability in other spheres, or by ignoring them altogether. The parameters of the problem as initially defined are deemed correct and there is no effort to make connections between or across problems. The assumption is of an unchanging reality providing the basis for 'objective' knowledge. But a fixed delimitation of the scope of inquiry and practice leads not to 'objective' knowledge but to the intellectual and practical hegemony of unnecessarily limited and distorted accounts of the social realm, in this case of international relations.

CRITICAL INTERNATIONAL THEORY

Given the countervailing pressures of fragmentation and globalisation in the international system, the nature of political communities – their boundaries, the basis of their constitutions, the relationships between them – needs to be rethought. Traditional forms of problem-solving theory are no longer adequate for such a task. What is needed is a theoretical account of how the relationships and interactions between different societies, cultures and communities, between 'insiders' and 'outsiders', are structured, of how we might alternatively structure them, and of what the practical implications of moving from one set of relationships towards another might be. One such possibility exists in the form of critical international theory, drawing on the traditions of the Frankfurt school and the ideas of Jurgen Habermas.

Critical theory starts with an understanding of a deep interconnection between theory and practice. As Cox has put, 'theory is always for someone and for something'; it is linked to a particular set of interests.[5] But a critical theory seeks to be more than the expression of a mere perspective or set of interests. It is critical in the sense that it stands apart from a prevailing order and asks how it came about. Unlike problem-solving theory, it does not take institutions and social and power relations for granted or accept them as given and predetermined but calls them into question by concerning itself with their origins and whether they are in the process of or amenable to changing. It seeks to assess the very framework which problem-solving accepts as its parameters. It is directed at the social whole rather than its separate parts. Thus critical theory is concerned with history: not as a source of empirical validation of an unchanging world, but as a process of continual but contingent change. The underlying purpose of critical theory is the promotion of a set of emancipatory interests through an exploration of the possibilities of and constraints upon human autonomy that are immanent with existing practices and structures.[6]

Critical theory correlates with John Dunn's characterisation of the purpose of theory as diagnosing 'practical predicaments and (showing) us how best to confront them'. This requires that we first ascertain the 'social, political and economic setting of our lives' and an 'understanding of why it is as it is'; second, that we develop ideas about 'how we could coherently wish that world to be or to become'; and third, that we attempt to judge 'how far, and through what actions and at what risk' we might hope to move from the world as it is to the world as we hope it might be.[7]

In the context of international relations, critical theory is concerned with the logics of inclusion and exclusions in world politics. Following Dunn's tripartite structure, it is characterised by: (1) an historical-sociological investigation of how it is that we arrived at the current practices and institutions of the international system, what ideas and practices became marginalised as the system developed and why; (2) a philosophical task of constructing viable future world orders which incorporate those features which we deem desirable; and (3) a practical politics of outlining paths from the past to the future which places emphasis on the open-textured nature of the future, that is, that are not simply a projection of the past as read by the present into the future.[8]

As characterised by Linklater, a critical international theory requires both a recovery of and movement beyond political realism, on the one hand, and the projects developed by Kant and Marx on the other.[9] Political realism provides a thorough-going account of the structural constraints on the realisation of emancipatory interests, offering-up 'repetition and recurrence' in a Wightian world of 'necessitous action'.[10] However, it lacks an 'account of the modes of political intervention which would enable human beings to take control of their international history'.[11] Kant and Marx, on the other hand, each provided an account which seeks to do precisely that. However, each is open to serious critique: Kant to charges of ahistoricism; Marx to an over-emphasis on the proletarian class as the vehicle for emancipatory politics.

Notwithstanding the limitations of political realism, Kantian liberalism and Marxism, a critical international theory entails a recovery and extension of various traditions of thought in both political and international theory. Taking seriously the economic, political and social logics of the international system, critical international theory provides the framework for an understanding of how far and in what ways these logics, and the dominant forms of state they produce in any given epoch, constrain or enhance the possibilities for the extension of moral obligation and political community.[12]

Critical international theory, thus, has a strong humanist component in that it seeks to re-establish the role of human agency or human action in the political world. Given its commitment to this emancipatory concern, and the philosophical task of articulating alternative world orders, it also contains an important utopian component. As Machiavelli noted, 'where there is no vision, the people shall perish'. In other words, utopias are a necessary part of the enabling process in the social construction of the world in which we live, since they point to the gap between human potential and the reality of human practices.

IRONIC COSMOPOLITANISM

Within critical international theory, this utopianism is manifested in the articulation of coherent alternative social and political orders. In its commitment to articulating alternatives world orders, critical international theory limits the range of choices to alternatives that are immanent within, and feasible transformations of, the existing world. A principal objective is to identify and clarify this range of alternatives. The utopianism of critical international theory is one that is mediated by a sense of the contexts within which it is being articulated and pursued. It contains a self-awareness of its historicity, of a need for self-reflection and a sense of the difficulties entailed in putting utopias into action. It rejects improbable alternatives just as it rejects the problem-solving view that there are no alternatives.

Equally important, the utopianism of critical international theory entails a commitment to a cosmopolitan ethic[13] which seeks to avoid ethnocentric or imperialist meta-narratives. It is a form of cosmopolitanism which takes seriously the idea of *cosmopolis* as the embodiment of diversity. In opposition to cosmopolitanism as an 'imperialism' of certain culturally specific practices, values, norms and institutions, it points to the practical forms of cosmopolitanism manifest in some modern cities and in many universities. It is a form of cosmopolitanism in which there is a recognition of features which we share in common, which recognises the contingency of this solidarity and which recognises the reality and desirability of diversity.

The cosmopolitanism of critical international theory is 'ironic'[14] in its recognition of the reality and possibility of world of multiple identities which are neither fixed nor self-evident. It is an irony which belongs to the international system itself and is aptly captured in the phrase 'one world, many worlds'.[15] Rather than seeking to undermine cultural diversity or eliminate the particularisms of local identities or communities, the ironic cosmopolitanism of critical international theory provides a framework for addressing the tensions between these multiple identities: between universalism and particularism, inclusion and exclusion, self and other. As Linklater argues:

> The intention is to defend a moral inclusion and equality without positing a single human identity, and to value difference without subscribing to doctrines of innate superiority and inferiority and correlative forms of moral exclusion.[16]

Such an approach seeks to extend the boundaries of normative discourse and practice through a deeper understanding and (re)articulation of identities and political communities, of the nature of 'otherness'. It opens up political discourse, actions and communities to internal and external scrutiny and provides the basis for a new politics of intervention which seeks to undermine exclusionary practices and discourses. In short, ironic cosmopolitanism provides the basis for a politics of inclusion which makes political communities answerable to one another.[17] Indeed, this element of scrutiny becomes essential to the practical interventionary dimensions of the ethics of a critical international theory.

Most importantly, an 'ironic cosmopolitanism' implies that membership within a community is never wholly inclusive or exclusive; that the sovereign state does not set the limits to, or exhaust, our moral and political identities and obligations. The political fragmentation and globalisation of the international system extends these beyond those obligations associated with the sovereign state to those which arise out of our multiple subnational, national and transnational identities.

THE SOVEREIGNTY OF STATES

The idea of the state, and of sovereignty as its essential defining characteristic, is often taken as a given within international relations. It is a foundational premise which provides the starting point for traditional international theory. And yet, as Halliday has noted, within international relations this core concept has been under-theorised and unscrutinised.[18] The same holds true for traditional political theory, where the territorial state enjoying sovereignty is a vital background assumption for its consideration of questions regarding 'the good life'.[19] Thus in both disciplines, the state is frequently taken as a settled expression, defined largely in legal terms.

Such a jurisprudential account of sovereignty effectively removes the concept from the dialogue and discourse regarding the nature and constitution of political communities; it leaves it uncontested. Instead of taking sovereignty as the given, as the fundamental starting point for a discussion of the ethics of intervention, we need to open up the idea of sovereignty to an interrogation. There are two complementary strands to such an interrogation, both of which argue that the meaning and nature of the sovereign state can only be understood by engaging with the political practices that constitute its stabilised core meaning.

The first focuses on sovereignty as a 'social construction'. Rejecting the traditional agency–structure dichotomy in favour of structuration theory, Wendt, for example, has argued that sovereign states need to be conceived of as socially constructed 'distributions of knowledge'.[20] Since sovereign identities are socially constructed or socially learned through interaction with other states, sovereignty is best understood as a practice and an institution. It is the practice of political communities that generated the idea of the sovereign state; it is an institution because these practices instantiate relatively stable rules regarding the nature of states, their interactions and the nature and functioning of international society. Sovereign states are thus inherently social actors whose identities are articulated within the confines of an international society which they instantiate.

The implication of this argument is that the nature of the international system depends on the practices of its members. As Wendt argues, the nature of anarchy in international society is what states make of it;[21] insecurity, and the pressures and practices it generates, is socially constructed. The anarchic features of international relations, which are seen as constitutive of the international system, are a product of state practices rather than an objective feature of the system. The self-help, egoistic practices of state are historically contingent and endogenous to the practices of international society itself. By extension, the problem of intervention is not exogenous, but is also socially constructed by the actions and practices of states themselves. As these practices change, so too does the 'problem' of intervention.

The second strand of thought adopts a more historical sociological approach, and challenges the use of 'grand narratives' of sovereignty. Instead, as Ruiz argues, the 'interrogation of sovereignty must be contextualised', and examined in the social and political practices in which it has come to dwell.[22] The key developments to focus upon are: the simultaneous processes of global integration and fragmentation; the resulting 'unevenness' of economic development and political identity; and the theoretical debate regarding sovereignty itself.[23] These three developments highlight that the historical and intellectual conditions and contexts which gave rise to the concept and practice of sovereignty no longer obtain.

The traditional rationalisation and justifications for the sovereign state were that it served as an intermediary form of political life, mediating 'otherness' internally and externally. Yet this role is increasingly being called into question. Externally, the state is increasingly vulnerable to what takes place beyond its sovereign reach.[24] Internally, the sovereign state is seen as a form of domination, of 'enclosure', which denies, marginalises and ignores the 'local' as the loci of the everyday life and politics of resistance and invention.[25] The efforts to resist these dynamics through the continued invocation of the 'normal' politics of enclosure generates territorial and extraterritorial forms of subjugation and harm.

The assumption that politics is impossible without enclosure has to be relinquished because it ignores the possibility that there might be forms of political community which resist or are stifled by enclosure. Moreover, these 'non-enclosed forms of political community' might provide the basis for extended or inclusive political communities. The consequence of the contradictory pressures of the effort to centralise power within the state in the face of the decentralisation of authority and the fragmentation of the international system is that the sovereign state, 'once the great agent of modernity, has now become its victim'.[26]

On this reading, the principle of state sovereignty has become incompatible with the way political life is organised. It has become an arbitrary limitation on the possibilities for political community. But sovereignty does not have a fixed meaning or characterisation, nor can one particular manifestation be a foundational starting point for an understanding of international relations. Instead, it constitutes the site of continual political struggle over the meaning of the boundaries and constitution of identities, and these can never be fixed. As Walker notes, the concept of 'sovereignty' becomes the focal point for critical discursive politics, rather than the 'silent' but constitutive code at the core of international relations. Behind these concerns lies a deeper set of questions regarding the character of political life, how political practices are to be understood, how they are to be transformed, and what actually constitutes the 'political'. In short, we need to readdress the question, who are 'we'?[27]

As this question makes clear, the underlying issue is the constitution of political community.[28] Within the existing discourse of international and political theory the question of political community is solved through recourse to the sovereign state. Both argue that the realisation of political community is possible only within the spatial and temporal boundaries of the modern sovereign state. But as the intellectual and practical boundaries of the state are increasingly contested, so too is the limitation of community to the confines of the state's authoritative domain.

The givenness of sovereignty, of state boundaries and the location and nature of political community is particularly called into question by acts of intervention. It might be possible to see acts of intervention (or non-intervention) as the affirmation of existing boundaries and their constitution. But this attempt at seeing them as the articulation of existing patterns misses the degree to which each act of intervention or non-intervention is also a reinscription, rearticulation and redefinition of sovereign identities and political community which are slowly corrosive of the 'fixed' meanings which constitute the core of political and international theory. Rather than starting with fixed definitions of sovereignty, political community and intervention, these important conceptualisations must be seen as political practices whose meaning and location are contested. Interventionary activity does not necessarily constitute a form of 'closure', sustaining existing sovereign identities, but also opens up the possibility of questioning existing boundaries and of constructing alternatives identities.

If the sovereign state no longer is, or should be, the linchpin to the resolution of the tensions between universality and diversity, of the answers to the question what constitutes the political community, what alternative accounts of sovereign identities can we pursue? Answering such a question requires an acceptance of multiple identities that are not crisply delineated. It also entails the exploration and rearticulation of new political spaces, new political practices, new ways of knowing and being, and new ways of acting across borders.[29] Two possibilities have been recently identified within critical international theory: the notion of an international citizenship and the development of critical social movements. Both provide the basis for forms of intervention which seek to extend the boundaries of political community while undermining systems of exclusion.

International Citizenship[30]

The idea of citizenship has a dual nature: it is the basis for both progressivist inclusionary and conservative exclusionary political practices. The tension between these contradictory characterises are all too readily evident in the modern state where the efforts at improving political, economic and social arrangements within a particular society via the extension of citizenship has often come at the expense of 'non-citizens', both within and outside that society.

But the theoretical and practical expansion of the idea of citizenship over the last two hundred years also provides the basis for locating in the concept of citizenship a radicalizing potential for questioning forms of exclusion. Initially promulgated with respect to civil rights, the idea of citizenship created the momentum for further demands – political, economic and social – applied more widely and evenly within society. The progressive expansion and extension of citizenship served to undermine exclusionary practices within the state.

The notion of an *international* citizenship entails an effort to extend this radicalising critique beyond the state. Its genesis can be located in a movement from Kant to Foucault. It builds on the former's identification of multiple axes of citizenship and the latter's argument that it provides the basis for the recovery of local power and identities in the face of the monopoly of power reserved for governments. It is characterised by the attempt to articulate conceptions of the self that are 'inclusionary' rather than 'exclusionary'. It seeks to promote a politics which is 'other-regard-ing'; where the interests of the community, of the other, are part of how the self is defined. It is the product of what Wendt has characterised as 'a recursive, non-individualistic social ontology in which forms of identity and community are the ongoing effect of social practices'.[31]

Extending Bull's arguments in the Hagey Lectures,[32] Linklater argues that these ongoing social practices are evident in the progressive extension of the membership of international society: first in the form of post-colonial states, later in the form of international governmental organisations (IGOs) and international non-governmental organisations (INGOs) and most re-cently with the individual via human rights.[33] Each can be seen as an indicator or manifestation of a gradual extension of political community in an effort to dismantle the exclusionary practices of a European-derived international order. The result is an international system that in-cludes multiple forms of citizenship, political organisation and political identities, none of which can claim exclusive sovereignty. Within this international system of multiple identities and sovereignties exists the po-tential for the realisation of an 'ironic cosmopolitanism' and the 'moral learning' associated with such a development.

Critical Social Movements[34]

Connected to the idea of an international citizenship, a critical international theory places great emphasis on the potential role of what are often referred to as 'new' or 'critical' social movements[35] in bringing about change and transformation. Critical social movements offer a fundamentally different account of the possibilities of change and transformation from the top-down perspective of traditional political and international theory. Instead, atten-tion is focused on activity at the margins and fringes of dominant patterns of political discourse and practice, on connecting the personal and the political.[36]

Critical social movements act with regard to single issues – such as nuclear weapons/power, the environment or gender – but also in the effort to identify the connections that exist between structures, processes and people, and to build coalitions which seek to expand or extend the horizons of our political imaginations. Thus, new social movements seek to promote change and transformation in the system by identifying or creating new openings, new political spaces and new understandings of what it means to act 'politically'.

Although it is easy to dismiss such social movements as being marginal to the 'stuff' of politics, this perceived 'weakness' allows them to engage in specific struggles while connecting with other movements in order to articulate alternative possibilities for the future. It enables them to challenge the constitutive principles of the existing order and to articulate new forms of political community, new senses of peace and justice. They are not 'powerful' in the traditional understandings of the term, but they have the power of ideas – to sow the seeds of new understandings, of the capacity to rearticulate and redefine the meaning of political space, of 'sovereignty'. As Rob Walker has argued, 'critical social movements are important not because they have the immediate capacity to induce existing élites to pursue more enlightened politics but because they participate in a more far-reaching reinvention of political life'.[37]

THE PRACTICAL CONSEQUENCES OF IMPRACTICAL UNIVERSALISM

What are the practical implications of adopting an ironic cosmopolitanism? What does it have to say about justified intervention? Primarily, the commitment to the realisation of human potential, the undermining of unjustified systems of exclusion and the expansion of political community, means that a critical international theory would locate justified intervention within a range of practices which would seriously address these concerns. In effect, it would engage in or support interventionary action that promoted the potential for the realisation of those goals that are immanent within existing practices and situations, acting within new political space and via new political agents.

One area that would clearly fall within the frame of reference of a critical international theory would be the practical realisation of human rights. This would connect strongly with critical international theory's utopianism and commitment to emancipatory interests. But recalling the 'ironic' nature of critical international theories' cosmopolitanism, it would not be wedded to the promotion of a set of finitely defined human rights. Its initial commitment is more likely to take the form of support for something along the lines of Shue's basic rights of subsistence and security, and to seek to promote their realisation. A long-term goal would be the promotion of forms of radical democratic political communities in which all inhabitants would have an equal right and opportunity to participate in a way that would not entail any enforced denial of identity.

The denial of human rights – basic or otherwise – by unjustified systems of exclusion, be they political, economic, social, cultural, ethnically, racially or gender based, would also create a set of obligations to act. The most extreme form of the denial of human rights – genocide – would require immediate and quite probably military responses. Such interventionary activity could be supported, even if it was unilateral as in the case of Vietnam in Kampuchea, not because it was deemed desirable, but because it may be the only effective option available to stop massive, unwarranted killings. Moreover, critical international theory would promote a shift in such actions toward the humanitarian end of the spectrum, as occurred in the case of the Kurds in northern Iraq. The less immediate, more structural but equally deadly denial of human rights, particularly subsistence rights,[38] via economic or political institutions would also create obligations for action. But in such cases critical international theory is more likely to act through forms of international citizenship or via new social movements.

Perhaps the most novel form of interventionary activity that would flow from a critical international theory would be that of third party facilitation in protracted social conflicts. This form of intervention is unique in both its purposes and process. Unlike more traditional forms of intervention, third party facilitation seeks to advance forms of practical reason and communicative rationality through a process of undistorted dialogue between conflicting parties in an effort to promote a self-generated and self-sustaining resolution to the conflict.[39] The role of the external intervention is to promote integrative outcomes that are mutually acceptable to all the parties to a conflict. It operates in a co-operative, non-hierarchical fashion to promote the resolution of a conflict via a collaborative approach aimed at increasing the capacity of the actors involved to determine and choose courses of actions that avoid recourse to violence, direct or structural. In the process it performs an important transformative function, promoting an awareness of common needs that can only be realised through redefined, restructured and rearticulated political relationships and institutions.[40]

CONCLUSIONS

The central concern of critical international theory is with the articulation and rearticulation of political space, of political society, of political community, of identity. This is evident in the reworking of cosmopolitanism, the problematising of political community and of identity, best encapsulated in the rearticulation of 'sovereignty', not as a legal construct but as a political practice, not just in relation to the state but in terms of a wide range of social practices. Indeed, the paradoxical nature of 'sovereignty', entailing as it does the notion of closure but also the possibility of community, becomes the focal point for critical international theory and practice.

This opens up the possibility of the realisation of individual autonomy, of an ethic of ironic cosmopolitanism that embraces difference and diversity, of the articulation and promotion of new political spaces and new political actors in the form of an international citizenry, new social movements and facilitative third parties which promote open, inclusive forms of political community.

But a critical international theory would also take seriously the central paradox of late-modernity: that the universalising and globalising tendencies of economic, political and informational change have also produced a heightened perception of economic, political and cultural differences. Indeed, this may be characterised as the defining feature of contemporary global politics: the tensions between universalism and particularism; between systems of inclusion and exclusion; the process of (re)affirmation and denial in the creation of identity, self and otherness. From this flows an indeterminacy which will act as a major constraint on the realisation of any critical international theory project, and should be the animating focus of international political theory.

We should therefore not be sanguine about the possibilities which result from adopting a critical international theory which seeks to extend the boundaries of political community via the rearticulation of sovereign identities. Rather than seeing an inevitable alignment and interconnection between the empirical, the practical and the normative dimensions of the critical theory project, the existence of a series of multiple and competing logics in the (post)modern international system must be recognised. These push in contradictory directions: some consolidating the particularism of the state and its exclusionary practices, others undercutting the power of the state and opening up new political spaces and identities and forms of action. But within such contradictory dynamics, a critical international theory would challenge the state monopoly of power by challenging its role as the constructor of identity. This would entail a redefinition of the relationships between insiders and outsiders by focusing on the emergence and potential of local, subnational and transnational solidarities. Above all it would maintain an ethic of universalism that does not overlook the merits of cultural diversity.

Notes

1.   Onuf argues that the presumption of anarchy as the core feature of international relations is an extension of the liberal paradigm – how egoistic, self-interested agents are capable of coexistence – to the international. But, Onuf argues, international relations was never a matter of anarchy, any more than domestic societies could have been. In Hobbes's time, social relations displayed evidence of being ruled arrangements (order) which nevertheless lacked central authority and were thus formally anarchic. It is not until the seventeenth century that political theorists transform anarchy from being the absence of guidance to the absence of central authority in the state. And it is only in the nineteenth century that we began to equate the centralisation of politics in the state with the centrality of the state for politics. The conceptions of anarchy and the state at the core of international theory are thus intimately connected with the development of modernity and the rise of liberalism's individualist ontology. See N. Onuf, *World of Our Making* (Charlotte, NC, 1990) chs 4 and 5. The issue of sovereignty is discussed more fully in the text of this essay.

2.   This constitutes a major theme for much of postmodern and critical international theory. Its implications for international theory are discussed in N. J. Rengger, 'Incommensurability, International Theory and the Fragmentation of Western Political Culture' in J. Gibbons (ed.), *Contemporary Political Culture* (Beverly Hills, 1989). Its implications for the question of sovereign identities are discussed in the essays in R. B. J. Walker and S. Mendolvitz (eds), *Contending Sovereignties: Redefining Political Community* (Boulder, CO, 1990).

3.   For a fuller discussion of these uneven interdependencies, though not the theme of inclusion and exclusion, see J. Rosenau, *Turbulence in World Politics: Toward a Theory of Change and Continuity* (Brighton, 1990).

4.   R. W. Cox, 'Social Forces, States and World Order: Beyond International Relations Theory', *Millennium: Journal of International Studies*, Vol. 10, No. 2 (Summer 1981) pp. 126–155.

5.   Ibid., p. 128.

6.   For discussions of critical theory and international relations, see R. W. Cox, 'Social Forces, States and World Order: Beyond International Relations Theory'; A. Linklater, 'Realism, Marxism and Critical International Theory', *Review of International Studies*, Vol. 12, No. 2 (1986) pp. 301–12; M. Hoffman, 'Critical Theory and the Inter-Paradigm Debate', *Millennium: Journal of International Studies*, Vol. 16, No. 2 (Summer 1987) pp. 231–49; M. Hoffman, 'Conversations on Critical International Theory', *Millennium: Journal of International Studies*, Vol. 17, No. 1 (1988) pp. 91–5; Y. Lapid, 'The Third Debate: On the Prospects of International Theory in a Post-Positivist Era', *International Studies Quarterly*, Vol. 33, No. 2 (1989) pp. 234–54; A. Linklater, *Men and Citizens in International Theory*, 2nd edn (London: 1990), particularly the 'Postscript'; A. Linklater, *Beyond Realism and Marxism: Critical Theory and International Relations* (London, 1990); A. Linklater, 'The Problem of Community in International Relations', *Alternatives*, Vol. 15, No. 2 (1990) pp. 135–53; and M. Hoffman, 'Restructuring, Reconstruction, Reinscription, Rearticulation: Four Voices in Critical Inter-

national Theory', *Millennium: Journal of International Studies*, Vol. 20, No. 2 (1991) pp. 169–85.

7. John Dunn, *Interpreting Political Responsibility* (Cambridge, 1990) p. 193. Similar views on the nature of theory as entailing this threefold project are identified in R. Bernstein, *The Restructuring of Social and Political Theory* (Cambridge, 1979).

8. See A. Linklater, 'Realism, Marxism and Critical International Theory', and M. Hoffman, 'Critical Theory and the Inter-Paradigm Debate'.

9. See A. Linklater, *Beyond Realism and Marxism*, on which the following discussion draws.

10. See M. Wight, 'Why Is There No International Theory?' in M. Wight and H. Butterfield (eds), *Diplomatic Investigations* (London, 1966).

11. A. Linklater, *Beyond Realism and Marxism*, p. 14.

12. For a fuller discussion of these issues see A. Linklater, *Beyond Realism and Marxism*, and A. Linklater, 'The Problem of Community in International Relations'.

13. On cosmopolitanism and international relations, see C. R. Beitz, *Political Theory and International Relations* (Princeton, 1979). For an argument that connects cosmopolitanism with critical international theory, see M. Hoffman, 'States, Cosmopolitanism and Normative International Theory', *Paradigms*, Vol. 2, No. 1 (1988) pp. 60–75. For a critique of this position, see C. J. Brown, 'Cosmopolitan Confusions', *Paradigms*, Vol. 2, No. 2 (1988–89) pp. 102–11; and C. J. Brown, 'The Modern Requirement', *Millennium: Journal of International Studies*, Vol. 17, No. 2 (1988) pp. 339–48.

14. The sense of 'irony' being deployed here draws on R. Rorty, *Irony, Contingency and Solidarity* (Cambridge, 1989). However, there are certain affinities with the senses of irony deployed in W. Connolly, 'Identity and Difference' in J. Der Derian and M. Shapiro (eds), *International/Intertextual: Postmodern Readings of World Politics* (Lexington, 1989), pp. 323–42; and J. Baudrillard, *The Evil Demon of Images* (New York, 1987).

15. See R. B. J. Walker, *One World, Many Worlds: Struggles for a Just World Peace* (Boulder, CO, 1989).

16. A. Linklater, 'The Problems of Community in International Relations', p. 141.

17. This theme, couched in terms of the principle of *ius gentium inter ser*, forms part of the concluding argument in R. J. Vincent, *Human Rights and International Relations* (Cambridge, 1986), and is developed in A. Linklater, 'The Problem of Community in International Relations'.

18. See F. Halliday, 'State and Society in International Relations: A Second Agenda', *Millennium: Journal of International Studies*, Vol. 16, No. 2 (1987) pp. 215–30.

19. Two pertinent, though different, examples of the reliance on this background assumption can be found in J. Rawls, *Theory of Justice* (Cambridge, MA, 1971) and M. Walzer, *Spheres of Justice* (Oxford, 1983).

20. See A. Wendt, 'Sovereignty and the Social Construction of Power Politics', manuscript (November 1990) on which the following discussion draws. For a discussion of the agent-structure debate in international relations, see A. Wendt, 'The Agent-Structure Problem in International Relations Theory', *International Organization*, Vol. 41, No. 3 (1987) pp. 335–70, and D. Dessler,

'What's at Stake in the Agent-Structure Debate?', *International Organization*, Vol. 43, No. 3 (1989) pp. 441–74.

21.   A. Wendt, 'Sovereignty and the Social Construction of Power Politics', p. 3.

22.   L. E. J. Ruiz, 'Sovereignty as Transformative Practice' in R. B. J. Walker and S. Mendolvitz (eds), *Contending Sovereignties*, pp. 79–96.

23.   Ibid., p. 80.

24.   See R. Falk, 'Evasions of Sovereignty' in R. B. J. Walker and S. Mendolvitz (eds), *Contending Sovereignties*, pp. 61–78.

25.   See W. Magnusson, 'The Reification of Political Community', pp. 45–60; L. E. J. Ruiz, 'Sovereignty as Transformative Practice', pp. 79–96; and A. Nandy, 'The Politics of Secularism and the Recovery of Religious Tolerance', pp. 125–44. All these articles are in R. B. J. Walker and S. Mendolvitz (eds), *Contending Sovereignties*.

26.   See J. Camilleri 'Rethinking Sovereignty in a Shrinking, Fragmented World' in R. B. J. Walker and S. Mendolvitz (eds), *Contending Sovereignties*, pp. 13–44.

27.   See R. B. J. Walker 'Interrogating State Sovereignty', pp. 1–12 and 'Sovereignty, Identity, Community', pp. 159–85, in R. B. J. Walker and S. Mendolvitz (eds), *Contending Sovereignties*.

28.   Despite the important differences between postmodern and critical international theory on questions of epistemology, it is this question which points to a shared ontological concern. This theme is developed in M. Hoffman, 'Restructuring, Reconstruction, Reinscription, Rearticulation: Four Voices in Critical International Theory'.

29.   These questions and themes are developed more fully in R. B. J. Walker 'Interrogating State Sovereignty'.

30.   The idea of an international citizenry is taken from the later writings of Foucault on the green movement and the Vietnamese boat people. It is more fully discussed in the chapter by I. Forbes in this volume and in A. Linklater, 'What is a Good International Citizen?', manuscript (1991). The following section draws on the arguments developed in these two pieces.

31.   A. Wendt, 'Sovereignty and the Social Construction of Power Politics', pp. 9, 11.

32.   H. Bull, 'Justice in International Relations', *The Hagey Lectures*, The University of Waterloo, Ontario (1983–4).

33.   A. Linklater, 'What is a Good International Citizen?'. It is worth noting that Linklater places a considerable emphasis on the possibilities immanent within the rationalist tradition in international theory, particularly within the 'English school' and the idea of international society, for its own restructuring as part of the core of a critical international theory.

34.   For a fuller discussion of critical social movements and in the role and impact on international relations theory and practice, see S. Mendolvitz and R. B. J. Walker (eds), *Towards a Just World Peace: Perspectives from Social Movements* (London, 1987), on which the following section draws.

35.   They have also been referred to as 'lifestyle politics'. See W. Chaloupka, 'Immodest Modesty: Antinuclear Discourse, Lifestyle Politics, and Intervention Strategies', *International Studies Quarterly*, Vol. 34, No. 3 (September 1990) pp. 341–52.

36.   The need for, and consequences of, focusing on the margins and fringes of

political discourse and practice is the theme of the articles in R. K. Ashley and R. B. J. Walker (eds), 'Speaking the Language of Exile: Dissidence in International Studies', *International Studies Quarterly*, Vol. 34, No. 3 (1990).

37. R. B. J. Walker, 'Sovereignty, Identity and Community'.
38. On subsistence rights, see H. Shue, *Basic Rights* (Princeton, 1980).
39. The idea of communicative rationality and undistorted dialogue is developed most fully by J. Habermas, *Communication and the Evolution of Society* (Boston, 1979), and *Theory of Communicative Action*, Vol. 1 (Boston, 1981).
40. This approach to third party intervention is most widely associated with the work of John Burton. See, for example, J. W. Burton, *A Handbook for Resolving Deep Rooted Conflicts* (Lanham, MD, 1987). On the transformative nature of facilitative third party interventions, see J. Rothman, 'Supplementing Tradition: A Theoretical and Practical Typology for International Conflict Management', *Negotiation Journal*, Vol. 5, No. 3 (1989) pp. 265–77. The role of practical reason and conflict theory is discussed in T. Nardin, 'Theory and Practice in Conflict Research' in t. R. Gurr (ed.), *Handbook of Political Conflict: Theory and Research* (NY: 1980). For an effort at extending Habermas's ideas into mediation processes, see J. S. Dryzek and S. Hunter, 'Environmental Mediation for International Problems', *International Studies Quarterly*, Vol. 31, No. 1 (1987) pp. 87–102.

17 Beyond the State

Ian Forbes

In the discussion thus far, 'intervention' as a category has appeared as one kind of *action* (*not* activity) by one actor (usually a state) against another actor (another state). Even though a number of different examples of intervention have been considered, these have remained state versus state actions as examples of a single, undifferentiated genre. Intervention is presumed to be an empirical act over which we may conduct a discourse on ethical themes.

Indeed, the notion of *having* an ethical concern is to a large extent seen as non-problematic. In general, discussions on the ethics of intervention presume that ethics – the realm of political philosophy, or political morality, or idealism – can be counterposed to intervention – the realm of *realpolitik*, the practical world of action and consequence. The links between the two are held to be tenuous and difficult to conceptualise, and an ethical concern, however constructed and justified, is thought to be virtually impossible to implement. However resolute and sustained the effort to generate understanding on the issue of ethics and intervention, the variety of perspectives only serves to make clear the unsatisfactory nature of the basic assumptions.

The difficulty with all these ethical positions is that they maintain the fiction that power is actually discontinuous with the conduct of a normative discourse at all. A corollary of this is that our professional discourse is not seen to serve that exercise of power we have labelled intervention. What should be analysed is the way that interventionary activity displaces knowledge. In general, it displaces it in the direction of the fiction that states have legitimate uses of centralised authority, and that force may be used against the weak.

Disenchantment with traditional approaches to the ethics of intervention indicates the need for a new perspective, exemplified by the work of Michel Foucault. He was a strong critic of traditional theory, and attempted to transcend its limitations, if necessary by parting company with it altogether. His approach enables discussion to negotiate the barriers so rigidly separating social science disciplines, such as political theory and international relations.

In fact, there are significant points of contact between the traditional moralist and realist accounts and Foucault's understanding of the grounds for action. Although Foucault is critical of terms such as 'rights' and 'the state', he is nevertheless forced to use them. He recognises that they are essential to modern political reality and understanding. However, as one might expect, Foucault invests these terms with double meaning, with dual tasks. In so doing, he indicates at once the impossibility of the discourse and the lack of any hope of further progress within it, as well as the absence of any alternative.

Foucault's enterprise is apposite to discussions of ethics and intervention in a number of ways. While his approach does not necessarily provide all the answers, it does provide a radical as well as cohesive context which goes beyond the superficially intractable components of the consideration of the ethics of intervention. Conceptualising the relation between ethical theory and interventionary practice from a Foucauldian perspective, a clear set of issues and themes begin to emerge. These are: the problem of the state and sovereignty; the problem of the human subject; and the problem of ethnocentrism.

THE STATE OF POWER

There appears to be no notion of the state which is valid for political theory and international relations alike. Social and political theory seems unable to transcend its own conceptions of the state. Liberal and realist thought especially is locked into a static conception of the state, and at the international relations level assumes a state of nature and reverts to stale contractarian formulae, or relies on the dubious authority of the jurisprudence model.[1] Marxism, on the other hand, maintains the fiction that proletarian state sovereignty is conceptually and practically different to that of a class state, as well as ethically superior. While this may produce interesting histories, it does not have a great deal of intellectual or predictive validity.

In discussions of intervention, the concept of the state has been used in different ways. The state has sometimes been seen as the subject, the key actor that carries out interventionary activity. However, the state has also been the object, the target of interventionary action. The state has even been seen as an idea, suggesting a teleological function. Sometimes the state is an abstract embodiment under the protective wing of governments, or international society, or the customary practice of international law, or an ethical concern. At other times it has been endowed with the properties of an agent, something which has interests and which can act in respect of its own population and the interests of other states. There are other variations on the conception of the state, but all views accept two things: first, that the definition of the state is largely unproblematic; and second, that the state must and will continue to exist. In addition, discussions of intervention are further muddied by the tendency for unacknowledged shifts to occur between these various meanings. All these confusions precipitate debates about the nature of the state, agency and sovereignty.

The problem for conventional discourses is that the concepts of the state employed masquerade as a single universal category. Foucault's contribution here is that he enables us to get beyond the confusions associated with contemporary definitions of the state by concentrating on relations of power that were previously presumed to reside in their most distilled and interesting form in the entity of the state. In other words, these power relations are intimately bound up with the nature and the activity of the state.

By focusing on power relations, Foucault identifies that which is, broadly speaking, universal in our experience and in our practice. For him, the state is composed of, and assisted in being by, power relations, amounting to a great negative form of power. It is a dominating, disciplining state. But, if the state is the only item for discussion, then there is the danger of ignoring all the other power relations which exist regardless of the state, in contradiction to the state, outside the realm of the state apparatus.

For Foucault, 'power is not an institution, and not a structure; neither is it a certain strength we are endowed with; it is the name that one attributes to a complex strategical situation in a particular society'.[2] This view of power, exercised in the state 'through disciplinary mechanisms and the stipulation of norms for human behaviour' requires a radical redefinition of the conception of the state and its relation to violence.[3] It establishes that the dominant theoretical traditions, premised on the legal and territorial construct of the post-Westphalian state, cannot produce a satisfactory theory of power and violence. The modern state is then reconceived as a system of disciplinary power and surveillance, in that new forms of power over workers are extended administratively. This amounts to an account of the internal pacification of the populace such that violence of the kind perpetrated against the criminal even 100 years ago is now deemed unnecessary. This view of the state, which is no longer reliant on the idea of the state as a *geographical* entity, throws into question the historical continuities that are essential to the intellectual underpinnings of international relations theory. Power relations do not reside any more in the entity of the state; the state does not generate, but is the result of power relations.

The deconstruction of conventional interpretations of the state has ramifications for the concept of state sovereignty in international studies. If the state does not exist in the way that traditional thought presumes, then the notion of state as power relations is severely corrosive of sovereignty. It is worth noting that state sovereignty is already a particular problem for international relations discourse. The idea that the state is in sovereign control over its population and territory is an empirical simplification.[4] It precludes analysis of just how control is exercised and developed and how other factors, including international ones, can modify and affect a state's capacity to control.

Nevertheless, it is clear that the state dominates political theory discourse as well. As Foucault puts it in *Power and Knowledge*:

> sovereign, law and prohibition formed a system of representation of power which was extended during the subsequent era [i.e., post-monarchical times] by the theories of right. Political theory has never ceased to be obsessed with the person of the sovereign.

This kind of philosophy produces and relies on law, on the discipline and the control of the individual in the population. Foucault rejects it, and reaches beyond the state, for a number of reasons. First, the legal conception of the state cannot capture all that is important in terms of power relations. Second, the state, in any event, is a superstructural phenomenon based on a whole mass of power relations. Third, analysis should bring about change in the political, economic, and institutional regime of truth. At the heart of this approach is a concern with social science as an activity contributing to power relations and the production of truth in society. Effectively, Foucault stresses the responsibility of social scientists to be critical about their intellectual practice. His demands are clear, as are the implications for the study of international relations.

> In short, it is a question of orienting ourselves to a conception of power which replaces the privilege of the law with the viewpoint of the objective, the privilege of prohibition with the viewpoint of tactical efficacy, the privilege of sovereignty with the analysis of a multiple and mobile field of force relations, wherein far-reaching, but never completely stable, effects of domination are produced. The strategical model, rather than the model based on law. And this, not out of a speculative choice or theoretical preference, but because it is in fact one of the essential traits of Western societies that the force relationships which for a long time found expression in war, in every form of warfare, gradually became invested in the order of political power.[5]

AGENTS AND SUBJECTS

Another feature of traditional approaches to international relations is the way that the human agent or subject is virtually ignored. The key components tend to be states, systems or structures. Even where individuals appear to be taken into account, such as foreign policy decision-making, agency is defined in terms of the states and international organisations being served. In the political theoretical approach, however, the individual tends to be over-emphasised. Indeed, the central concern of traditional political theory has been the relationship between individual and collective human and social identity. Political theory appears to offer a corrective to international theory on the basis of its highly developed understanding of agency and subjectivity.

However, the utility of these notions of agency and subjectivity for explaining ethics and intervention is open to question. The focus on the individual by the human rights model is a good example of the problems that beset talk of action and ethics in international relations. The search is for universalisable propositions concerning ethical thought and action based on a transculturally conceived individual with basic and general human rights. Leaving aside the cogency of human rights, this is a model which must stay embarrassingly silent with respect to one of the key parts of the rights, duties and obligation formula, namely, the state. It cannot shed any light on questions about the nature of the state. Is it an actor, is it an agency, does it represent individuals, or groups? Moreover, how is it to be judged? The individual in these models is an abstraction, seen in isolation from the real conditions of existence which stimulate intervention and gain our concerned attention.

Three consequences flow from this kind of focus on the individual. Although the human rights model may be used to establish grounds for the generation of rules of international behaviour,[6] this is nothing more than an enhancement of the international law approach. Second, if a human rights model is used in a cosmopolitan way, to create a normative milieu, then the options for action are limited to justified intervention. Third, any insistence on the primacy of human rights operates to undermine the principle of non-intervention. On the one hand, it constructs a universalism which suggests that individuals and not just states have rights in international law or international society. This makes states vulnerable in the context of external claims regarding their own population. On the other hand, there is no corresponding responsibility created with respect to any new agencies or actors in the international system. Individuals are taken to have rights, but there is no ascription of responsibility or duties beyond borders to these same individuals. Raymond Plant has suggested that logical and moral obligations and claims are created, but this falls a long way short of their recognition in international law and in international relations. The net effect is to legitimate interventionary activity by states in respect of other states *and* individuals, understood as subjects and objects.

These outcomes are unsatisfactory, because there remains a great deal of difference between the individual as an abstract repository of rights and the real individuals who are the subjects of intervention. By conceptualising individuals as rights-holders, political theory ultimately reinforces the rights of states over such individuals. Thus political theorists tend to concentrate on the internal reorganisation of states as a solution to the problems of denial and violation of rights. Ironically, nothing precipitates interventionary activity, or threats of it, quicker than changes to the internal reorganisation of a state. The postulation of change within the state as an ethical solution to intervention can only be a small part of a much more complicated story.

ETHNOCENTRISM

Normative considerations of intervention and sovereignty sometimes assume that the values and actions of another society are beyond the judgemental realm of those outside that society. This leads to a considerable degree of moral and practical reticence. Some commentators want to avoid ethnocentrism, treating it as a matter of sensitivity but not theory; at worst, it is regarded as a conceptual cul-de-sac, preventing us from judging and acting at all. Ethnocentrism may even be reduced to an 'interests of the strong' argument. Put unkindly, a concern with ethnocentrism looks a bit like guilt over past and present imperialism rather than a recognition and validation of other cultures and an acknowledgement of the shortcomings of our own moral and political analyses. In other words, ethnocentrism is a term which sanitises the reality of the dominance of Western values and habits in the exercise of power. The kind of ethnocentrism that is problematic is much more accurately described as Eurocentrism. Crucially, an approach to power which privileges a certain conception of law and sovereignty is deemed to constitute a universal rather than contingent and peculiarly Western norm.

THE SUBJECTIVITY OF OPPRESSION

The problems posed by the nature and existence of states in the international system, the concept of the human subject with rights, and ethnocentrism act like centrifugal forces on the attempt to generate a normative account of intervention. Following Foucault, these problems can be shown to be inter-related because each entails specific relations of power. Power relations are the central element in the activity of intervention as well as the principal focus of ethical constraints. His understanding offers new ways to theorise the relationship between power, norms and action. Three particular aspects of his thought offer a means to negotiate the barriers that stand in the way of progress on the question of ethics and intervention. These are: his conception of power; the connection between power, knowledge and truth; and his focus on the body as the site of history and of power.

Power, for Foucault, is not as we have been given to understand it. It is ubiquitous, but not unitary; it is exercised but not possessed; and its exercise is multiple rather than binary.[7] Foucault put it this way:

> Power is everywhere: not because it embraces everything, but because it comes from everywhere . . . power is not an institution, nor a structure, nor a possession. It is the name we give to a complex strategic situation in a particular society.[8]

This view of power challenges the traditional understanding of power as unitary and juridical. However, the traditional view predominates, perpetu-ating 'the notion of a correspondence between forms of power and political structures'.[9]

> Hence the importance still accorded in the theory of power to the prob-lems of right and violence, law and illegality, will and liberty and, above all, the state and sovereignty (even if sovereignty is no longer embodied in the person of the sovereign, but in a collective being). To conceive of power in these terms is to do so from within a historical form – juridical monarchy -that is peculiar to our own societies.[10]

These are some of the very terms, of course, that are the currency of the language of both ethics and intervention. More generally, this language permeates most normative political theory as well as the conduct of interna-tional relations. It should be noted that Foucault is drawing attention to the inadequacy of a formulation of power which is predominantly Western. Nevertheless, his critique applies to any system which accepts and perpetu-ates a view of power which is not only peculiar but also parochial. More-over, Foucault's position is more than just critical of traditional views of power, because he attacks the notion of sovereignty at its core.

Who exercises power? And in what sphere? . . . We know that it is not in the hands of those who govern. . . . Everywhere that power exists, it is being exercised. No one, strictly speaking, has an official right to power; and yet it is always exercised in a particular direction, with some people on one side and some on the other. It is often difficult to say who holds the power in a precise sense, but it is easy to see who lacks power.[11]

This deconstruction of the usual assumptions of the centres and controllers of power has a number of radical implications. It undermines conventional interpretations of the state, because power comes as much from below as from above. The ubiquity of power means that power relations are immanent in all other types of relations, and that, wherever power is exercised, there will always be resistance to that power. Far from just being used to subdue, the exercise of power is much more interestingly complex. Power is a strategic relation in social situations. As Sheridan puts it:

Power relations depend on a multiplicity of points of resistance, which serve at once as adversary, target, support, foothold. Just as there is no centre of power, there is no centre of revolt, from which secondary rebellions derive, no unified class that is the seat of rebellion.[12]

The multidirectionality and the numerous possibilities of the exercise of power are accompanied by the idea that power *needs* resistance. Furthermore, Foucault disturbs traditional concepts of possession, cause and effect, and agency.

We must cease once and for all to describe the effects of power in negative terms: it 'excludes', it 'represses', it 'censors', it 'abstracts', it 'masks', it 'conceals'. In fact power produces; it produces reality; it produces domains of objects and rituals of truth. The individual and the knowledge that may be gained of him belong to this production.[13]

Foucault, therefore, is not a thinker for whom power is something to be set against liberty, as something to be constrained and controlled. Power is both positive and negative; it is like a mechanism. It is something that can be exercised at the local or micro-level, against the apparent power-holders, against the structures that exist in society. This means that new conglomerations of power are always possible, even among the weak, the dispossessed and the poor – 'power relations are always potentially unstable and potentially reversible'.[14]

Power is productive in another important and systematic sense, too. In producing reality, power produces the objects of knowledge, and knowledge itself. The close relationship between power and its product is what Foucault refers to as the power/knowledge discourse. It has three features: power is immanent and diffused throughout society; knowledge is not ideal and abstract, but material and concrete, and inevitably connected to the workings of power throughout society; science cannot be divorced from ideology, since science is a form of knowledge.[15] In particular, the human sciences 'are rooted in non-rational, contingent and frequently unsavoury origins'.[16] Foucault has in mind psychiatry, medicine and political economy, but these are held to be representative of the modern social science disciplines, among which must be numbered political theory and international studies. Moreover, the human sciences have been instrumental in the transformation of unstable power relations into general patterns of domination based on reason and norms of human functioning. Thus state power based on the rule of law has 'mutated into its current disciplinary and normalising form'.[17]

Even though Foucault theorises this at the state level, the point has wider application. The production of knowledge and truth is intimately associated with the exercise of power: 'we are subjected to the production of truth through power, and we cannot exercise power except through the production of truth'.[18] Our knowledge is actually a political activity, because it seeks to conceal the way that power constructs that knowledge.

> Power is not caught in the alternative: force or ideology. In fact every point in the exercise of power is at the same time a site where knowledge is formed. And conversely every established piece of knowledge permits and assures the exercise of power.[19]

There are two questions that arise out of the power/knowledge discourse, whenever one is faced either with knowledge or truth claims, or with power and control. Where is the effect of power in this knowledge? Where is the displacement of knowledge in this power tactic? These are questions that can be addressed to ethical claims (which are a form of ideology or knowledge claim) and to interventionary practice (which is certainly about force and control).

The third aspect of Foucault's thought is the importance of the body. The body is the principal empirical object of investigation because it became the focus of the development of the liberal age. This age saw 'the development of strategies for controlling for political purposes the bodies of potential workers'.[20] In *Discipline and Punish*, Foucault sets out the proposition most clearly. The body is the site of oppression; it is the target of political tactics

INTERVENTION AS OPPRESSION

These questions challenge the key assumption that the intellectual framework of a discourse on ethics, conducted in the rarified atmosphere of academic circles, is to be regarded as quite distinct from the hard practice of intervention on the cross-border ground. This assumption deserves to come under complete challenge, because intervention in practice and ethics in theory share precisely the same assumptive base. Consequently, it is conceptually impossible to rule out or justify or decide upon the validity of an intervention on ethical grounds. Such explorations should take on an entirely different character.

This can be demonstrated by an alternative account of intervention. Interventionary activity is a phenomenon of concern to the West in a quite particular way. The West is concerned with control, with administering the world in such a way that its own power hierarchies are maintained intact and can flourish. The West has been able to build an international system in its own image, with its own apprehension of the power/knowledge discourse becoming dominant. This means that the international system, like the modern western state and its less developed counterparts is a collection of systems of domination with a range of activities and agencies designed to sustain a certain kind of order in the world. Intervention is one of the means of generating and spreading control. It is especially a great power notion, a great power capability *vis-à-vis* non-great powers, and a great power practice.[25] For the great powers and their agents, intervention is not an ethical issue, but a recognised practice for definable ends. If this were not so, the great powers would not be able to observe as well as break 'rules' of military intervention, nor would they want to.[26]

Thus intervention is an exercise of power which aims to control. This formulation has the virtue of addressing the *activity* of intervention as well as the *objects* of intervention. This requires a simultaneous consideration, not of consequences intended or not, but of the necessary constituents of the problem designated as ethics and intervention. Not all acts of intervention are the same, just as those who exercise power, and those who lack power, are variables. Nevertheless, the activity remains the same – to focus oppression on the site of the body. Intervention needs bodies. It is bodies who populate cross-border areas, it is bodies who operate military hardware.

This is a generalisation with greater potency than the rights argument, because it is the actual human powers of individuals which are empirically rather than conceptually being subjugated and used as a strategy for an overall controlling exercise of power. Moreover, it allows for uncertainty over the outcome. The bodies chosen as the site of interventionary oppression may upset expectations, and produce a result that is liberating for themselves.

This formulation also avoids the problem of ethnocentrism, of trying to appreciate the different perspectives involved. The ubiquity of power model assumes that there are systems of domination that are in place and that operate on a global basis. The international system, composed as it is of states defined almost entirely according to Western precepts, is also a hierarchy of domination. It is not ethnocentrism to acknowledge such a hierarchy, or to argue that from this hierarchy flow specific patterns of domination that are Western in their form and content.

It is necessary, therefore, when examining ethics and intervention, to investigate the strategies for revealing the truth of the distortions of power in respect of intervention. But this is not done from any superior or *a priori* position, because it is always the case that events like intervention are the situations in which knowledge and power reinforce each other in the practices of social actors. Intervention produces knowledge in the sense that it disciplines bodies as a tactic of control, and is also a discipline relating to sets of rules within the international system. That is, intervention produces its effect and reinforces the interventionary practice.

For these reasons, intervention is a proper empirical object of historical research to be examined with respect to the regulatory mechanisms at work in the international system. It is important to see that intervention is not *just* an objective or empirical question – politically defined, or economically motivated, or a matter of realism – but it is also a *subjective* practice not conceptually or practically dissociated from the fundamental act of domination of bodies. Therefore, intervention is tactical in that it always applies knowledge (of the practice itself, of bodies, of *power*) for a *political* purpose.

This presumes that it is not possible to have a pure ethical element or foundation to a political purpose. An ethic is not knowledge or power, but it may be a part of the power/knowledge discourse which serves to actualise and perpetuate global systems of domination.

BEYOND THE STATE: POWER/KNOWLEDGE POLITICS

Applying Foucault so freely beyond the boundaries of his own discourse and beyond the realm of the state is an exercise replete in ambiguities. First, it must be recognised that the alternative account of intervention offered above is itself an ethnocentric product that seeks to produce a solution, to sort out a programme of right thoughts which might find their way into right action. Foucault is a necessary corrective, especially to ethnocentrism. His thought allows the problem of the state to be articulated in a more challenging and productive fashion. This leads to a rejection of the validity of the sovereignty of the Western state in the name of human rights or on pragmatic or prudential grounds relating to order within international society. Such a state, to survive, must inevitably discipline and control its population; new states will have as bloody a history of repression as to do those in the West.

Given the ubiquity of power, the focus on power relations at the extremities of its exercise reveals that ethics cannot be pre-ordained or created out of our intellectual efforts. The ethics of intervention arise out of the struggle itself, which is conducted at the margins of the global system of domination. It is there that the insights into the nature of the system, its provisionality and conditionality, its fragility, are available. And yet, individuals and their bodies cannot be abandoned to interventionary actions and consequences in the existing system of states. The human subject, no matter how intellectually bankrupt a notion, is a deeply ingrained concern. The subjects of intervention offer hope for resistances to those exercises of power which lock us into a system of domination and its power/knowledge discourse. Since power is exercised in order to render bodies active, to make them productive, then the outcome must always be uncertain, and there is always the possibility of a reversal of that power. Therefore, far from this being a bleak prognosis, Foucault establishes the possibility and probability of myriad countermovements.

A Foucauldian view of the world does not mean that political action is ruled out. An emphasis on the resistance by the victims and subjects of intervention may operate to silence conventional criticisms of interventionary practice or unethical behaviour which focus on states and their agents. This would be a misapplication of Foucault's contribution. It is not possible to sidestep the language and the action realities which have shaped material and historical outcomes, namely states as they are, governments as they behave. Nor can the dominant conceptual discourse in terms of rights, sovereignty, duties, and morality be evaded. In other words, there is a discourse, which, however unsatisfactory, is as inescapable as the reality of intervention.

For Foucault this means dispensing with all the standard bases of human rights. Like Althusser, he rejects humanism conceived as a universal human essence, and, like Feyerabend, denies the possibility of social scientific knowledge about humans. For Foucault there are no justifications for values that are based on transcendental, normative or historicist principles. For Nietzschean post-humanists, such as Foucault, values arise out of our activity, our constant need to choose and evaluate. This is not a claim about human nature; rather, to choose and evaluate is intrinsic to ordinary existence. As these values are employed, so they are constantly called into question. Events force us to consider and reconsider choices and evaluations. Values also arise out of perceptions of individuals involved in power relations. It is in this sense that agency and subjectivity have meaning and content. The 'body' is also an individual person. In this respect, Foucault develops a unique neo-Kantian concept of individuality. The commonality of bodiliness is a kind of foundation for a universality of humans, but it is not yet enough to establish any link between humans on an ethical level. It is the transformation of that bodiliness in specific historical and material circumstances understood as power relations into individual agency and subjectivity which generates the possibility of a shared ethical dimension.

RIGHT ACTION BEYOND BORDERS

Such a shared ethical dimension existed when Foucault formed, with other individuals, a group to raise money to send non-governmental naval vessels into the South China Sea to protect Vietnamese boat people from piracy.[27] One of the things that associated or 'combined' him with other individuals was 'a shared difficulty' with what was happening. Nothing more. Nothing unites such individuals in terms of nature, but there are those who share a difficulty with specific situations. No one empowers such individuals to act; no one gives them the task or the responsibility. Indeed, part of what makes it their right to intervene arises from no one doing these things. Foucault's action rests on three main points. First:

> There exists an international citizenry, which has its rights, which has its duties, and which promises to raise itself up against every abuse of power, no matter who the author or the victims. After all, we are all governed and, to that extent, in solidarity.[28]

Foucault's brief theorisation or account of the call to intervene demonstrates that there are duties beyond borders. Moreover, it is possible to intervene in what we take to be an international situation without recourse to the state or a model of human rights based on positive rights or needs or a normative imperative arising from religious or naturalistic perspective. Regardless of Foucault's critique of the state and rights-based theories, he still offered grounds for action, and a requirement to act. That requirement is a direct challenge to the concept of the state, government by law and formal rights. The argument hinges on the exercise of force: it must not be assumed that 'the state, the form of the law, or the over-all unity of domination are given at the outset, these are only the terminal forms power takes'.[29] Attention has to be turned to the 'moving substratum of force relations, which, by virtue of their inequality, constantly engender states of power'.[30] This means that all citizens find themselves within a *local* 'state of power', a government which functions to replace 'war' with 'politics'. It is this commonality which creates the international citizenry and which can threaten the existing patterns of force relations. Foucault's second point illustrates the connections between individuals that governance constructs.

> Because they claim to concern themselves with the welfare [*bonheur*] of their societies, governments have arrogated to themselves the right to draw up a balance sheet, to calculate the profit and losses, of the human misfortune [*malheur*] provoked by their decisions or tolerated by their negligence. It is a duty of this international citizenry always to make an issue of this misfortune, to keep it in the eyes and ears of governments – it is not true that they are not responsible. People's misfortune must never be a silent remainder of politics. It founds an absolute right to rise up and address those who hold power.[31]

Effectively, this is to argue that the inclusion of relations of power associated with war into governmental and political power has been accompanied by the practice of judging the effects of power relations, such as intervention. The implication of Foucault's response, however, is that the state is not the ultimate and highest arbiter of action and judgment, since there is a citizenry beyond the state, capable of speaking and acting against the convenient silences which disguise suffering. That citizenry must act against the constant transgression of states beyond their legitimate sphere, and the persistent relegation of individual agents to subjected and emasculated beings.

> We must reject the division of tasks which is all too often offered: individuals can get indignant and speak out, while it is governments which reflect and act. It is true that good government likes the hallowed indignation of the governed, provided it remains lyrical. I believe that we must realise how often, though, it is the rulers who speak, who can only and want only to speak. Experience shows that we can and must reject the theatrical role of pure and simple indignation which we are offered. Amnesty International, Terre de Hommes, Médecins du Monde are

initiatives which have created a new right: the right of private individuals actually to intervene in the order of politics and international strategies. The will of individuals must inscribe itself in a reality over which governments have wanted to reserve a monopoly of power for themselves – a monopoly which we must uproot little by little every day.[32]

The requirement to act is thus based on three precepts. First, an international citizenry is said to exist, because all people are in the same relationship to existing power structures, namely they are all governed. This common situation establishes a relationship that can be generalised. The second principle concerns the nature of governments and their activity in constructing the discourse about truth. Governments tend to assume the right to respond or not respond to what happens in the world. In the process they ignore human misfortune. The responsibility falls to people who are under governments continually to point out to governments what they are doing. As long as people's misfortune are a silent remainder of politics, there exists the foundation of an absolute right to rise up and to address those who can exercise power. The third principle rejects the idea that governments rather than individuals have duties, and that their right to act requires us to remain silent. However, it is precisely in this power relation that individuals have constantly to act against and to uproot those unequal power relations in which they find themselves. This amounts to a non-state, interventionary activity which uses the language of state and rights without reproducing a repressive power/knowledge discourse.

There is no simple panacea, then, no ready remedy to apply to the problem of intervention in the international system. There is the possibility for action, however. This is beyond the realm of the state, while addressing the culpability of state actions. This shift in the nature of the analysis, away from legal interpretation and traditional approaches to political theory and international relations alike, has significant implications for the study of an increasingly internationalised politics. It means relinquishing hitherto productive but all too comfortable assumptions about statehood and sovereignty in favour of a practice which recognises the relational character of power, the significance of subjectivity and the responsibility of individual agency.[33]

Notes

1. See C. Beitz, *Political Theory and International Relations* (Princeton, 1979).
2. M. Foucault, *The History of Sexuality. Volume I: An Introduction* (Harmondsworth, 1978) p. 93.
3. M. Philp, 'Michel Foucault', in *The Return of Grand Theory in the Human Sciences*, Q. Skinner (ed.) (Cambridge, 1985) p. 67.
4. F. Halliday, 'State and Society: A Second Agenda', *Millennium*, Vol. 16, No. 2 (1987); I. Forbes, 'Fred Halliday's Second Agenda: The State of International Relations Discourse', *Millennium*, Vol. 17, No. 1 (1988), pp. 61–6.
5. Foucault, *History of Sexuality*, p. 102.
6. H. Bull, 'Conclusion', *Intervention in World Politics*, H. Bull (ed.) (Oxford, 1984) pp. 182–3.
7. A. Sheridan, *Michel Foucault: The Will to Truth* (London, 1980) pp. 138, 183.
8. Foucault, *History of Sexuality*, Vol. I, p. 93.
9. M. Foucault, 'Power and Norm: Notes', in *Michel Foucault: Power, Truth, Strategy*, M. Morris and P. Patton (eds) (Sydney, 1982) p. 59.
10. Foucault, *History of Sexuality*, pp. 88–9.
11. M. Foucault, 'Intellectuals and Power', in *Language, Counter-Memory and Practice: Selected Interviews by Michel Foucault*, D. Bouchard (ed.) (Ithaca, 1977), p. 213.
12. A. Sheridan, *Foucault*, pp. 184–5.
13. M. Foucault, *Discipline and Punish*, trans. A. Sheridan (London, 1977), p. 194.
14. Philp, 'Michel Foucault', p. 75.
15. G. Lemert and G. Gillan, *Michel Foucault: Social Theory as Transgression* (New York, 1982), p. 136.
16. M. Philp, 'Michel Foucault', p. 70.
17. Ibid., p. 75.
18. M. Foucault, *Michel Foucault: Power/Knowledge*, C. Gordon (ed.) (Hassocks, 1980), p. 93.
19. M. Foucault, 'Power and Norm: Notes' in *Michel Foucault: Power, Truth, Strategy*, M. Morris and P. Patton (eds) (Sydney, 1982), p. 62.
20. Lemert and Gillan, *Michel Foucault*, p. 128.
21. Ibid., p. 136.
22. Sheridan, *Michel Foucault*, p. 136.
23. Foucault, *History of Sexuality*, p. 102.
24. Sheridan, *Michel Foucault*, p. 126.
25. I see no contradiction in moving from a statement about the West to a consideration of great power activity. The notion of state power on a world scale is fundamentally European in nature. See I. Forbes, 'Warfare without War: The Problem of Intervention in the International System', *Arms Control*, Vol. 8 (May 1987), pp. 52–67.
26. N. Matheson, *The 'Rules of the Game' of Superpower Military Intervention in the Third World 1975–1980* (Washington, 1982); R. Allison and P. Williams, *Superpower Crisis Management in the Third World* (Cambridge, 1989).
27. M. Foucault, 'Face aux gouvernements, les droits de l'Homme', *Liberation*,

22, (1984) quoted in T. Keenan, 'The "Paradox" of Knowledge and Power: Reading Foucault on a Bias', *Political Theory*, Vol. 15, No. 1 (1987) pp. 5–37.

28. Ibid.
29. M. Foucault, *History of Sexuality*, p. 92.
30. Ibid., p. 93.
31. M. Foucault, 'Face aux gouvernements'.
32. Ibid.
33. For an account of individual agency in history see I. Forbes, *Marx and the New Individual* (London, 1990).

Bibliography

Africa Contemporary Record, 17 (1984/5)

M. Akehurst, 'Humanitarian Intervention' in H. Bull (ed.), *Intervention in World Politics* (Oxford, 1985)

R. Allison and P. Williams, *Superpower Crisis Management in the Third World* (Cambridge, 1989)

S. Amin, *Imperialism and Unequal Development* (Brighton, 1977)

N. Angell, *After All* (London, 1951)

R. K. Ashley and R. B. J. Walker (eds), 'Speaking the Language of Exile: Dissidence in International Studies', *International Studies Quarterly*, Vol. 34, No. 3 (1990)

M. Banks, 'The Evolution of International Relations Theory' in M. Banks (ed.), *Conflict in World Society* (Brighton, 1984)

E. Barker, *Translation of The Politics* (Oxford, [1946] 1977)

J. Barnes, M. Schofield and R. Sorabji (eds), *Articles on Aristotle* (London, 1975–9)

J. Baudrillard, *The Evil Demon of Images* (New York, 1987)

C. Beitz, 'Bounded Morality: Justice and the State in World Politics', *International Organization*, Vol. 33 (1979)

C. Beitz, 'Nonintervention and Communal Integrity', *Philosophy and Public Affairs*, Vol. 9 (1980)

C. Beitz, *Political Theory and International Relations* (Princeton, 1979)

C. Beitz, M. Cohen, T. Scanlon and M. Simmons (eds), *International Ethics* (Princeton, 1985)

M. Beloff, 'Reflections on Intervention' in *The Intellectual in Politics and Other Essays* (London, 1970)

C. F. Bergston, R. O. Keohane and J. S. Nye, 'International Economics and International Politics: A Framework for Analysis', *International Organization* (Winter, 1975)

I. Berlin, 'The Originality of Machiavelli', in *Against the Current: Essays in the History of Ideas* (Oxford, 1981)

R. Bernstein, *The Restructuring of Social and Political Theory* (Cambridge, 1979)

M. Billig, *Ideology and Social Psychology* (Oxford, 1982)

J. Blodgett, 'Vietnam: Soviet Pawn or Regional Power?' in R. W. Jones and S. A. Hildreth (eds), *Emerging Powers: Defence and Security in the Third World* (New York, 1986)

D. Bradshaw, 'After the Gulf War: the Kurds', *The World Today*, Vol. 47, No. 5 (May 1991)

J. Brebner, 'Laissez-Faire and State Intervention in Nineteenth Century Britain' in 'The Tasks of Economic History', *Journal of Economic History, Supplement VIII*, (1948)

C. J. Brown, 'Cosmopolitan Confusions', *Paradigms*, Vol. 2, No. 2 (1988–89)

C. J. Brown, 'The Modern Requirement', *Millennium: Journal of International Studies*, Vol. 17, No. 2 (1988)

L. C. Buchheit, *Secession: The Legitimacy of Self-Determination*, (New Haven, 1978)

H. Bull, *The Anarchical Society* (London, 1977)

H. Bull, 'Conclusion', in H. Bull (ed.), *Intervention in World Politics* (Oxford, 1984)

H. Bull (ed.), *Intervention in World Politics* (Oxford: 1984)

H. Bull, 'Justice in International Relations', *The Hagey Lectures*, The University of Waterloo, Ontario (1983–4)

H. Bull, 'The Emergence of A Universal International Society' in H. Bull and A. Watson (eds), *The Expansion of International Society* (Oxford, 1985)

H. Bull and A. Watson (eds), *The Expansion of International Society* (Oxford, 1985)

John W. Burton, *A Handbook for Resolving Deep Rooted Conflicts* (New York, 1987)

John W. Burton, *World Society* (Cambridge, 1972)

President George Bush, Speech to the American Academy for the Advancement of Science, 15 February 1991, *Financial Times*, 16–17 February 1991

J. Camilleri, 'Rethinking Sovereignty in a Shrinking, Fragmented World' in R. B. J. Walker and S. Mendolvitz (eds), *Contending Sovereignties* (Boulder, CO, 1990)

F. Cardosa and E. Faletto, *Dependency and Development in Latin America* (Berkeley, CA, 1979)

E. H. Carr, *The Twenty Years' Crisis, 1919–1939* (London, 1939, 1946)

A. Carty, *The Decay of International Law? A Reappraisal of the Limits of Legal Imagination in International Affairs* (Manchester, 1986)

W. Chaloupka, 'Immodest Modesty: Antinuclear Discourse, Lifestyle Politics, and Intervention Strategies', *International Studies Quarterly*, Vol. 34, No. 3 (September 1990)

R. Cohen, *Theatre of Power* (London, 1987)

A. Cohen, 'Lackey on Nuclear Deterrence: A Public Policy Critique or Applied Ethics Analysis?', *Ethics*, No. 97 (January 1987)

M. Cohen, 'Moral Skepticism and International Relations', in C. R. Beitz, M. Cohen, T. Scanlon and A. J. Simmons (eds), *International Ethics* (Princeton, 1985)

W. Connolly, 'Identity and Difference' in J. Der Derian and M. Shapiro (eds), *International/Intertextual: Postmodern Readings of World Politics* (Lexington, 1989)

Corfu Channel case, ICJ Reports (1949)

G. A. Cornia, R. Jolly and F. Stewart, *Adjustment with a Human Face*, 2 vols. (Oxford, 1987)

R. W. Cox, 'Social Forces, States and World Order: Beyond International Relations Theory', *Millennium: Journal of International Studies*, Vol. 10, No. 2 (Summer 1981)

B. Croce, *Politics and Morals* (New York, 1945)

'Declaration on the Granting of Independence to Colonial Countries and People's, 14 December 1960 in I. Brownlie (ed.), *Basic Documents in International Law*, 2nd edn (Oxford, 1972)

D. Dessler, 'What's at Stake in the Agent-Structure Debate?', *International Organization* Vol. 43, No. 3 (1989)

M. Donelan, 'The Political Theorists and International Theory' in M. Donelan (ed.), *The Reasons of State* (London, 1979)

M. Donelan (ed.), *The Reason of States* (London, 1978)

J. Donnelly, *The Concept of Human Rights* (New York, 1985)

G. Doppelt, 'Walzer's Theory of Morality in International Relations', *Philosophy and Public Affairs*, Vol. 8, (1978)

J. S. Dryzek and S. Hunter, 'Environmental Mediation for International Problems', *International Studies Quarterly*, Vol. 31, No. 1 (1987)

B. Duner, *Military Intervention in Civil Wars: The 1970s* (Aldershot, 1985)

T. M. Franck and E. Weisband, *World Politics: Verbal Strategy Among the Superpowers*, (New York, 1971)

John Dunn, *Interpreting Political Responsibility* (Cambridge, 1990)

S. Dutt, *India and the Third World: Altruism or Hegemony?* (London, 1984)

L. Dutter and R. Kania, 'Explaining Recent Vietnamese Behaviour', *Asian Survey* (September 1980)

R. Dworkin, *Taking Rights Seriously* (London, 1977)

A. Ellis (ed.), *Ethics and International Relations* (Manchester, 1986)

R. Falk, 'Evasions of Sovereignty' in R. B. J. Walker and S. Mendolvitz (eds), *Contending Sovereignties* (Boulder, 1990)

R. Falk, *A Study of Future Worlds* (New York, 1975)

T. J. Farer, 'Harnessing Rogue Elephants: A Short Discourse on Foreign Intervention in Civil Strife', *Harvard Law Review*, Vol. 82 (1969)

J. Finnis, *Natural Law and Natural Rights* (Oxford, 1980)

I. Forbes, 'Fred Halliday's Second Agenda: The State of International Relations Discourse', *Millennium*, Vol. 17, No. 1 (1988)

I. Forbes, *Marx and the New Individual* (London, 1990)

I. Forbes, 'Warfare without War: The Problem of Intervention in the International System', *Arms Control*, Vol. 8 (May 1987), pp. 52–67

M. Foucault, *Discipline and Punish*, trans. A. Sheridan (London, 1977)

M. Foucault, 'Face aux gouvernements, les droits de l'Homme', *Liberation*, 22, (1984)

M. Foucault, *The History of Sexuality. Volume I: An Introduction* (Harmondsworth, 1978)

M. Foucault, 'Intellectuals and Power', in *Language, Counter-Memory and Practice: Selected Interviews by Michel Foucault*, D. Bouchard (ed.) (Ithaca, 1977)

M. Foucault, *Michel Foucault: Power/Knowledge*, C. Gordon (ed.) (Hassocks, 1980)

M. Foucault, 'Power and Norm: Notes' in *Michel Foucault: Power, Truth, Strategy*, M. Morris and P. Patton (eds) (Sydney, 1982)

J. Gallagher and R. Robinson, 'The Imperialism of Free Trade', *Economic History Review*, Vol. 6 (1953)

E. Gellner, 'Islam and Marxism: Some comparisons', *International Affairs*, Vol. 67, No. 1 (January 1991)

A. Gewirth, 'The Epistemology of Human Rights', in E. F. Paul, F. D. Miller, Jr., and J. Paul (eds) *Human Rights* (Oxford, 1984)

A. Giddens, *Central Problems in Social Theory* (London, 1979)

R. Gilpin, *The Political Economy of International Relations* (Princeton, 1987)

R. Gilpin, *War and Change in World Politics* (Princeton, 1981)

J. L. S. Girling, *America and the Third World: Revolution and Intervention* (London, 1980)

T. H. Green, *Lectures on the Principles of Political Obligation* (London, 1941)

A. Guelke, 'Force, Intervention and Internal Conflict' in F. S. Northedge (ed.), *The Use of Force in International Relations* (London, 1974)

J. Habermas, *Communication and the Evolution of Society* (Boston, 1979)

J. Habermas, *Theory of Communicative Action* Vol. 1 (Boston, 1981)

D. L. Hafner, 'Castlereagh, the Balance of Power, and Non-Intervention', *The Australian Journal of Politics and History*, Vol. 26 (1980)

J. Hall, *Powers and Liberties: The Causes and Consequences of the Rise of the West* (Oxford, 1985)

F. Halliday, 'State and Society in International Relations: A Second Agenda', *Millennium: Journal of International Studies*, Vol. 16, No. 2 (1987)

S. Hampshire (ed), *Public and Private Morality* (Cambridge, 1978)

G. W. F. Hegel, *Philosophy of Right*, trans. T. M. Knox (Oxford, 1952)

R. Higgins, *International Law and the Reasonable Need of Governments to Govern*, Inaugural Lecture, London School of Economics, 1982

R. Highway (ed.), *Intervention or Abstention: The Dilemma of American Foreign Policy* (Lexington, KY, 1975)

F. H. Hinsley, *Power and The Pursuit of Peace* (Cambridge, 1963)

T. Hobbes, *Leviathan*, ed. with introduction by C. B. Macpherson (Harmondsworth, 1968)

M. Hoffman, 'Conversations on Critical International Theory', *Millennium: Journal of International Studies*, Vol. 17, No. 1 (1988)

M. Hoffman, 'Critical Theory and the Inter-Paradigm Debate', *Millennium: Journal of International Studies*, Vol. 16, No. 2 (1987)

M. Hoffman, 'Restructuring, Reconstruction, Reinscription, Rearticulation: Four Voices in Critical International Theory', *Millennium: Journal of International Studies*, Vol. 20, No. 2 (1991)

M. Hoffman, 'States, Cosmopolitanism and Normative International Theory', *Paradigms*, Vol. 2, No. 1 (1988)

J. Hoffman, 'Should Britain impose Sanctions against South Africa?', *Social Studies Review* (November 1989)

J. Hoffman, *State, Power and Democracy* (Brighton, 1988)

S. Hoffmann, *Duties Beyond Borders* (New York, 1977)

S. Hoffmann, 'The Problem of Intervention', in H. Bull (ed.), *Intervention in World Politics* (Oxford, 1984)

K. J. Holsti, *International Politics*, 2nd edn (Englewood Cliffs, NJ, 1972)

N. M. Hung, 'The Sino-Vietnamese Conflict – Power Play Among Communist Neighbours', *Asian Survey* (October, 1979)

Rt Hon. Douglas Hurd CBE, MP, Lord Mayor's Banquet, London, 10 April 1991. *Verbatim Service*, VS008/91

R. Jackson and C. Rosberg, 'Sovereignty and Underdevelopment: Juridical Statehood in the African Case', *The Journal of Modern African Studies*, Vol. 24, No. 1 (1986)

R. Jackson and C. Rosberg, 'Why Africa's Weak States Persist: The Empirical and the Juridical in Statehood', *World Politics*, Vol. 35, No. 1 (1982–83)

M. A. Kaplan and N. de B. Katzanbach, *The Political Foundations of International Law* (New York, 1961)

T. Keenan, 'The "Paradox" of Knowledge and Power: Reading Foucault on a Bias', *Political Theory*, Vol. 15, No. 1 (1987)

Keesings Contemporary Archives, 1974 (Bristol, 1974)

I. Kende, 'Twenty Five Years of Local Wars', *Journal of Peace Research*, No. 8 (1971)

I. Kende, 'Wars of Ten Years', *Journal of Peace Research*, No. 3 (1978)

G. F. Kennan, *American Diplomacy 1900–1950* (London, 1952)

R. O. Keohane and J. S. Nye, *Power and Interdependence* 2nd rev. edn (Boston, 1991)

J. M. Keynes, *The Economic Consequences of the Peace* (London, 1922)

M. Kirswani, 'Foreign Interference and Religious Animosity in Lebanon', *Journal of Contemporary History*, Vol. 15, No. 4 (1980)

M. T. Klare, *Beyond the 'Vietnam Syndrome': U.S. Intervention in the 1980s*, (Washington, DC, 1981)

J. van der Krof, 'Kampuchea: the diplomatic labyrinth', *Asian Survey* (October 1982)

L. Kuper, *On the Prevention of Genocide* (Harmondsworth, 1979)

D. P. Lackey, *Moral Principles and Nuclear Weapons* (Totowas, NS, 1984)

Y. Lapid, 'The Third Debate: On the Prospects of International Theory in a Post-Positivist Era', *International Studies Quarterly*, Vol. 33, No. 2 (1989)

M. Leighton, 'Perspectives on the Vietnamese–Cambodia Border Conflict', *Asian Survey* (October 1978)

G. Lemert and G. Gillan, *Michel Foucault: Social Theory as Transgression* (New York, 1982)

M. J. Levitin, 'The Law of Force and the Force of Law: Grenada, The Falklands and Humanitarian Intervention', *Harvard International Law Journal*, Vol. 27, No. 2 (1986)

A. Linklater, *Beyond Realism and Marxism: Critical Theory and International Relations* (London, 1990)

A. Linklater, *Men and Citizens in International Theory* 2nd edn (London, 1990)

A. Linklater, 'The Problem of Community in International Relations', *Alternatives*, Vol. 15, No. 2 (1990)

A. Linklater, 'Realism, Marxism and Critical International Theory', *Review of International Studies*, Vol. 12, No. 2 (1986)

A. Linklater, 'What is a Good International Citizen?' manuscript (1991)

R. Little, *Intervention: External Involvement in Civil Wars* (Oxford, 1975)

E. Luard, 'Collective Intervention' in H. Bull (ed.), *Intervention in World Politics* (Oxford, 1984)

D. Luban, 'Just War and Human Rights', *Philosophy and Public Affairs*, Vol. 9 (1980), reprinted in C. Beitz, M. Cohen, T. Scanlon and M. Simmons (eds), *International Ethics* (Princeton, 1985)

D. Luban, 'The Romance of the Nation-State', *Philosophy and Public Affairs*, Vol. 9 No. 4 (1980), reprinted in C. Beitz, M. Cohen, T. Scanlon and M. Simmons (eds), *International Ethics* (Princeton, 1985)

R. Macfarlane, 'Intervention and Regional Security', *Adelphi Paper* No. 196, 1985

A. MacIntyre, *After Virtue* (London, 1981)

A. MacIntyre, *The Relevance of Moral Enquiry* (London, 1990)

A. MacIntyre, *Whose Justice? Which Rationality?* (London, 1988)

W. Magnusson, 'The Reification of Political Community', in R. B. J. Walker and S. Mendolvitz (eds), *Contending Sovereignties* (Boulder, CO, 1990)

M. Mann, *The Sources of Social Power: From the Beginning to AD 1700* (Cambridge, 1986)

N. Matheson, *The 'Rules of the Game' of Superpower Military Intervention in the Third World 1975–1980* (Washington, 1982)

J. Mayall and C. Navari (eds), *The End of the Post-War Era: Documents on Great-Power Relations, 1968–75* (Cambridge, 1980)

J. McMahan, 'The Ethics of International Intervention' in A. Ellis (ed.), *Ethics and International Relations* (Manchester, 1986)

S. Mendolvitz and R. B. J. Walker (eds), *Towards a Just World Peace: Perspectives from Social Movements* (London, 1987)

E. B. F. Midgley, *The Natural Law Tradition and the Theory of International Relations* (London, 1975)

J. S. Mill, 'A Few Words on Non-Intervention', *Dissertations and Discussions* (London [1867] 1973)

J. S. Mill, *On Liberty* (Harmondsworth, 1982)

J. S. Mill, *Consideration on Representative Government* (London, 1986)

J. D. B. Miller, 'Morality, Interests and Rationalisation', in Ralph Pettman (ed.), *Moral Claims in World Affairs* (London, 1979)

D. Miller, *Social Justice* (Oxford, 1976)

A. J. M. Milne, 'Human Rights and the Diversity of Morals: A Philosophical Analysis of Rights and Obligations in the Global System' in M. Wright (ed.), *Rights and Obligations in North-South Relations* (London, 1986)

W. Minter, 'South Africa: Straight Talk on Sanctions', *Foreign Affairs*, 65 (Winter 1986–7)

H. J. Morgenthau, *Politics Among Nations*, 6th edn with K. W. Thompson (New York, 1985)

A. F. Mullins, *Born Arming: Development and Military Power in New States* (Stanford, CA, 1987)

E. Mysliwiec, *Punishing the Poor: The International Isolation of Kampuchea* (Oxford, 1988)

A. Nandy, 'The Politics of Secularism and the Recovery of Religious Tolerance', in R. B. J. Walker and S. Mendolvitz (eds), *Contending Sovereignties* (Boulder, CO, 1990)

T. Nardin, 'Theory and Practice in Conflict Research' in T. R. Gurr (ed.), *Handbook of Political Conflict: Theory and Research* (New York, 1980)

R. Niebuhr, *Moral Man and Immoral Society* (New York, 1932)

J. Noel, *Le principe de non-intervention: théorie et pratique dans les relations inter-américaines* (Paris, 1981)

N. Onuf, *World of Our Making* (Charlotte, NC, 1990)

D. Parfit, *Reasons and Persons* (Oxford, 1984)

Pascal, *Pensées*, trans. with an introduction by A. J. Krailsheimer (Harmondsworth, 1976)

Barrie Paskins, *Goodwill in Ethics and Politics* (forthcoming)

C. Payer, *The Debt Trap* (Harmondsworth, 1986)

C. Payer, *The World Bank: A Critical Assessment* (London, 1982)

F. S. Pearson, 'Foreign Military Intervention and Domestic Disputes', *International Studies Quarterly*, Vol. 18 (1974)

F. S. Pearson, 'Geographic Proximity and Foreign Military Intervention', *Journal of Conflict Resolution*, Vol. 18 (1974)

J. Peck (ed.), *The Chomsky Reader* (London, 1988)

J. A. Perkins, 'The Right of Counter-intervention', *Georgia Journal of International and Comparative Law*, Vol. 17 (1987)

J. Petras, 'U. S. Foreign Policy: The Revival of Interventionism', *Monthly Review* (Feb. 1980)

M. Philp, 'Michel Foucault', in *The Return of Grand Theory in the Human Sciences*, Q. Skinner (ed.) (Cambridge, 1985)

D. Pike, 'A Voyage into Unchartered Waters', *Far Eastern Economic Review* (11 June 1982)

D. C. M. Platt, *Finance, Trade and Politics in British Foreign Policy 1815–1914* (Oxford, 1963)

D. C. M. Platt 'Further Objections to an Imperialism of Free Trade', *Economic History Review*, Vol. 26 (1973)

D. C. M. Platt, 'The Imperialism of Free Trade: Some Reservations', *Economic History Review*, Vol. 21 (1963)

L. Pratt, 'The Reagan Doctrine and the Third World', *Socialist Register* (1987)

J. H. A. Quitter, 'Editor's Foreword', Special Issue on Intervention, *Journal of International Affairs*, Vol. 22 (1968)

D. D. Raphael, *Political Theory and the Rights of Man* (London, 1967)

J. Rawls, *Theory of Justice* (Cambridge, MA, 1971)

G. A. Raymond and C. W. Kegley, 'Long Cycles and Internationalized Civil War', *The Journal of Politics*, Vol. 49 (1987)

N. J. Rengger, 'Context and Interpretation in International Theory' in N. J. Rengger and M. Hoffman (eds), *Critical Theory and International Relations: Beyond the Inter-Paradigm Debate* (Hemel Hempstead, 1993)

N. J. Rengger, 'The Fearful Sphere of International Relations', *Review of International Studies*, Vol. 15, No. 4 (October, 1990)

N. J. Rengger, 'Incommensurability, International Theory and the Fragmentation of Western Political Culture' in J. Gibbons (ed.), *Contemporary Political Culture* (Beverly Hills, 1989)

N. J. Rengger (ed.), *Treaties and Alliances of the World* (Harlow, 1990)

'Report to the Export Committees for Drugs: Bangladesh' *World Development*, Vol. 11 (1983)

R. Rorty, *Irony, Contingency and Solidarity* (Cambridge, 1989)

R. Rorty, *Philosophy and The Mirror of Nature* (Oxford, 1980)

J. N. Rosenau, 'The Concept of Intervention', *Journal of International Affairs*, Vol. 22 (1966)

J. N. Rosenau, *Turbulence in World Politics: Toward a Theory of Change and Continuity* (Brighton, 1990)

J. Rothman, 'Supplementing Tradition: A Theoretical and Practical Typology for International Conflict Management', *Negotiation Journal*, Vol. 5, No. 3 (1989)

J. J. Rosseau, *The Social Contract and Discourse*, rev. edn (London, 1973)

L. E. J. Ruiz, 'Sovereignty as Transformative Practice' in R. B. J. Walker and S. Mendolvitz (eds), *Contending Sovereignties* (Boulder, CO, 1990)

A. Sayer, *Method in Social Science: A Realist Approach* (London, 1984)

S. J. Schleffer (ed.), *Consequentialism and Its Critics* (Oxford, 1988)

S. J. Schleffer, *The Rejection of Consequentialism* (Oxford, 1982)

U. Schwarz, *Confrontations and Intervention in the Modern World* (New York, 1970)

A. Sheridan, *Michel Foucault: The Will to Truth* (London, 1980)

H. Shue, *Basic Rights: Subsistence, Affluence and US Foreign Policy* (Princeton, 1980)

H. Sidgwick, *The Elements of Politics*, 2nd rev. edn (London, 1897)

H. J. Simons, and R. E. *Class and Colour in South Africa, 1850–1950* (Harmondsworth, 1983)

Q. Skinner, *The Foundations of Modern Political Thought*, 2 vols (Cambridge, 1978)

J. Slater and T. Nardin, 'Nonintervention and Human Rights', *Journal of Politics*, Vol. 48 (1986)

M. Small and J. D. Singer, *Report to Arms: International and Civil Wars* (Beverly Hills, 1982)

A. D. Smith, *Nation and State-Building in the Third World* (Brighton, 1984)

T. Smith, *The Patterns of Imperialism: The United States, Great Britain and the Late-industrializing World Since 1815* (Cambridge, 1981)

J. E. Spence, 'The Most Popular Corpse in History', *Optima* 43:1 (1986)

A. J. Taylor, *Laissez-Faire and State Intervention in Nineteenth-Century Britain* (London, 1972)

F. R. Teson, *Humanitarian Intervention: An Inquiry into Law and Morality* (London, 1987)

F. R. Teson, 'Le People, C'est Moi! The World Court and Human Rights', *American Journal of International Law*, Vol. 81, No. 1 (1987)

C. Thayer, 'Vietnamese Perspectives on International Security: Three Revolutionary Currents' in D. H. McMillen (ed.), *Asian Perspectives on International Security* (London, 1984)

C. Thomas, 'Challenges of Nation-Building: A Case-study of Uganda', *India Quarterly* (July–December 1985)

C. Thomas, *In Search of Security: The Third World in International Relations* (Brighton, 1985)

C. Thomas, *New States, Sovereignty and Intervention* (Aldershot, 1983)

H. K. Tillema, *Appeal to Force: American Military Intervention in the Era of Containment* (New York, 1973)

H. K. Tillema and J. Van Wingen, 'Law and Power in Military Intervention: Major States After World War II', *International Studies Quarterly*, Vol. 26, No. 2 (1982)

C. Tilly (ed.), *The Formation of National States in Western Europe* (Princeton, 1975)

A. de Tocqueville, *Democracy in America*, Vol. 2 (London, 1965)

R. J. Vincent, 'Grotius, Human Rights and Intervention' in H. Bull, B. Kingsbury and A. Roberts (eds), *Hugo Grotius and International Relations* (Oxford, 1990)

R. J. Vincent, *Human Rights and International Relations* (Cambridge, 1986)

R. J. Vincent, *Non-intervention and International Order* (Princeton, NJ, 1974)

R. B. J. Walker and S. Mendolvitz (eds), *Contending Sovereignties: Redefining Political Community* (Boulder, CO, 1990)

R. B. J. Walker 'Interrogating State Sovereignty', in R. B. J. Walker and S Mendolvitz (eds), *Contending Sovereignties* (Boulder, CO, 1990)

R. B. J. Walker, *One World, Many Worlds: Struggles for a Just World Peace* (Boulder, CO, 1989).

R. B. J. Walker, 'Sovereignty, Identity, Community', in R. B. J. Walker and S. Mendolvitz (eds), *Contending Sovereignties* (Boulder, CO, 1990)

K. Waltz, *Theory of International Politics* (Reading, 1979)

M. Walzer, *Just and Unjust Wars: A Moral Argument with Historical Illustrations* (New York, 1977)

M. Walzer, 'The Moral Standing of States: A Response to Four Critics' C. Beitz, M. Cohen, T. Scanlon and M. Simmons (eds), *International Ethics* (Princeton, 1985)

M. Walzer, 'Political Action: The Problem of Dirty Hands', *Philosophy and Public Affairs*, No. 2 (Winter 1973)

M. Walzer, *Spheres of Justice* (Oxford, 1983)

A. Wendt, 'The Agent-Structure Problem in International Relations Theory', *International Organization*, Vol. 41, No. 3 (1987)

A. Wendt, 'Sovereignty and the Social Construction of Power Politics', manuscript (November 1990)

M. Wight, *Systems of States*, ed. by H. Bull (Leicester, 1977)

M. Wight, 'Why Is There No International Theory?' in M. Wight and H. Butterfield (eds), *Diplomatic Investigations* (London, 1966)

M. J. Wilks, *The Problem of Sovereignty in the Later Middle Ages* (Cambridge, 1963)

B. Williams and J. J. C. Smart, *Utilitarianism: For and Against* (Cambridge, 1973)

P. Williams, 'Intervention in the Developing World: A View from the North', in C. Thomas and P. Saravanamuttu (eds), *Conflict and Consensus in South/North Security* (Cambridge, 1989)

P. Windsor, 'The Justification of the State', in M. Donelan (ed.), *The Reason of States: a study in international political theory* (London, 1978)

J. Van Wingen and H. K. Tillema, 'British Military Intervention', *Journal of Peace Research*, Vol. 17 (1980)

A. Wood, 'Nationalism and Poverty in the Breakdown of Sino-Vietnamese Relations', *Pacific Affairs*, Vol. 52 (1979)

M. Wright (ed.), *Rights and Obligations in North–South Relations* (London, 1986)

Yearbook of the UN, 1974 (New York, 1975)

M. Zuberi, 'Intervention in Developing Countries: A View from the South' in C. Thomas and P. Saravanamuttu (eds), *Conflict and Consensus in South/North Security* (Cambridge, 1989)

Index